The Driver's Story

EARLY AMERICAN STUDIES

Series editors: Kathleen M. Brown, Roquinaldo Ferreira,
Emma Hart, and Daniel K. Richter

Exploring neglected aspects of our colonial, revolutionary, and early national
history and culture, Early American Studies reinterprets familiar themes
and events in fresh ways. Interdisciplinary in character, and with a special
emphasis on the period from about 1600 to 1850, the series is published
in partnership with the McNeil Center for Early American Studies.

A complete list of books in the series is available from the publisher.

The Driver's Story

*Labor and Power in
the World of Atlantic Slavery*

Randy M. Browne

PENN

UNIVERSITY OF PENNSYLVANIA PRESS

PHILADELPHIA

Published by
University of Pennsylvania Press
Philadelphia, Pennsylvania 19104-4112
www.upenn.edu/pennpress

Printed in the United States of America on acid-free paper
10 9 8 7 6 5 4 3 2 1

Hardcover ISBN: 978-1-5128-2586-2
eBook ISBN: 978-1-5128-2587-9

A catalogue record for this book is available
from the Library of Congress.

For Mafe and Pedro

CONTENTS

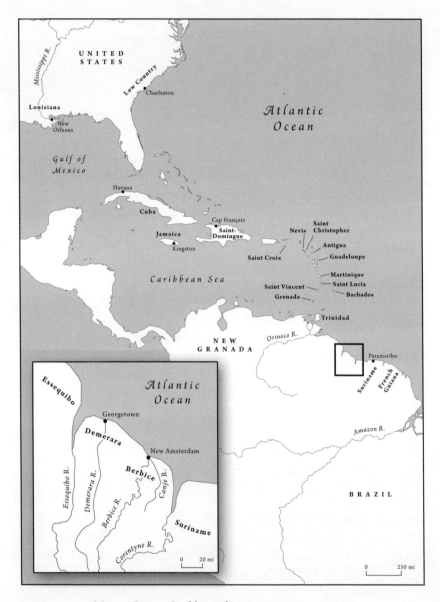

Map 1. Greater Caribbean plantation societies, ca. 1800

Within the map:

UNITED STATES

Mississippi R.

Low Country
Charleston

Louisiana
New Orleans

Atlantic Ocean

Gulf of Mexico

Havana

Cuba

Cap Français
Saint-Domingue

Jamaica
Kingston

Saint Croix

Nevis

Saint Christopher

Antigua

Guadeloupe

Martinique
Saint Lucia
Barbados

Saint Vincent
Grenada

Caribbean Sea

Trinidad

NEW GRANADA

Orinoco R.

Paramaribo

Suriname
French Guiana

Amazon R.

BRAZIL

0   250 mi

Inset:

Atlantic Ocean

Essequibo

Georgetown

Demerara

New Amsterdam

Berbice

Essequibo R.

Demerara R.

Berbice R.

Canje R.

Suriname

Corentyne R.

0   20 mi

Introduction

The story of the driver is the story of Atlantic slavery.[1] It is a story of racial capitalism: a story about the exploitation of enslaved Africans and their descendants in the name of profit, the strategies enslavers used to force the people they enslaved to work to the utter limits of their endurance, and the human costs of plantation production.[2] It is also a story of resistance and resilience: a story about people who fought back in spite of brutal consequences, built families and communities to sustain one another, organized strikes and rebellions, and insisted that their lives meant more than their status as enslaved laborers. Above all, it is a story of existential horror: a story about how people coped when they found themselves at the very center of the never-ending war between enslavers and the enslaved.[3]

The "driving system," as it was known, dominated plantation societies throughout the Americas from the beginning of large-scale sugar production in the seventeenth-century English Caribbean to the final abolition of slavery in the late nineteenth century.[4] Its purpose was straightforward: to extract the maximum amount of labor from enslaved workers and thwart their resistance. Once established, the driving system's basic dynamics were surprisingly stable and similar throughout the Americas. Everywhere, the figure that had to make the system work in practice was the driver. This was an enslaved person—usually but not always a man—appointed by white plantation authorities to supervise, manage, and punish other slaves.[5]

The earliest references to drivers come from late seventeenth-century Barbados, the small island where English planters revolutionized the production of sugar by developing a new model of labor organization and social control that would be replicated time and again as the plantation system spread throughout the Americas—the division of enslaved laborers into multiple, highly regimented work "gangs."[6] Those gangs were supervised not by white employees but by enslaved Black people who came to be called drivers, a term until then used to describe people who drove working animals.

If the plantation was, as some planters liked to imagine it, a "machine," drivers were the ones tasked with making it work—and preventing other enslaved people from sabotaging it.[7] The driving system thus turned the fundamental problem of plantation production into the problem of the driver.

To tell the story of the driver is to illuminate the lives of the people at the very heart of the plantation world. This is a story not only about labor extracted and withheld, about how plantations were managed, or about the ways enslaved people fought to negotiate the terms of their labor, tested the limits of their enslavers' power, and struggled to survive—although it is a story about all of those things. First and foremost, this is a story about drivers themselves—their predicament, their motivations, their harrowing struggles. It is a story about the life-and-death stakes of trying to get by on "slave labor camps" from which escape was all but impossible.[8] It is also a story told, as closely as possible, from the driver's own point of view. How did drivers themselves understand their predicament and ordeal? How did they try to reconcile their status as enslaved laborers with their role as enforcers of labor discipline? How did they respond to, perpetuate, and resist the driving system?

The title of this book draws on two distinct meanings of "story." On many West Indian plantations, enslaved people used the word "story" not only as it is commonly understood today, to refer to a narrative or sequence of events, but also as shorthand for conflict, trouble, or struggle.[9] As one enslaved man put it after a violent confrontation in a Caribbean cotton field, "I have story with the driver."[10] Drivers inevitably found themselves at the center of conflicts with everyone around them because their role trapped them between the insatiable labor demands of white plantation authorities and the resistance of other enslaved laborers. As a result, many of the stories about different drivers told here are necessarily stories of struggle.

Struggle defined the life of the driver. Drivers struggled to meet the impossible expectations of their enslavers, to protect themselves from brutal reprisals when they failed, and to maintain a position that helped them outlive their peers. They struggled to get other slaves to obey their orders and respect their authority—and to calibrate their response when people defied them. Drivers struggled to develop social roles that transcended their official status as agents of planter power, building families and serving as leaders for the communities to which they belonged. They struggled to maintain their authority among the enslaved even when their enslavers tried to humiliate them through demotion. And when resistance morphed into rebellion, drivers struggled with others to decide what kind of revolution they wanted.

The driver's story played out on plantations across the Atlantic world for more than three hundred years. To understand that story, I scoured a wide range of sources and scholarship on different Atlantic slave societies, from the precursors of the driving system in early seventeenth-century São Tomé and Brazil to the antebellum United States. I concentrated on Caribbean plantation societies in the eighteenth and nineteenth centuries—when the plantation complex and the driving system that made it possible were at their height—including the French colonies of Martinique and Saint-Domingue (Haiti), the Dutch Guianas (including Suriname), Cuba, and the British West Indies. Comparing various kinds of evidence from different places and periods allowed me to see that even as plantation societies changed over time and varied widely in their states of development, demographics, political and legal systems, and dominant crops, drivers' roles and the challenges they faced were remarkably consistent.

Many of the individual stories told here, however, took place in a particular time and place: the early nineteenth-century British Caribbean. That is because in this era the shifting politics of slavery and abolition produced an explosion of new and unique types of evidence about slavery and plantation production. In the decades after Britain abolished its transatlantic slave trade in 1807, the metropolitan government orchestrated a series of uneasy compromises between abolitionists and planters designed to gradually reform slavery through new laws meant to "ameliorate" the treatment of enslaved people, grant them limited legal rights, and better surveil plantation management. During this period of so-called amelioration, which lasted until the end of slavery in the British Caribbean in 1834, established colonies like Jamaica and Barbados successfully resisted metropolitan pressure, while newly acquired territories with less legislative autonomy were forced to reform their legal systems and adopt new forms of recordkeeping.[11]

Among the most important consequences of this expanding surveillance apparatus for Trinidad, St. Lucia, and the Guiana colonies of Berbice and Demerara-Essequibo was the appointment of legal officials known as fiscals and protectors of slaves.[12] In the process of adjudicating enslaved people's complaints and investigating alleged violations of the law, the fiscals and protectors created a remarkable body of evidence with no parallel in other plantation societies: extensive first-person testimony from thousands of enslaved people themselves, including hundreds of drivers.

Enslaved people went to the fiscals and protectors with a wide range of grievances and goals, and their testimony ultimately produced an extraordinary archive that spans tens of thousands of pages. Many of the complaints they made stemmed from conflicts about work—conflicts that often revolved around the actions of drivers. People claimed that drivers punished them excessively, arbitrarily, or to settle some personal grudge, and that drivers pushed them to work beyond customary limits or their physical capacity. Complaining about drivers was always risky, since colonial authorities tended to privilege testimony from drivers and white plantation authorities. Drivers themselves described field laborers who refused to obey their orders, challenged their authority, and even physically attacked them. They also complained about white plantation authorities who gave them impossible workloads and then punished them for unavoidable shortfalls. And sometimes, white plantation authorities complained about drivers who sabotaged production or conspired with other enslaved people to resist the labor regime they had been appointed to support.

Taken together, the records of the fiscals and protectors of slaves compose the single largest archive of first-person testimony from and about enslaved people in the Americas and bring us as close as we can hope to come to the voices of drivers and other enslaved people.[13] This archive thus offers an unusually raw and intimate view of the driving system as described by enslavers, drivers themselves, and the other enslaved people drivers flogged and fought, befriended and married, protected and organized.

Rich as this archive is, it is also limited. Complainants, defendants, and witnesses made difficult decisions about what to disclose, when to stay silent, and what kinds of narratives and evidence to offer. As a result, they told conflicting stories that often make it hard to know what really happened in any given case.[14] At the same time, colonial authorities often paraphrased, summarized, and translated spoken testimony—especially from enslaved people—into the kind of English that they and their peers understood. Inevitably, this archive reveals more about some aspects of enslaved peoples' lives than others. Most cases that came before the protector or fiscal had to do with intense and violent conflicts about working conditions, resistance to the labor regime, and punishment.[15] Consequently, this evidence may exaggerate the extent of conflict between drivers, other enslaved laborers, and white plantation authorities. A final challenge in using this archive is that it contains important gaps and silences, most notably the near-total absence of female drivers.[16] Nonetheless, enslaved people's testimony archived in the records of the fiscals and protectors offers an unparalleled view of drivers and the driving system in one of the largest slave systems in the Americas.

Because the basic patterns that emerge from this archive correspond to what I have learned about drivers from other sources and in other places, *The Driver's Story* is not organized around comparisons between different slave systems or change over time. Instead, it is organized thematically around different dimensions of drivers' lives. To center drivers and the problems they faced, each chapter highlights the unstable, triangular relationships drivers negotiated with white plantation authorities and with other enslaved laborers. This approach also allows me to explore the multiple roles drivers played at the center of other enslaved people's working lives, social relationships, and struggles against slavery.

The Driver's Story begins with the origins of the driving system and the driver's fundamental predicament, emphasizing both the relentless surveillance and brutal discipline drivers faced at the hands of white plantation authorities and the marginal advantages of being a driver rather than a field laborer. I then turn to the different strategies drivers used to negotiate insatiable labor demands from above and constant resistance from below, highlighting the existential horror that drivers faced in trying to do a job that was all but impossible in a world where failure could be deadly. Then, I shift away from labor and explore drivers' efforts to build families and exercise leadership within the communities to which they belonged, where drivers drew on broadly shared African-Atlantic understandings of politics to negotiate social relationships. I then focus on drivers who were demoted, particularly those who continued to be seen as leaders by other enslaved people and provoked explosive confrontations with enslavers. Finally, I explore the agonizing dilemmas drivers faced during rebellion, which crystallized their politics and revealed that their aspirations were not necessarily the same as those of most other enslaved people.

The figure of the driver has been of enduring interest to writers for more than two centuries. In the late eighteenth and early nineteenth centuries, antislavery activists on both sides of the Atlantic depicted drivers as simple-minded agents of planter power, corrupted by the brutal realities of slavery. More recently, historians, reggae artists, and novelists alike have tried to make sense of drivers' role in plantation management and complicated position in the slave community.[17] Drivers appear as key antagonists in Marlon James's *Book of Night Women* (2009), a powerful historical novel that centers on a group of enslaved women and girls on a Jamaican sugar plantation at the turn of the nineteenth century.[18] In a slave society where white residents were vastly outnumbered by enslaved Black people and the threat of revolt loomed large, drivers helped enslavers maintain control and made plantations productive through relentless surveillance and shocking violence.

But if drivers were oppressors, they were also oppressed. At the most fundamental level, they were trapped in the same hellish world of slavery and capitalism that they were coerced into supporting. At the same time, as several historians have recognized over the past half century, drivers also faced the special challenges that came with being "the men between" the fundamentally opposed demands of enslavers and other enslaved laborers.[19] Drivers thus found themselves, as the historian John Blasingame put it, "caught in the no-man's-land between management and labor."[20]

Exploring the driver's predicament offers a new approach to one of the enduring questions in the study of Atlantic slavery: How did enslavers manage to extract so much labor from the people they enslaved in the face of relentless resistance? Efforts to answer this question have taken many forms, but generally fall into two basic camps. Economic historians and other scholars who have focused on the business of slavery and its relationship to capitalism have demonstrated that plantations—especially those that produced sugar—were some of the most complex businesses of their time.[21] Slave owners were ruthless capitalists.[22] Seeking ever-greater profits, they experimented with different strategies of management, accounting, and surveillance. The strategies they pioneered to exploit enslaved workers, moreover, would later be adapted to coerce nominally free wage laborers under industrial capitalism.[23] Meanwhile, some historians more focused on the experiences of enslaved people themselves have argued that labor—and labor resistance—was at the center of enslaved people's daily lives.[24] Enslaved laborers developed a range of strategies to exert some degree of control over the ways they worked, from collective bargaining and strikes to more dangerous acts of resistance such as *marronage*—attempted escape from slavery—and rebellion.[25] As a result, they endured both routine violence and spectacular torture as enslavers tried to terrorize them into submission.[26] Surprisingly, drivers have received relatively little attention from most historians of slavery, even as they commonly acknowledge that drivers played a central role in extracting labor and managing resistance.[27]

Focusing on drivers thus offers an opportunity to integrate the approaches and insights of two fields of study usually addressed separately: first, the business of slavery and, second, the social and cultural history of the enslaved.[28] To understand how the plantation labor regime worked in practice and how enslaved people experienced, resisted, and shaped it, *The Driver's Story* develops a human history of the driving system. Doing so opens new and productive lines of inquiry. How did drivers negotiate the impossible problem of balancing pressure from above and resistance from below? How did they try to resolve labor conflicts in ways that allowed them to maintain their authority and a position that facilitated their survival? What happened when they failed? And how stable—or fragile—was a labor regime in which ground-level supervisors were drawn from the ranks of the enslaved? What emerges from my efforts to answer such questions is neither a straightforward story about the totalizing power of enslavers nor an account of enslaved people's heroic resistance. It is a messier story about fraught negotiations, contingent alliances, and difficult compromises.

In foregrounding stories of individual people, *The Driver's Story* also builds on the robust tradition of scholarship on enslaved people's social relationships. For more than half a century, historians have shown that enslaved people responded to the threat of "social death" and natal alienation by developing strong social ties, building families and communities, and adapting African cultural practices to meet new needs.[29] In many places, displaced Africans from the same broad geographic region came together to create new identities as members of diasporic "nations," such as Coromantees or Congos, which became important social and political communities.[30] Enslaved people were not only coerced laborers but also husbands and wives, parents and children, shipmates and friends, youths and elders, spiritual healers and midwives, recent African arrivals and creoles. In the complex communities they built, cooperation and conflict coexisted as enslaved people struggled both against their enslavers and against each other.[31]

In the slave community, drivers were often at the center of enslaved people's interpersonal relationships. Here, I focus on drivers' leadership and explore their efforts to draw on the unique opportunities provided by their official status, the negotiating skills they developed as intermediaries, and widely shared African political practices to construct impressive social authority. To what extent did drivers' formal role at the top of the occupational hierarchy and close connections to white authorities compromise—or facilitate—their efforts to get their fellow slaves to see them as community leaders? How did male drivers try to adapt the political practices of their African homelands, where would-be "Big Men" worked to recruit and retain followers (especially women) by offering scarce resources and protection, to the very different conditions of chattel slavery in the Americas?[32] When African-born drivers sought roles as kings or other leaders of diasporic "national" groups, what happened when their political aspirations clashed with those of other leaders? Exploring drivers' leadership ultimately illuminates new dimensions of the social worlds enslaved people created as they sought solace, belonging, and material support.

Finally, *The Driver's Story* intervenes in ongoing debates about slave resistance. In particular, focusing on the painful decisions drivers had to make both in their day-to-day lives and in moments of crisis exposes the limitations of the domination and resistance framework that continues to shape much scholarship. The analysis of drivers' politics I develop here underscores an important argument worth repeating: that a narrow focus on enslaved people's resistance to slavery is too simplistic to fully appreciate the complex power relationships of Atlantic slavery. It obscures the reality that the actions of many enslaved people—including and perhaps especially drivers—were motivated by other considerations, especially survival.[33]

Drivers' complex political calculations were laid bare when the ever-present possibility of rebellion forced them to choose sides. I focus on the pivotal roles that drivers played in rebellion both to see enslaved people's war against slavery with fresh eyes and to better understand drivers' politics. What role did drivers' leadership in African national groups play in forming—or undermining—the kind of political communities and solidarities that were necessary to organize a successful rebellion? What motivated individual drivers to support, avoid, or oppose enslaved rebels? And when drivers did organize or lead rebellions, how did their previous experiences and investment in hierarchical political structures shape their goals and aspirations?

Approaching resistance and rebellion from the driver's point of view ulti-mately reminds us that enslaved people did not share a common political vision. That drivers and other enslaved people disagreed on crucial questions of strat-egy, leadership, and goals, even when it came to revolution, reveals that enslaved people had a wide range of understandings about their world and about what sort of alternatives were possible or desirable. More broadly, centering drivers in histories of resistance to slavery allows us to see that the politics of the enslaved were, as much as those of any people, complex, contingent, and contested.

Sources and Method

To tell the driver's story is to confront the same basic problem all historians of slavery face trying to recover enslaved people's experiences. The overwhelming majority of the records in which enslaved people appear were produced by slave owners, merchants, and governments for their own purposes. The archives of Atlantic slavery, which reproduce the extreme imbalance of power between enslavers and the people they enslaved, were not generally designed to document enslaved people's own perspectives or voices. As a result, surviving records tend to offer only fleeting, fragmentary, and distorted glimpses of enslaved people's lives.[1]

When I set out to understand everything I could about drivers and the worlds they inhabited, I knew it would involve painstaking research. My search for drivers took me across the Atlantic world, from archives in Guyana, Cuba, and the United Kingdom to rare-book libraries in the United States. I have also benefited immensely—especially as the COVID-19 pandemic made research travel all but impossible—from the explosion of digitized primary sources now available online. Fortunately, drivers appeared virtually everywhere I looked for them. In hindsight I am not surprised, since drivers were at the center of plantation production, enslaved people's social lives, and resistance to slavery.

Early on, I realized that one of the richest bodies of evidence for this project was an unusual set of legal documents from the British Caribbean: the records of the Crown officials known as fiscals and protectors of slaves. These records were the result of a series of major legal and political transformations in the early nineteenth century. The period between the abolition of Britain's transatlantic slave trade in 1808 and emancipation in 1834 was one of the most well documented eras in the history of Atlantic slavery. During this period of "amelioration," the metropolitan government pressured colonies to gradually reform slavery through new laws meant to grant slaves limited legal rights, improve their working and living conditions, and better regulate relationships between enslavers and the enslaved.[2] While established West Indian colonies like Jamaica and Barbados were largely able to resist pressure to enact legislative reforms, colonies that Britain seized from other European powers in the late eighteenth and early nineteenth centuries—Trinidad (from Spain), St. Lucia (from France), and the Guyana colonies of Berbice and Demerara-Essequibo (from the Netherlands)— were not. Those colonies also inherited different legal systems, based on Roman law, that recognized enslaved people's personhood and provided opportunities to seek redress by appealing to colonial officials.

Under British rule, the responsibility for adjudicating enslaved people's complaints and documenting the progress of amelioration fell first on preexisting legal officers, such as the fiscals in Guyana, and then on new Crown officials known as protectors of slaves. Today, the records of the fiscals and protectors are part of the British Colonial Office (CO) series at the British National Archives, where they are organized into nearly fifty large, bound volumes. Together, they compose tens of thousands of pages.[3]

The most unusual and valuable part of this archive are the first-person complaints from thousands of enslaved people. The records of those complaints—and the investigations, prosecutions, and correspondence that sometimes followed— vary widely, from a few sentences of terse summary to several dozen pages of carefully transcribed, near-verbatim testimony. Taken together, these records offer extraordinary insights into the experiences and concerns of different enslaved people in several British Caribbean colonies, including many drivers and the people they worked, lived, and otherwise interacted with.

Like any archive, the records of the fiscals and protectors present several challenges. While the ostensible purpose of colonial authorities' adjudication of complaints was to uncover the truth, the very nature of the legal system in which they operated and the larger power dynamics of slavery had the opposite effect and pushed people to tell conflicting stories. When people testified, whether they were enslaved or free and whether they appeared as complainants, defendants, or witnesses, they had to make fraught decisions about what to disclose, when to stay silent, and what kinds of narratives and evidence might lead to favorable outcomes or at least protect them from the worst consequences.[4] As a result, it is not always possible to tell what really happened in a given case.

But, unlike the legal officials who were interested only in deciding whether a particular law had been violated and what verdict to reach, my reading of this evidence aims to understand not only what drivers did (and what was done to them) but also how drivers and the people they interacted with understood their world and their relationships. Rather than smoothing over conflicting claims or pretending that we can always separate fact from fiction, I foreground the competing stories that emerge from this archive in order to explore the motivations, goals, and perspectives of different actors. And, while I find it both necessary and productive to speculate beyond empirical certainty, I try to make clear the difference between what I believe we can know, what we can reasonably infer, what we can only imagine in light of other evidence, and what we ultimately cannot know.

Moreover, while the most extraordinary thing about this archive is just how close it brings us to the actual voices of enslaved people, recorded testimony was not always a direct transcription of what people actually said. Colonial scribes often, though not always, paraphrased, summarized, and translated what they heard—especially when it came to enslaved people's speech—into the kind of English that they and their peers understood. As a result, when reading this evidence, I have attempted to distinguish testimony that is mostly paraphrased from that which appears to be relatively unfiltered by paying close attention to clues such as the use of the first-person, the length and the level of detail, and the presence of African and West Indian terms, idioms, and syntax. I have also attempted to directly quote testimony only when I am relatively confident that doing so comes close to what people actually said and how they said it.

At the same time, this archive documents some aspects of enslaved peoples' lives better than others. The kinds of grievances enslaved people brought to the protectors and fiscals were shaped not only by their own concerns but also by the legal system itself, which encouraged certain types of complaints. Most of them involved conflicts about working conditions, resistance to the labor regime, and punishment. This is not surprising, since these were some of the major issues that amelioration-era legal reforms were designed to address. Accordingly, this archive emphasizes conflicts that revolved around the driver's role as enforcer of plantation discipline and may exaggerate the scale of conflict between drivers, other enslaved laborers, and white plantation authorities. Even so, when read against the grain, many cases also contain illuminating glimpses about other dimensions of drivers' lives, including their family roles and social relationships with other enslaved people.

A final challenge in using this archive is that it can be hard to assess its representativeness. There are some obvious ways in which, at least when it comes to drivers, it is clearly not representative. Among the most glaring examples is the absence of female drivers. While enslaved men served as drivers more often than enslaved women, something like a quarter of all drivers in the Caribbean may have been women. Enslaved women were especially prominent as drivers of specialized "children's gangs," but they also sometimes supervised adult field laborers. Nonetheless, among the thousands of enslaved people who appear in the records of the fiscals and protectors of slaves, I only found a handful of enslaved women identified as drivers, which led me to look elsewhere to understand the role and experiences of such women. A broader issue with this unusual archive concerns the extent to which the very presence of a fiscal or protector of slaves shaped enslaved people's political calculus and ground-level power dynamics. In many slave societies, including much of the West Indies before and during the era of amelioration, enslaved people never had the opportunity to appeal to colonial officials for redress.

To contextualize and assess what I learned about drivers from the records of the fiscals and protectors—and to understand the driving system over a wider chronological and geographic span—I explored a broad range of other sources, too. These include other types of records from the British Caribbean, especially Barbados and Jamaica, and an array of sources produced in other slave societies and non-English languages.[5] To help interpret this evidence, especially when it relates to places and periods beyond my own primary area of expertise in the British Caribbean, I have gratefully relied on the work of scholars who study different parts of the Atlantic world.

To understand how enslavers wanted the driving system to work and the pressures drivers faced from above, I analyzed the written instructions that planters provided to their employees as well as the guides or manuals they published to offer other planters advice. Those produced during the early years of the driving system in the seventeenth century, such as Henry Drax's "Instructions" (ca. 1679) for the management of his Barbados plantations, allowed me to see how the position of the driver and the gang system emerged and evolved in tandem.[6] To see how the driver's role changed—or did not change—as the plantation complex matured and spread, I compared publications from different eras, including Samuel Martin's *Essay on Plantership* (1750), Poyen de Sainte-Marie's *De l'exploitation des sucreries* (1802), Thomas Roughley's *Jamaica Planter's Guide* (1823), and several others. Taken together, this evidence also offered a range of insights into how planters tried to coerce, incentivize, and assess drivers. I also read through enslavers' private journals or diaries, including those of the notorious eighteenth-century Jamaican overseer Thomas Thistlewood and of Pierre Dessalles, a planter in nineteenth-century Martinique, which contain revealing glimpses of different incidents involving drivers.

Planters' idealized depictions of plantation production contrasted sharply with the accounts of newcomers, who were shocked and sometimes disgusted by the brutality of the driving system. Travel narratives from European visitors to the Caribbean, such as George Pinckard's *Notes on the West Indies* (1807) and Henry Whiteley's *Three Months in Jamaica* (1833), often contain detailed descriptions of plantation labor and in some cases disturbing accounts about the experiences of individual drivers. The observations such writers made about the physical and emotional violence of the driving system also became an important part of abolitionist propaganda, which proved to be another useful body of evidence. Antislavery activists such as William Wilberforce and James Stephen seized on the driver's whip as the epitome of slavery's barbarity and centered the driving system in debates about slavery, amelioration, and emancipation.

Another series of particularly valuable records were slave registers (or slave registration returns) from the early nineteenth-century British Caribbean. These records, which the metropolitan government forced colonial slaveholders to adopt, starting with Trinidad in 1813, were originally designed to curb the illegal importation of slaves to and between the West Indies after Britain abolished its transatlantic slave trade in 1808. Officials reasoned that if they were able to compile a complete register of each colony's slave population and then document any subsequent "additions" or "deductions"—whether from birth, death, sale, purchase, marronage, or manumission—they could then identify anyone who was imported illegally. With some variation by colony, slave owners or their representatives recorded the total number of people they owned on each plantation and described them according to standard categories, including name (and sometimes surname), sex, age, "colour," birthplace, height, "employment" (or "occupation"), "conspicuous natural marks" (that is, country marks) and "remarks tending further to identify" (scars, missing limbs, and so on). In some cases, slave owners also recorded enslaved people's kinship ties and purported African ethnicity or "nation."[7] Today, copies of these records sent to the Slave Registry Office in London between 1813 and 1833—some 671 volumes in all—are archived as part of the Treasury series (T 71) at the British National Archives.[8] They contain information on hundreds of thousands of enslaved people throughout the British Caribbean, including thousands of drivers on hundreds of plantations.

Slave registration returns provide two distinct and important types of evidence. Most obviously, they contain useful demographic or statistical information about drivers as a category. On that front, I have relied mainly on B. W. Higman's massive, quantitative analysis of these records, which reveals that drivers across the West Indies generally lived healthier, longer lives than most other enslaved people (findings confirmed by Richard Dunn's longitudinal analysis, based on different records, of enslaved laborers on plantation Mesopotamia in Jamaica).[9] At the same time, when read with a biographer's eye and triangulated with other evidence, slave registration returns also offer revealing snapshots of individual drivers' lives.[10] Wherever possible, I have located drivers and other enslaved people who appear in other documents (such as cases adjudicated by the protectors of slaves) in the registration returns to learn more about their biographies, kinship ties, and experiences. Doing so has, in many cases, allowed me to see not only where different drivers were born and how old they were at different points in time but also what occupations they previously held, how long they served as drivers, and what sort of families they had. In some cases, I have been able to trace drivers over decades.

One of the most surprising discoveries I made during my research came when I turned my attention to drivers in rebellion. I knew, from the work of other historians, that drivers played key roles in rebellions and conspiracies across the Americas, from seventeenth-century Barbados to nineteenth-century Cuba, both as leaders and as whistleblowers who betrayed rebel plots. But nothing prepared me for the wealth of materials I found about a little-known rebellion organized, led, and ultimately betrayed by drivers in Berbice in 1813–14, during the final days of Dutch rule. Among some one hundred thousand documents from the National Archives of Guyana that were recently digitized by the National Archives of the Netherlands—records that were previously unavailable to me and other researchers in Guyana, in part because they were in such fragile condition—I found some six hundred handwritten pages of evidence, including testimony from more than one hundred enslaved people, including about twenty drivers. These records allowed me to explore, in extraordinary detail, the complicated relationships that various drivers had to rebellion and, in this case, to the African "nations" that served as a locus of rebel organizing.

My journey into the world of drivers also led me to explore a wide range of other archives and evidence. At the National Archives of Cuba, I spent several weeks combing through criminal court records, where I found several prosecutions involving drivers—both as victims and as defendants—in violent conflicts with white plantation authorities and other enslaved people. That experience deepened my appreciation for the scholarship that historians of Cuba have produced under very difficult conditions and provided further evidence that the problems drivers negotiated were common across the Caribbean. To better understand how drivers themselves and their fellow slaves understood the pressures they faced, I also explored narratives by formerly enslaved people, like Mary Prince, and the handful of first-person narratives from drivers themselves, such as Solomon Northup's *Twelve Years a Slave* (1853).[11] Also useful were the diaries and correspondence of missionaries who lived on Caribbean plantations, including the London Missionary Society's John Wray and John Smith, who worked in nineteenth-century Guyana, and Moravian missionaries in eighteenth-century Jamaica.

Immersing myself in these different bodies of evidence and reading a range of scholarship on different plantation societies led me to see just how ubiquitous drivers were—and how heavily the slave system relied on them. Having looked at drivers across a wide sweep of time and space, it also seems to me that the basic dynamics of the driving system and the predicament of the driver were surprisingly stable. Other historians may or may not reach the same conclusion, but they will find plenty of evidence about drivers in slave societies across the Americas.

CHAPTER I

The Driving System

When most people think about the violence at the heart of Atlantic slavery, the image that usually comes to mind is the whip—but it could just as easily be the tally stick.[1] By the early nineteenth century, enslaved drivers in the Caribbean used wooden tallies to keep track of the work performed by the field laborers they supervised. At regular intervals, white plantation authorities inspected those tally sticks to see if drivers were pushing the people below them to work as hard as they demanded. When tallies indicated that drivers fell short, the consequences could be brutal.[2]

One such incident horrified an English visitor to a Jamaican sugar plantation in 1832. Early one afternoon, a driver of about sixty years old with "silvery locks," who had lived on the plantation "a great number of years" and had likely worked as a driver for decades, walked to the overseer's door to give his customary "account of the half-day's work." The driver handed the overseer his "tally," which showed the amount of work his gang had done that morning on a "bit of notched stick." The overseer "said it was insufficient" and ordered the driver to be flogged. The driver protested that getting more work out of the gang was impossible. "Well, Busha," he told the overseer, "me could have done no better, had you been standing by." Nevertheless, the driver resigned himself to a humiliating punishment. "Groaning deeply," he set down his staff and whip and then stripped. One of his fellow drivers then flogged him. Afterward, "the other drivers looked at each other and shook their heads, but uttered not a word. They dared not."[3] They likely knew all too well what it felt like to be brutalized for failing to meet impossible demands.

The tally stick epitomized the desperate predicament of the driver, caught in the middle of the relentless labor struggle between white plantation authorities and enslaved field laborers. Enslavers constantly pressed drivers to do more—to make the people below them cut more sugarcane or pick more coffee. With tallies and work logs, as well as direct surveillance, plantation managers and overseers tracked production and assessed drivers' performance with ruthless discipline.[4] Enslaved field laborers, meanwhile, resisted labor demands at every opportunity. There were also physical limits on just how hard human beings—often malnourished, diseased, and exhausted—could be pushed before breaking.

Enslavers took comfort in imagining that the plantation was, as Antiguan planter Samuel Martin described it in his *Essay on Plantership* (1750), a "well constructed machine" with "various wheels, turning different ways, and yet all contributing to the great end proposed."[5] In reality, it was a violent battlefield. And drivers were perpetually caught in the crossfire.[6]

The driving system developed in tandem with the rise of the large, integrated sugar plantation in the seventeenth-century English Caribbean. Over the next two centuries, the system spread to plantations throughout the Americas, from Suriname to South Carolina. At root, it was an attempt to solve the perennial problem enslavers faced: how to extract labor from people who vastly outnumbered them without losing control. When the driving system worked, it was ruthlessly effective. Enslavers used drivers to extract extraordinary amounts of labor and profit from the people they held captive under some of the most dire conditions imaginable. The driving system, however, was inherently unstable. To coerce enslaved people into the horrific work of supervising and discipling their fellow slaves, enslavers offered the people they appointed as drivers a range of incentives. Those incentives mitigated some of the worst parts of being enslaved, allowed drivers to outlive their peers, and pushed drivers to accept the structures of power and coercion that served planters' interests. But mainly, enslavers made the driving system work by subjecting drivers to relentless surveillance and brutal discipline. Drivers thus found themselves trapped at the center of the very labor system they were forced to uphold.

The Plantation's "Life and Soul"

At the height of Atlantic slavery, in the late eighteenth and early nineteenth centuries, everyone involved understood that plantation production relied on drivers. As the owner of one plantation in Saint-Domingue advised his resident managers in 1778, "Good order in the *atelier*," or gang, "depends absolutely on the intelligence, good conduct, activity and firmness of the *commandeurs*," or drivers.[7] Two and a half decades later, a planter in Guadeloupe agreed that the "success" of a plantation "always depend[ed]" on its drivers, who were the plantation's very "soul."[8] Other enslavers, from the British Caribbean to the United States, similarly described the driver as "the most important negro on the plantation" and "the most important personage in the slave-population."[9] As one Jamaican slave owner saw it, "Next to a good overseer, the welfare of a plantation depends mainly on a good driver."[10] Consequently, "*the head driver*" was, as another Jamaican planter put it, "the man responsible for all."[11]

During the early years of the Atlantic plantation complex, however, managerial structures were simple, and there was little need for low-level supervisors like drivers. In the early sixteenth century, sugar production on both sides of the Atlantic generally involved relatively small landholdings where a few dozen or so enslaved laborers worked directly under their enslavers. Even as the scale of production expanded and the locus of sugar production shifted from São Tomé (an island in the Gulf of Guinea, off the Central African coast) to northeastern Brazil, sugar was normally cultivated by small groups of enslaved workers owned by individual farmers or sharecroppers. Once harvested, sugar from multiple estates was transported to centralized mills (*engenhos*) where other enslaved laborers— under different ownership—processed it.[12]

Even during this early period of Atlantic slavery, enslaved and free Africans were sometimes given important supervisory roles. In the seventeenth-century transatlantic slave trade, England's Royal Africa Company used captive African men and women as "guardians" during the Middle Passage to supervise and discipline other captives.[13] In early colonial Brazil, sugar planters employed African men to oversee the complex industrial process of turning raw sugarcane into refined sugar. This included a figure known as the sugar master (*mestre de açucar*), a sort of foreman in charge of the boiling house and the specialized laborers who worked there.[14] In using enslaved laborers for such important roles, enslavers displayed their confidence in the managerial skill of enslaved Africans and pioneered the use of slave labor for specialized, supervisory tasks.

The position of driver itself was created by the rise of a new kind of plantation in seventeenth-century Barbados.[15] There, English planters built on Brazilian precedents and revolutionized the production of sugar by building their own mills, combining for the first time the growing and manufacturing processes.[16] The "integrated" plantations they established in the second half of the seventeenth century were larger and more industrial than previous ones there and elsewhere. By about 1680, planters thought an ideal plantation consisted of some two hundred acres of land, two or three mills, and a hundred enslaved laborers.[17] One consequence of what has often been called the "sugar revolution"

Figure 1. A driver, carrying a long whip, supervises enslaved laborers preparing
a field for the planting of sugar. This idealized view of plantation labor, devoid
of violence and with field laborers fully clothed, was based on a drawing
made by a British artist who worked as a plantation overseer and perhaps
attorney for several years in early nineteenth-century Antigua. "Digging, or
Rather Hoeing, the Cane-Holes," hand-colored aquatint in *Ten Views in the
Island of Antigua . . . From Drawings Made by William Clark . . .* (London:
Thomas Clay, 1823). Paul Mellon Collection, Yale Center for British Art.

was the rise of new methods of labor management that would transform the way
enslaved laborers worked and were supervised.

Around the same time that English planters shifted away from using white
indentured servants and embraced African slavery, they developed a new model
of labor organization by dividing enslaved field workers into multiple work units
or "gangs." To supervise, manage, and coerce those gangs, planters increasingly
turned to enslaved people they came to call drivers, adopting a term until then
used to describe people who drove working animals.[18] Under the gang system,
field laborers worked from sunup to sundown—and during harvest season, well
into the night—at the same collective task under the constant supervision of
drivers. With military-like discipline, drivers stood where they could observe the
gang and threatened, cajoled, and whipped the people below them to work in

unison at monotonous, back-breaking tasks assigned by the plantation managers or overseers immediately above them.[19]

The gang system soon became the standard form of labor organization on plantations throughout the Caribbean and beyond because planters found it profitable. It proved to be an effective way of coercing large numbers of people into providing the maximum amount of labor, of synchronizing the complex tasks involved in the production of sugar, and of supervising field laborers at low cost.[20] As sugar cultivation spread to other colonies and came to dominate the Caribbean economy by the early eighteenth century, so, too, did the gang system. While some enslaved people—especially on estates that produced other crops, like coffee—worked under the task system, where people were assigned individual daily tasks and were allowed to leave the field once their tasks were complete, the gang system remained paramount. Even where the task system dominated, moreover, such as the rice plantations of the Carolina Lowcountry, drivers were ubiquitous.[21]

As a result, by the early nineteenth century most enslaved people in the Americas worked on rural plantations under the driving system. In the Caribbean, plantations typically had something like one driver for every fifty to seventy-five slaves. Small plantations (by Caribbean standards) like Berbice's Woordsburg coffee estate—with just seventy-six enslaved people—might have a single driver.[22] The largest, like the Best and Phoenix sugar plantation in Demerara, had more than five hundred enslaved people and six or more drivers.[23] Most Caribbean plantations had between one hundred and three hundred and fifty enslaved laborers and two to four drivers.

Field laborers were usually organized into three basic gangs, based on their age, physical condition, and perceived labor capacity. Enslavers expected everyone in the same gang to keep the same pace. Each gang worked under the supervision of one or more drivers, depending on its size and the specific tasks assigned. Head drivers, who had the most experience, normally supervised the first gang, also known as the "Great Gang," "strong gang," or "working gang." The first gang was composed of the most able adults who could do the most physically demanding and important labor, such as digging holes to plant sugarcane and, during the harvest, chopping the cane with razor-sharp "bills" or cutlasses. More junior drivers—sometimes called second drivers—normally supervised the second, or "middling," gang, made up of adults who were too young, too old, or too weak to do the hardest tasks.[24]

Beyond the field, enslaved people assigned to trade work also labored under drivers or enslaved supervisors often called "heads." A "head carpenter" or "first carpenter," for example, supervised the other carpenters on the plantation. Large plantations employed significant numbers of enslaved tradespeople, primarily as carpenters, coopers, masons, and, on sugar estates, as sugar boilers and rum distillers. Senior tradespeople were, like field drivers, recognized as labor supervisors and sometimes known as "officers," rather than common field laborers. Sometimes, an enslaved person might hold overlapping roles, such as a boiler who worked as a driver out of crop season or a man who was both "head carpenter and driver."[25]

Although the first and second gangs were normally supervised by male drivers, most of the field workers in those gangs were enslaved women. This gendered division of labor resulted from white plantation authorities' belief that only men were suited to supervisory roles, including the position of driver. Men also enjoyed a near monopoly on trade work and specialized tasks associated with the manufacture of sugar and rum. By one measure, enslaved women on British Caribbean sugar plantations accounted for only 7 percent of tradespeople. Women were excluded from most skilled trades other than sewing, midwifery, and washing, and consequently they worked mainly in the fields or at domestic tasks.[26]

Nevertheless, a surprising number of enslaved women worked as drivers. Female drivers primarily supervised the "small gang," "grass gang," or "children's gang," made up of children between about six and fourteen years old. Such children performed comparatively light work under the supervision of an older enslaved woman sometimes known as the "driveress."[27] On the Mesopotamia sugar plantation in Jamaica, for instance, female drivers supervised a "grass gang" or "third gang" of between thirteen and thirty-eight children, aged six to sixteen.[28] Enslaved children weeded around cane plants, threw manure into cane holes as fertilizer, and cut grass for livestock—work that helped make Caribbean plantations productive and profitable.[29]

As drivers in charge of children just beginning to enter their working years, female drivers also played an essential role in acculturating enslaved children to the intensity of plantation labor. Enslavers believed that as soon as they were old enough, enslaved children needed to be forced to work so that they could be molded into industrious, compliant laborers. As Robert Renny put it in his *History of Jamaica* (1807), children needed to be supervised by a "careful old woman" and given "gentle exercise . . . to preserve them from habits of idleness."[30] Planter David Collins similarly argued that if such children were not put to work, they would "escape from their nurses, and employ themselves in mischief, such as in breaking canes, or pilfering from the absent negroes, or in setting fire to their houses."[31] A sugar planter from Guadeloupe explained more explicitly how female drivers were expected to shape children into enslaved laborers. It was their job to teach the children under their care "how to perform all their duties well," to "stimulate the quick-witted to make the effort to conform," to "instruct them to obey orders without question and to resist bickering among themselves." Female drivers thus played a crucial role, the planter stressed, as "authority figures" responsible for shaping children "into either good or bad subjects."[32]

In short, female drivers like Madeleine Spencer, the fifty-four-year-old "Driver [of the] little Grass Gang" on a sugar estate in St. Lucia, or Sylvia, the thirty-eight-year-old "Driver of [the] Small Gang" on a Demerara sugar plantation, were expected to show enslaved children what it meant to be an enslaved worker.[33] They were supposed to teach children how to work with sugar, coffee, or whatever crop was grown on the plantation where they lived; to work collectively at a certain pace; to respect official authority figures; and to avoid punishment by obeying orders.[34] As Jamaican slave owner Thomas Roughley explained, a woman appointed "to superintend, instruct, and govern" the "gang of pupils," as he liked to imagine the children's gang, should be "armed with a pliant, serviceable twig," whose primary purpose was "to create dread." When such children turned twelve, they would be "fit subjects to be drafted into the second gang, going on thus progressively from one gang to the other, till they [were] incorporated with the great gang."[35] In describing the planter's ideal of the female driver, Roughley and other writers ignored the possibility that such enslaved women may have also taught the children they supervised how to subvert enslavers' orders in subtle enough ways to avoid drawing attention.

Enslaved women also sometimes worked as drivers in charge of adult laborers in the second and first gangs. Surviving work logs from especially well-documented plantations in Barbados, for instance, reveal that enslaved women sometimes supervised their own sub-gangs carved out of the first gang. On the Prospect sugar plantation in 1785, between seven and twenty-two laborers—probably adult women—worked under an older woman named Jubar. Just over a decade later on Newton plantation, a fifty-year-old woman named Molly, the mother of the first gang driver, supervised a gang that ranged in size from six to thirty-one field laborers.[36] Scattered records from other plantation societies suggest that similar arrangements existed elsewhere. When British physician George Pinckard traveled to Demerara in the 1790s and observed female drivers armed with whips, "a gentleman of the colony" told him "that it was by no means uncommon" to use women as drivers and that, far from being "too tender" to maintain control in the field, women drivers "were sometimes particularly severe, and often corrected the stoutest slaves with no feeble arm."[37] Decades later, references to female drivers in the colony continued to appear, such as one that identified a woman named Lucy as plantation Blankenburg's "woman driver."[38]

Assessing the extent to which women like Lucy, Molly, and Jubar supervised enslaved adults is difficult because of the nature of surviving records. For the Caribbean, some of the best evidence we have for enslaved people's working lives appears to systematically underrepresent the number of women drivers. In the early nineteenth century, British colonial governments required slave owners or their representatives to register every person they owned on triennial slave registers, listing them by name, sex, and official "occupation."[39] In these records, the number of female drivers varies significantly across colonies, from zero in Trinidad and Anguilla to a handful in St. Lucia and Berbice to a large number in Barbados, where a striking 80.6 percent of second-gang drivers and 94.7 percent of third-gang drivers were women.[40] Other evidence, however, suggests that these records did not always accurately reflect enslaved people's actual work assignments. In some cases, even when women were appointed as drivers, enslavers listed them as having other occupations. Take, for instance, a fifty-year-old African woman named Asia from plantation Le Resouvenir in Demerara. Asia was listed in a registration return in 1817 as a field laborer but, according to a white missionary who lived on the plantation for several years, Asia served as driver of the "feeble gang" (probably the second gang) for at least two and a half decades.[41] In Trinidad, similarly, where registration returns do not identify any female drivers, an 1832 complaint to the colony's protector of slaves involved a woman named Marie Louise who supervised adult field laborers on a sugar plantation and was explicitly identified as "the Driver."[42]

Overall, it seems that although white plantation authorities refused to acknowledge female drivers in many of the records they created, in practice they recognized that enslaved women were perfectly capable of working as drivers. Placing women in an official position of authority—especially in a role that involved supervising and discipling other adults and even adult men— threatened their gender ideology. And yet, enslavers sometimes did so, perhaps because they had trouble finding enslaved men they thought could fulfill such an important role.[43] In such cases, practical considerations overrode sexist assumptions about women's supposed unsuitability for supervisory work. This contrast between ideology and practice helps us better understand why enslaved women's archival erasure was so pervasive.[44]

While enslavers had a clear preference for using enslaved men as drivers, gender was only one of many qualities they looked for when appointing a driver. What mattered even more was an individual person's experience, personality, and reputation. As Thomas Roughley explained, the "proper choice" of a driver was an important task that required "circumspection, and an intimate knowledge" of a prospective driver's "talents and capacity." The ideal driver, Roughley continued, was "an athletic man; sound and hardy in constitution; of well-earned and reputed good character; of an age, and, if possible, an appearance to carry respect; perhaps about thirty-five years old; clean in his person and apparel; if possible a native or Creole . . . long used to field work."[45] Roughley's fellow planters agreed with this list of qualifications. A man appointed as a driver, one slave owner wrote, should be "an old grey-headed man, selected in consideration of his good conduct, intelligence, and established character for sobriety, attention, and honesty, and the influence he possesses among the other slaves on the property."[46] Other planters said that a driver should be "selected from the others for his superior intelligence, and his general knowledge of the culture of the cane," and that he needed "to be perfectly skilled in work of every kind."[47]

Due to enslavers' preference for people with extensive experience and demonstrated capacity for leadership, most people appointed as drivers were older than the average enslaved laborer. Male drivers were usually appointed in their thirties, and many head drivers were in their forties or even fifties. Female drivers were even older, since they were usually appointed when they were in their forties and deemed to be too weak for the first or second gang.[48] And, while some planters expressed a preference for using Creoles, Africans were also commonly appointed as drivers.

With the right drivers, the driving system worked well for planters and their white employees. On any plantation there were, as Roughley observed, "so many points to turn to, so many occasions for his skill, vigilance, steadiness, and trustworthiness." That was because "the head driver manage[d] every thing on the estate." In fact, such a driver was nothing less than "the life and soul of an estate."[49]

What planters like Roughley did not acknowledge, of course, was that for drivers themselves, being tasked with making the driving system work was a nightmare. Day in and day out, that system trapped drivers between the insatiable labor demands of their enslavers and the limits of how hard the field laborers they supervised could—or would—be forced to work. Why would anyone take on such an impossible, precarious role?

Surviving the Driving System

If a man enslaved on a Caribbean plantation managed to stay alive until he was about thirty years old, he would have seen hundreds of "shipmates," friends, strangers, and kin die. How much longer, he may have wondered, can I survive?

Enslaved men who worked in the field routinely died in their early forties, literally worked to death by the ruthless driving system.[50] Those who made it into their fifties or sixties generally held positions that spared them the rigors of field labor. Usually, they were tradesmen or drivers.[51] For enslaved people trapped in this horrific world, becoming a driver—rather than remaining among the driven—was one of the surest ways to prolong one's survival.[52]

Caribbean plantations were notorious deathtraps. African captives who managed to survive the Middle Passage were especially vulnerable during the so-called seasoning period, their first few years after arrival. Their immune systems weakened by the horrific conditions of the Atlantic crossing, "saltwater" slaves struggled to adjust to new disease environments, to resist their enslavers' violent domination, and to endure more grueling work conditions than they had ever known.[53] Some planters estimated that almost half of all captives died during seasoning; others thought the average life expectancy of a recently arrived African was about seven years.[54] Modern scholarship suggests that up to a third of all captives died within a year of their arrival.[55] Children born on the plantation were also at especially high risk. In nineteenth-century Jamaica, for instance, more than half of all babies died within days of birth.[56]

Adults who survived the seasoning period and children who survived into their working years continued to suffer greatly and died at high rates, due in large part to the rigors of field work. Gang labor, especially on a sugar plantation, was more intense and more debilitating than any sort of agricultural work in early modern Africa or Europe.[57] Enslavers forced field laborers to exert themselves to—and beyond—the utter limits of human endurance.[58] Over the course of their often short lives, enslaved workers spent thousands or tens of thousands of hours working outdoors with inadequate clothing, performing repetitive motions at breakneck speed. With bodies weakened by poor diets and little rest, they dug holes, swung cutlasses, pulled weeds, spread manure, and carried heavy loads of cane, coffee, and cotton. The work they did often made them sick—by one measure, male field laborers were ill nearly half their lives.[59] It also broke their bones and tore their muscles. One study found that one in every four enslaved adults suffered herniated discs before they died.[60]

Slave labor was, as one historian called it, "killing labor."[61] That was because enslavers made the cruel calculation, especially before the abolition of the transatlantic slave trade, that they could afford to work people to death and then replace them.[62]

In a world where enslaved laborers were treated as disposable, drivers stood for their remarkable longevity. Throughout the Americas, drivers outlived other

enslaved people. Detailed demographic evidence from West Indian sugar plantations—the most dangerous places for enslaved people—shows just how much
more deadly it was to be a field laborer than a driver. A careful analysis of slave
registration returns from St. Lucia between 1815 and 1819 found that the death
rates of (Creole) field laborers over thirty years old were more than double those
of drivers (as well as skilled tradespeople and "domestics").[63] A similar pattern
emerges from the unusually extensive records of Mesopotamia, a large Jamaican sugar plantation, which make it possible to trace enslaved men's working
lives between 1762 and 1833. There, drivers lived longer than enslaved men in any
other occupational category. On average, field laborers died at the age of forty-
two, while drivers died at just over sixty.[64] Summarizing similar patterns across
the West Indies, one historian concluded that "there is no doubt that field laborers, especially those living on sugar estates, suffered significantly higher mortality
than privileged drivers."[65]

Enslaved men appointed as drivers lived significantly longer than other
slaves because their position brought an escape from the brutal physical toll of
fieldwork and because being a driver came with a range of other important practical advantages, some of which were immediately apparent from the driver's
physical appearance. On Caribbean plantations, field laborers worked barefoot
and nearly naked, saving most of their precious clothing for their nonworking
hours. Men and women alike often worked naked above the waist and wore
only basic "wraps," or what one observer described as "a mere rag around their
loins."[66] The sight of such exposed bodies was so shocking to European observers
that when artists depicted plantation labor they often represented enslaved field
laborers as fully clothed rather than mostly naked. Even against this romanti-
cized backdrop, the driver stood out. He typically wore good-quality pants, a
shirt, and even a hat and boots. Drivers regularly received larger "allowances"
of clothing—or fabric to make clothing—than other enslaved people and their
clothing was often of a better quality.[67] Some drivers carried watches to better
keep track of the pace of work. And all drivers carried the distinctive tools of
their trade: a tall staff and a large whip, which were both weapons and symbols
of their authority.[68]

For enslavers, the stark physical contrast between drivers and field laborers was part of a deliberate managerial strategy designed to create an aura of
authority around the position of the driver by distinguishing him from what one
planter called "common" enslaved laborers.[69] As another West Indian planter
advised, "principal negroes" like drivers "should receive some other clothing, not
assigned to the others," including "a hat of somewhat superior quality" and a

Figure 2. This benign representation of field labor was produced by an
absentee British planter who visited his Jamaican sugar plantation in the
early 1820s. He shows field laborers working with ease and unrealistically
well dressed. In reality, the driver, with a large staff and whip, would
have likely been the only fully clothed enslaved person in the field.
"Jamaica Negroes Cutting Canes in Their Working Dresses," hand-
colored lithograph in Henry Thomas De La Beche, *Notes on the Present
Condition of the Negroes in Jamaica* (London: T. Caddel, 1825), frontispiece.
Courtesy of the John Carter Brown Library, Brown University.

different-colored coat "as a distinguishing ensign of their authority."[70] For drivers themselves, there were also more practical benefits to such clothing. Hats
and shirts shielded drivers' skin from the blazing tropical sun; boots provided
protection against cuts, snakebites, and infection.

Drivers received many other material advantages, too, that mitigated the
extreme material deprivations of slavery. Some drivers received occasional cash
rewards, "salaries," or "gratuities," which they could use to purchase various items
or hire other people to work for them.[71] Some drivers employed other enslaved
people as their personal servants, such as a driver in Berbice who had his own
"washerwoman" or a driver in Jamaica who had his own "servant boy."[72] In Suriname, one driver had other enslaved people fish for him and work his provision
ground.[73] Scattered evidence also indicates that some enslavers allowed their
drivers to own mules and even horses—major status symbols that also facilitated
drivers' mobility and helped them conserve energy.[74]

Figure 3. This unusual image highlights the symbolic contrast between
field laborers, who typically worked in only "laps," or loincloths, and the
driver, who is shown wearing trousers, a jacket, and shoes. Detail from
William Hilhouse, *Map of British Guiana* (Demerary [Demerara], 1827).
CO 700/BritishGuiana15, National Archives, Kew, United Kingdom.

Drivers also typically had better, larger houses than most enslaved people,
both because they had greater access to cash and goods to exchange for higher-
quality building materials and because their enslavers generally wanted drivers
to be, as one put it, "better housed" than others.[75] Because they were better constructed, drivers' houses were less vulnerable to storms and hurricanes, less likely
to catch fire, and better waterproofed—in short, they were safer and healthier
places to live in.[76] Their houses were usually better furnished, too, since drivers
owned more personal property than most enslaved people.[77] The head driver's
house on Spring Garden plantation in Jamaica, for instance, "was not inferior
in comfort to the overseer's," according to the resident physician.[78] Similarly, the
head driver on one Savannah River rice plantation lived in what Frederick Law
Olmstead described as "considerable luxury."[79]

Another major factor that facilitated drivers' longevity was their special
access to food. As a rule, drivers received significantly more food—and of better
quality—than most enslaved people. Throughout the Caribbean, slaves struggled
to meet their nutritional needs, subsisting on monotonous, starchy diets that only
barely provided enough calories and often lacked essential nutrients. During envi-
ronmental crises such as droughts or hurricanes, or when trade disruptions made
it impossible to import provisions, many people starved.[80] Drivers, however, were

much less vulnerable to malnutrition and food shortages. Most planters followed the sort of advice found in plantation manuals such as William Belgrove's *Treatise on Husbandry* (1755), which recommended that drivers be given twice the amount of salt fish—the primary source of protein for enslaved people throughout the Caribbean—given to other enslaved laborers.[81] Enslavers believed it was important that drivers received, as one absentee planter instructed his resident managers in Saint-Domingue, "an abundance of food."[82] On some plantations, drivers also had exclusive access to milk cows.[83] In addition, drivers often had larger provision grounds or garden plots than other enslaved people and were allowed to raise more livestock.[84] As a result, drivers subsisted on better diets than most enslaved laborers, which helped them maintain their health.

Drivers not only survived longer than other enslaved men but were also better positioned to avoid the "social death" of natal alienation.[85] For enslaved men who wanted to establish families or sexual relationships with enslaved women, one of the biggest obstacles was unfavorable demographics. In the transatlantic slave trade, men typically outnumbered women.[86] As a result, on most Caribbean plantations there were often many more enslaved men than enslaved women.[87] And with male majorities, relatively few enslaved men managed to form long-term intimate relationships with enslaved women.[88] In this regard, drivers stood out. They were much more likely than other enslaved men—especially men who worked in the field—to live with wives and children.[89] On two especially well-documented sugar plantations in Barbados, for example, only 15 percent of male field laborers had wives, while nearly 50 percent of drivers did. At the same time, compared to field laborers, drivers had about three times as many children.[90] Even more striking, drivers were some of the only enslaved men to establish polygynous marriages. Across the Caribbean, drivers sometimes had multiple wives and established large families that reflected—and reinforced—their social status as "Big Men."[91]

The connection between drivers' comparatively high socioeconomic status and ability to maintain large, polygynous families was recognized by enslavers from the earliest years of the driving system. As Henry Drax—one of the wealthiest sugar planters in seventeenth-century Barbados—advised his resident manager, it was important to provide an enslaved man named Moncky Nocco, the "head overseer" or driver, with more food than other men because his family was so large. In an unusually explicit acknowledgment by a planter of a driver's polygynous family, Drax specified that in addition to Moncky Nocco's "own diet in the house," his allowance should include ten additional pounds of "fish or flesh," which he was free "to dispose of as he [would] think fit to his mother[,] wives[,] and family."[92] For drivers like Moncky Nocco, then, one of the benefits that came with the additional material resources they received was that they could share them with their kin.[93]

Taken together, the many comparative advantages of being a driver had profound consequences for the enslaved men who held that role. Most drivers lived less precarious, healthier, and longer lives than other enslaved people. It is easy to understand why someone trapped on a Caribbean plantation may have wanted to be a driver or at least saw it as preferable to being a field laborer, even as the position necessarily required drivers to perpetuate the same structures of power that facilitated their enslavement. Nonetheless, the driving system subjected drivers to a particular kind of existential horror.

A Cycle of Violence

The driving system made the fundamental problem of plantation production—how to get as much work as possible out of an enslaved labor force—the problem of the driver. As one Jamaican enslaver put it, the driver's "duty" was straightforward: "to see that the people [did] their work" and to make sure that they were "diligent in the field."[94] If the plantation was a machine, drivers were, as one French Caribbean planter described them, nothing less than "the levers which move the gang." Therefore, any "disturbance" in the field or "indolence" within the gang was ultimately evidence of a driver's "bad maneuvers" or "incapacity."[95]

Because they saw drivers as the key to production and security, enslavers relentlessly assessed their performance. When drivers failed to extract the amount of labor from other slaves that their enslavers demanded, they could find themselves subjected to terrifying punishments. Most enslavers believed, as one wrote, that while it was in their best interest to offer "rewards" to drivers who kept production up and maintained control, they needed to "take it out boldly on" those who did not. It was "more profitable," he reasoned, and "less repugnant to punish two drivers than a hundred other negroes."[96]

While enslavers often asserted that it was counterproductive to punish drivers for anything other than the most egregious faults, since publicly degrading a driver could chip away at the authority he needed to do his job, plenty of evidence suggests that in practice white plantation authorities routinely punished drivers for a range of supposed faults.[97] Caught between their enslavers' drive to maximize profits and the resistance of their fellow slaves, drivers thus found themselves trapped at the very center of the same system of violent labor extraction they were tasked with upholding.

Exactly how white plantation authorities set labor expectations is not always clear. They read plantation-management manuals and compared notes with other planters to see how many hogsheads of sugar, pounds of cotton, or baskets of coffee they might compel the people they enslaved to produce in a certain period of time. They measured the amount of work completed in a given day, month, or season against past performance, using various tools like tally sticks and work logs.[98] And they routinely supervised drivers and field laborers at work to see how fast or how hard they appeared to be working.

Ultimately, whatever standard enslavers set or workload they assigned became the driver's nightmare. On the ground, it was the driver's responsibility to figure out how to get that amount of labor out of the people beneath him—or else. When drivers failed, the consequences were dire. Such incidents were sometimes severe enough to make it into the documentary record, revealing some of the otherwise hidden costs of the driving system for drivers themselves.

One such case, documented in a detailed investigation by Berbice's fiscal in 1826, concerned a driver named William on a sugar plantation ironically named Friends. According to the manager, William's poor performance was to blame for a major bottleneck in production. One Monday, William supervised a gang of workers responsible for cutting sugarcane and loading the canes into the punts (long, narrow boats) that would transport them from the field to the mill. That evening, the manager checked with William to make sure they had enough cane ready to begin the nonstop processing of sugar the following day. William's gang had managed to send seven fully loaded punts of cane to the mill. There were also, he supposedly told the manager, four more loaded punts waiting in the field. Satisfied that this was enough cane to "keep the work going," the manager gave orders to start the mill early the next morning.[99]

As Tuesday morning dawned, however, no one brought any more cane to the mill, so the manager went to the field to see what was wrong. There he found only "two punts half loaded"—not even half of what William had reported the previous evening. This was "so great a disappointment," he said, that he "feared the mill would run out of canes." He had to remove some people from the mill gang and send them into the field to cut and transport more cane. William tried to explain to the manager that he had not been given enough people—there had only been seven "hands" working under him, and they had done all they could. In effect, William tried to establish what he saw as a reasonable labor expectation given the constraints he faced.[100]

But the only thing that mattered to the manager was that William's gang had not provided the amount of cane he wanted. He beat William himself and then had another man give him "a good flogging." After fifteen or twenty lashes, the whip broke. Then, William was locked in the stocks for the rest of the day. From William's point of view, he had been "unjustly punished," which was why he appealed to the fiscal. From the manager's point of view, "the estate had suffered a loss of labour" that amounted to one hogshead of sugar, and William was the one responsible. Predictably, the fiscal agreed that William's punishment was justified and dismissed his complaint.[101] For drivers like William, the message colonial officials sent by rejecting their complaints was clear: managers had the right to hold drivers accountable for the work performed by the people under them.

Four years later, a different driver on the same plantation found himself in a similar predicament. According to the newly appointed manager, when he took over he noticed that a driver, Smart, was allowing the twenty-six women he supervised to leave some "canes uncut in the field." So, "to induce him to be more attentive, he found it necessary to have him punished." Over the next couple months, however, Smart's gang continued to cut less cane than the manager demanded. Or, as the manager framed it, "Smart still persevered with his negligence." The breaking point came one Monday when the manager ordered Smart to get twenty-four punt loads out of the women he supervised, and Smart only managed to get them to cut ten punt loads. In response, the manager had him flogged a second time. Smart was, as the manager saw it, ultimately responsible for "the Indolence of the cane cutting gang." And that "indolence" was cutting his sugar production in half. When Smart appealed to the protector of slaves, complaining that he was "punished whenever the gang of women under his charge fail[ed] to perform their tasks," the protector reinforced the manager's authority to hold his driver accountable.[102] While drivers like Smart objected to what seemed to them like being unfairly blamed for other enslaved people's productivity, white plantation authorities saw the driving system working as it was supposed to.

The experience of a head driver on a Berbice coffee plantation exemplifies the desperate lengths to which drivers went to meet impossible labor demands. By 1825, Sondag, who was in his mid-forties, had been a driver for the better part of a decade, at least—a long tenure that suggests he was an effective driver.[103] But, over several weeks in the middle of that year, Sondag ran into a series of conflicts with the manager, which he described in a long complaint to the fiscal. In each case, Sondag said, the manager gave him a task that his gang was unable to complete. Sondag had good reasons for not getting the people he supervised to complete their work, but the manager did not care. Three days in a row, Sondag and the eighteen men under him "did their utmost" to clear the coffee trees of overgrown grass and weeds but were unable to get as much work done as the manager required, so the manager locked him in the stocks each night.[104]

Several days later, Sondag failed once again to satisfy the manager's demands, even though he tried several tactics. Sondag modified work arrangements to be more efficient, putting three men on each coffee bed instead of one, as before, and even forced the people he supervised to skip the customary two-hour breakfast break to get more work done. The underlying issue, Sondag tried to explain, was that the grass was so tall that the men were "obliged to chop two or three times before they cut it to the ground," which slowed their progress.[105]

Rather than accept Sondag's explanation, the manager made good on an earlier threat and called a burgher officer, who sided with him and had everyone flogged. Sondag himself received more than fifty lashes—more than the law allowed managers to inflict and an especially humiliating punishment for a head driver. After this public ritual of violence, Sondag's gang resumed weeding and picking coffee for several days, finishing their new tasks while also trying to finish their "old rows," or previously unfinished work. But there was no way they could catch up during the normal six-day work week, so Sondag took the unusual step of working his gang on a Sunday—a major violation of custom and law that could lead to serious consequences for him and the manager.[106]

When the fiscal traveled to the plantation several days later to investigate, the manager defended the various forms of intimidation and violence he used to get Sondag to stamp out what he saw as the "troublesome" gang's "spirit of unwillingness" to work harder. As was typical, the fiscal sided with the manager (whose testimony was predictably supported by the overseer). He "seriously cautioned" Sondag "against making such an ungrounded complaint for the future."[107] Drivers like Sondag thus learned that no matter what working conditions they faced or how hard they tried to solve problems, at the end of the day all that mattered to their enslavers was whether they extracted enough labor from the people below them.

As they struggled to meet daily labor demands, drivers also had to deal with relentless surveillance. On plantations throughout the Americas, overseers, managers, and occasionally planters themselves made regular visits to the field to assess drivers' performance. Typically, they aimed to see whether drivers were pushing field laborers hard enough. British missionary Thomas Cooper described one such incident in 1817 on a Jamaican plantation. Accompanied by Cooper, the overseer rode "up to a place where the children's gang was at work" and determined "that the driver was not sufficiently vigilant" in extracting work from the children he supervised. "What is the use of your having the whip," the overseer demanded, "unless you make use of it?" "Attend to them," he commanded, and the driver "instantly obeyed," flogging several children.[108]

In a similar case from a Berbice coffee plantation in 1826, the manager went to the field one morning and concluded that the gang supervised by Marquis—an African man in his early fifties who had been a driver for at least nine years—was not working fast enough. In the manager's view, Marquis was being too soft.[109] So the manager took the stick he carried whenever he made his rounds and beat Marquis in front of everyone else. "This is the way," he barked, "you are to lay it on." Further humiliating Marquis, he added, "if you are afraid of them I am not of you." When Marquis protested that he was supposed to use a whip, not a stick, to discipline field laborers, the manager called him a "scoundrel." "Set the negroes to their work," he ordered. With no other choice, Marquis began beating the others with the stick.[110]

Many drivers worked under white plantation authorities who brutally punished them for supposedly being too soft on other enslaved laborers. One such case emerges from an official investigation into complaints against the owner of several sugar plantations in Cuba. There, according to one colonial official, the owner was in the habit of inflicting such "dreadful punishments" that he drove several slaves "to the brink of despair." Some even killed themselves to avoid further abuse. Things were especially bad for the drivers, according to the testimony of one enslaved man. If a driver so much as "let up because he became fatigued" while flogging someone, "he was subjected to the very same treatment himself, with his own whip." The result, the official said, was that the drivers "were punished more than any other slave."[111] On a plantation where the owner sometimes beat people to death, it is hard to imagine just how terrifying it must have been to be a driver.

Evidence from other colonies underscores the extent to which white plantation authorities terrorized drivers so that they would in turn terrorize other slaves. When a driver in Jamaica "seemed very reluctant" to follow the overseer's order to flog his fellow driver for having not worked his gang hard enough, the overseer swore "a rough oath or two" to compel him to carry out the punishment.[112] A driver in Nevis who momentarily "relax[ed] in his exertions" during a particularly severe flogging similarly prompted his owner to explode. "You damned rascal," he yelled, "did I not order you to flog him?" The owner then threatened to punish the driver himself with a cart whip—a notoriously feared weapon that caused severe lacerations with just a few strokes of its long lash.[113] The fact that such drivers hesitated to carry out the punishments they had been ordered to inflict, despite knowing the potential consequences, reminds us that they had to be continually disciplined into the role of driver.

Drivers who could not bring themselves to act as brutally as their enslav-ers demanded risked not only being physically attacked themselves but also demoted.[114] As one former driver in Nevis, named Tomma, told magistrates, his manager demoted him to watchman because he and the manager "never agreed together." The reason, Tomma explained, was that he "did not beat the negroes for every fault," as the manager demanded, or "beat the negroes enough."[115] A planter in Martinique documented a similar series of conflicts with his driver in his diary. When he observed to the driver that the pace of work under him "was very sluggish" and ordered him "to do something about it," the driver instead "sassed him." He had his "own way of working the negroes," he told his enslaver, and was "not in the habit of killing people." For daring to assert that he knew bet-ter than his owner how to manage the gang and suggesting that violence could be counterproductive, the driver wound up staked to the ground and given fifty lashes. Even then, he refused "to admit that he was wrong" or promise to follow future orders, so the planter had an iron collar locked around his neck and then replaced him with a new driver.[116]

Given the stakes of such resistance, most drivers complied with their enslav-ers' orders when it came to inflicting violence on other slaves. As one British trav-eler to Barbados asked rhetorically—after observing that the driver was likely to be flogged for any "deficit" in the day's work—"is it to be supposed, then, that he will spare the rod on the backs of those who are placed at his mercy?"[117] Drivers themselves were quick to point out that if they wanted to protect themselves, they had no other choice. James Williams, who worked for several years as a driver on an Alabama cotton plantation, recounted in his 1838 *Narrative* that he had "orders to apply the whip unsparingly to every one, whether man or woman, who faltered in the task, or was careless in the execution of it," and that if he instead dared to spare anyone, he knew he would "feel the accursed lash" on his "own back."[118] One driver in Berbice defended himself against a complaint from an enslaved man he beat in the field (for working too slowly) by pointing out the obvious: "He himself was responsible for the performance of [the man's] work."[119] Solomon Northup, who described his work as a driver on a Louisiana sugar plantation in *Twelve Years a Slave* (1853), similarly explained that when he was given a whip "with directions to use it upon any one who was caught standing idle," he knew that if he "failed to obey" those orders "to the letter, there was another" whip for his "own back."[120] Flog or be flogged—this was the driver's dilemma.

The cycle of violence that tied enslavers to drivers to field laborers was at the very heart of the driving system. It also struck some antislavery activists as one of the most disturbing aspects of West Indian slavery. As Charles Johnston, an abolitionist who had previously worked in Jamaica as a "bookkeeper," or junior overseer, explained, even when white authorities were not physically present, drivers felt intense pressure to terrorize other enslaved people to avoid being punished themselves. When enslaved people worked, Johnston explained to readers without firsthand experience of plantation slavery, drivers—rather than the white plantation authorities to whom they answered—had "all immediate power in the field." But drivers knew that the bookkeeper was always watching, or playing "his part of the drama, which is that of a spy on the drivers" and the people beneath them. Drivers were painfully aware that, sooner or later, they would be held accountable for the work of the field laborers they supervised. So, a driver who aimed to protect himself and maintain his position had little choice but to "flog, swear, and threaten."[121]

A similar story was recounted by Irishman Benjamin McMahon, who, like Johnston, worked on Jamaican plantations (for nearly two decades) before becoming an avowed abolitionist.[122] In his *Jamaica Plantership* (1839), McMahon described a horrifying incident on the Crawle sugar estate in 1822. One day, the "cruel tyrant" of an overseer—a man "ready to do any thing to get into favour with" the planters who employed him—"found fault with" a driver named John Clark. In the overseer's view, Clark had not "forced enough work out of the gang." The overseer gave Clark "a severe flogging." Afterward, Clark walked to a pond "to wash off the blood" and then announced, "'Never mind, I don't blame busha for this; but I will know what to do—I'm not going to take lick for all the gang in this way.'" Clark then "went to the field, and took ample revenge on the poor slaves," flogging them so severely that the next morning, several of them went to the hospital with fevers and "many were entirely lame and unable to walk."[123]

Abolitionists related such accounts mainly to emphasize the horrific violence that planters forced enslaved laborers to endure. William Wilberforce and others campaigned against the driving system because of the physical pain and emotional suffering it caused for field laborers, who were "subjected to the immediate impulse or present terror of the whip, and driven at their work like brute animals." For Wilberforce, the driving system was nothing short of "truly odious."[124]

Some observers also recognized that the driving system took a terrible toll on drivers themselves. The violence of the driving system, an English missionary to Jamaica concluded, not only "degraded" field laborers "from the rank of rational beings, to the condition of cattle in a team" but also "brutalized" the drivers who supervised them.[125] In the second volume of his widely read *Slavery of the British West India Colonies Delineated* (1830), abolitionist James Stephen similarly acknowledged the widespread contemporary view that drivers were, as planters readily admitted, "*hard-hearted.*" This was a logical consequence for people forced into a role that required repeated acts of violence against other human beings. "Who can doubt," he asked, "that such must be the ordinary effect of an office, the daily and hourly business of which is the inflicting [of] pain on their fellow-creatures?"[126]

The logic of the driving system doomed drivers to fail. Drivers were expected to turn their enslavers' fantasies—productive, profitable plantations where no one resisted the labor regime—into reality. They were the ones tasked with pushing other enslaved laborers to the very limits of human capacity. They faced severe consequences when the people they supervised failed to do "enough" work. And the capitalist nature of the plantation complex meant that, for enslavers, there was no such thing as "enough."

For drivers and the people below them, the fundamental problem was that no matter how well they did their job or how hard they worked, their enslavers always demanded more. As two desperate men from one Berbice plantation explained to the colony's fiscal in 1821, there was no amount of labor that could satisfy their manager. Like other enslavers, he was "in the habit of giving uncommonly large tasks" and then flogging anyone who could not finish them. If a person somehow did manage to finish the day's task, then the workload was simply "augmented . . . the next day."[127] Five years later, a man on a different Berbice plantation bitterly complained about the same dire dynamic. "Altho we exert ourselves to the utmost," he told the fiscal, "we are flogged every day." He emphasized that "we give the manager no trouble, but he is never satisfied."[128] At root, the problem was not so much any one manager but the capitalist slave system itself.

The driver's predicament was at once inescapable and insoluble. The desperate sense of hopelessness that drivers often felt was captured in a lengthy official investigation in 1826 into a years-long crisis on a Berbice River sugar plantation.[129] A year earlier, things became so bad that some three dozen enslaved people fled the plantation to protest the impossible demands their manager made and the punishments he doled out, only to be sentenced to even more severe public punishments designed to terrorize them into producing more sugar.[130] Instead, field laborers continued to struggle to cut as much sugarcane as the manager wanted, and the manager blamed the driver, Hussar. When the time came to harvest and process the cane, the manager pushed Hussar to deliver more and more cane over several days. He threatened, complained, and punished, demanding to know why Hussar did not "do enough" to get the people below him to chop more cane for the mill. Eventually, as Hussar passed through "the negro ground" one morning before dawn on his way to the field, the manager confronted him. As he had done many times before, he called for another driver to flog Hussar. It was then that Hussar reached his breaking point.[131]

"Very well," Hussar replied. After enduring years of abuse under a manager who made impossible demands, Hussar declared that he had "taken too much punishment" and could "bear it no longer." In open defiance, Hussar left the plantation to appeal to higher authorities in a last-ditch effort to get the manager to relent. But instead of the recourse he sought, Hussar received fifty lashes.[132]

On plantations across the Americas, drivers knew that there was nothing reasonable about the labor demands their enslavers made. They also knew that no matter what material and social advantages came with their position, there was no escape from the unrelenting violence of slavery. Such was the existential horror of the driving system.

CHAPTER 2

Driving

As the coffee berries on Essendam, a plantation on the Berbice River in what is now Guyana, ripened in mid-September 1824, plans for harvesting them began in earnest. The driver, Tobias, received orders from the manager one evening about the final preparations that needed to be completed over the next few days. Tobias was to supervise the weeding of two fields, clearing the coffee trees of vines, and pruning the water sprouts. And since the work was supposedly "very light"—the fields had been weeded previously not long before—Tobias was to put only three men on each bed of trees "instead of four, as was customary." That night, Tobias made his rounds among the people he supervised. He told them what to expect the next day, and no one objected. When he went to sleep that night, he had no way of knowing that the following morning he would face a crisis.[1]

Shortly after daybreak the next morning, Tobias walked into the first of the two fields, dissected by four long rows of coffee trees, and blew his horn to call the gang to order. He repeated the previous night's instructions. Before anyone could begin working, an African man named Max objected. Like Tobias, Max was about forty years old. "Brothers, you hear the order that is given," Max called out. "None of us must go three to a bed," he insisted, "but four of us." Tobias, like other drivers, was not one to shrink from a challenge. "You stand before my face, hear me give order, and you change it," he responded. "Do you want the people not to hear me but to hear you?" he demanded. Tobias threatened to report Max to the manager. But Max remained defiant, and the other people, following his instructions, began working four to a bed.[2]

When the overseers made their rounds a short time later, Tobias had still not regained control. He told them what had happened, and they told him to march Max to the manager's house. Tobias began to do so but only made it a few paces. Turning around, he saw that he was being followed by "the whole of the

Gang—men, Women, and Creoles [children]." Tobias demanded to know what they wanted. Their response made clear their determination to stand in solidarity with Max. "Before you carry that man home," they said, "better for us all to follow you."[3] What had begun as one man's protest had become a wave of defiance.

The showdown on Essendam was merely one episode in the never-ending labor struggle at the heart of Atlantic slavery. It is now commonplace to say that plantations—or slave labor camps—were sites of brutal work, continuous resistance, and shocking violence.[4] But such generalizations, as accurate as they are, often obscure the nuances of exactly how the plantation labor regime worked on the ground and make it difficult to grasp its true human cost. One way to better understand it is to focus on the drivers at its heart. As enforcers of labor discipline and also enslaved laborers themselves, drivers found themselves at the center of coercion, resistance, and terror—as both perpetrators and victims.

The constant challenge drivers faced in getting other enslaved people—people with no incentive to work for their enslavers—to comply with the labor regime was captured by a series of records created by the British imperial government in the early nineteenth century. As part of a broader effort to "ameliorate" colonial slavery through new mechanisms of surveillance, slave owners or their representatives in several West Indian colonies were required to keep "Punishment Record Books." Those records document the various "offenses" that individual enslaved people supposedly committed and the resulting punishments they endured.[5] For nearly a decade, colonial officials compiled them twice a year to prepare lengthy reports for the Colonial Office in Britain. As officials observed, the overwhelming majority of the several dozen offenses listed had to do with conflicts over work. Enslaved laborers were regularly flogged, locked in the stocks, confined in solitary cells, and otherwise tortured for everything from "not coming to work in proper time," "bad work," and "not finishing task" to "disobedience," "insubordination," and "idleness, laziness, and indolence."[6]

These records also reveal that drivers faced a wide range of sometimes violent resistance. Among the officially categorized offenses were things like "telling falsehood to driver" and "obstinately persisting in disregarding the orders of the driver." Other categories indicate that drivers also struggled to make other enslaved people respect their authority. Field laborers were punished for "cursing the driver," displaying "insolence to driver" and "disrespect to driver," "abusing driver & resisting [driver's] authority," and "instigating the other negroes in the field to curse and abuse the driver." And in some cases, drivers faced physical threats and violence, such as "holding and tearing driver's shirt," "striking driver," "biting driver," and "raising cutlass at driver."[7]

These records illuminate—in broad strokes—just how violent the driving system was for field laborers and drivers alike. But behind every name recorded on a plantation's punishment record book, or number tallied next to a particular category of offense, were actual people with their own stories. When those stories were captured by other kinds of evidence—as with the legal investigation into the crisis Tobias faced on Essendam—they offer opportunities to see, in intimate detail, how individual drivers tried to navigate the insatiable labor demands of their enslavers and the dogged resistance of the people they supervised.

Drivers used a variety of strategies to enforce labor discipline, but what happened when other enslaved people could not—or would not—be coerced into doing the work their enslavers demanded? Sometimes, field laborers resisted overtly, explicitly questioning drivers' authority and even physically attacking them. Faced with such direct threats, how did drivers respond? There were also times when drivers decided that the labor demands their enslavers made were so unreasonable that it was utterly impossible to fulfill them and consequently worth the risk of trying to negotiate with white plantation authorities. Under what circumstances did drivers decide to advocate on behalf of their fellow slaves despite the danger? And what happened when they failed?

Work! Work!

Henry Whiteley arrived on the northern coast of Jamaica in 1832, hoping to find work as a plantation "book-keeper," or junior overseer. By his own admission, the English newcomer had "no clear conception of the nature of Colonial Slavery." Naively, he assumed it was milder than British factory labor. So, as he rode a horse from St. Ann's Bay to New Ground plantation, a large sugar estate several miles inland, Whiteley focused on the "majestic and beautiful scenery" all around him—until, that is, he "came in sight of a gang of negroes at work . . . superintended by a driver." The "disgustingly dirty work" of fertilizing canes—people carrying baskets full of manure on their heads that weighed as much as eighty pounds, shit "dripping through the baskets, and running down [their] bodies"—shocked Whiteley. But the brutal reality of the driving system made an even stronger impression. "Just as I rode past," he wrote, "the driver cracked his whip and cried out, 'Work! work!'" In that moment, Whiteley's reveries were drowned out by "the thundering crack of the cart whip."[8]

The scene that shocked Whiteley was the driver's job distilled to its raw essence: relentlessly pushing field laborers to work under the threat of violence.

The challenge drivers faced was dire. With no real incentives to offer, they were expected to turn captive men, women, and children—people with every reason to resist a labor regime that they recognized was killing them—into a compliant, organized, and efficient labor force.[9]

What did drivers do with enslaved laborers who would not—or could not—keep up with the relentless demands they faced? In part, they turned to the same tools their enslavers favored: terror and violence. One driver from late eighteenth-century Barbados, when asked how he had "the heart to strike a person so hard," explained simply: "If [I] did not beat him he would not work."[10] Decades after the U.S. Civil War, a former driver in Louisiana remembered that violence was also essential for projecting authority. "I had to whip 'em," he said, "I had to show 'em I was boss, or the plantation would be wrecked."[11] A driver's recourse to violence was so important that when the British metropolitan government forced several colonies to adopt new slave codes in the 1820s that banned the use of the whip in the field as part of a broader campaign to make slavery less physically violent, drivers continued to rely on their whips. For drivers and the white plantation authorities to whom they answered, a driving system without violence was inconceivable.[12]

Drivers have long been associated with the whip for good reason, but their use of violence was not arbitrary. Contrary to certain sensationalist accounts from abolitionists, drivers did not spend all day flogging or beating everyone they supervised.[13] Instead, effective drivers knew that indiscriminate violence was counterproductive and that they had to calibrate their use of force. Some drivers also found the pressure to brutalize their fellow slaves deeply agonizing, especially when it came to punishing their own family members. As a driver named Henry—accompanied by his wife—told his fellow congregants at a Methodist prayer meeting in Antigua, "it was a horrid thing" to have "to beat his own wife or sister." And yet "he was compelled to obey the orders of his master" and could only pray that his fellow slaves—and God—"would forgive him."[14]

Surviving evidence suggests that drivers targeted people who posed direct threats to production, including those who failed to adhere to work schedules, did not complete the required quantity of labor, or performed what drivers saw as sloppy work. Drivers thus relied as much on discretion as brute force to extract labor from other enslaved people.

The driver-enforced disciplinary regime began early each morning with a series of rituals designed to force everyone into the same rigid schedule.[15] On most plantations, drivers or the white overseers immediately above them woke enslaved laborers up well before sunrise by ringing a bell, firing a gun, or cracking a whip.

Everyone was expected to be in the field, which was sometimes several miles away, soon after—usually no later than 5:00 or 6:00 A.M. As one driver in St. Christopher (a British colony in the Leeward Islands) told officials, field laborers "ought to be at their work as soon as they could see to work—the sooner the better—in the cool."[16] There, drivers blew a horn or conch shell, or cracked their whips, to call their gangs to order. Before they issued the day's work orders, they conducted roll call. Anyone who showed up late was likely to be flogged on the spot or later that day; those who were absent would face more severe punishments.[17] The meaning of such rituals was clear: drivers expected everyone to abide by the same schedule, and anyone who did not would be forced into compliance.

Even when field laborers had good reasons for not showing up on time, drivers felt intense pressure to punish them anyway. On a St. Lucian plantation one day in 1831, the drivers were forced to punish several field laborers—mostly women—who did not show up until 7:00 A.M. In this case, the manager, supervising everyone from atop his horse, threw his "riding whip" to one of the drivers and ordered him to give each of the latecomers "three or four blows." The women "tried to excuse themselves," the manager said, pointing out that they were still nursing. But the manager had lost what little patience he had with them. It had become "impossible for him to manage the female slaves," he later whined to the protector of slaves, who adjudicated the women's complaint. "They all put their heads together combine," the manager said, "to come late to work." The driver had already flogged them "several times of his own accord," he added, for the same reason.[18] Drivers who took the opposite approach paid a heavy price, such as a driver in Berbice who helped a woman he supervised sneak away from the field to nurse her "very young" infant, only to be "punished and locked in the stocks" himself.[19] In a system where enslavers had no tolerance for people who did not comply with their rules, no matter the reason, drivers often had to set aside their discretion and compassion.

Aware that shortfalls would be blamed on them, drivers constantly sought ways throughout the workday to set a fast enough pace of work.[20] Sometimes their efforts had the opposite result, especially when the people they supervised pushed back. On a sugar plantation in Berbice, for example, a driver named La Fleur—an African-born man in his mid-thirties—tried to get a field laborer named Louis to work more quickly. Louis objected because he and the rest of the people in La Fleur's gang had "got their task fixed," or received orders to do a specific quantity of work, that morning. Louis thought he should be able to complete his assigned task at his own pace. Soon, he lost patience with La Fleur for "constantly hurrying him" and told La Fleur "that as it was so early in the day, he ought not to hurry him *alone*, as he, as well as any other, would finish the task in proper time." La Fleur took this response—from a man who not only had a lower-status job but was also about a decade younger than him—"as an insult" and immediately flogged Louis. But that only prompted Louis to "make more remarks." La Fleur eventually called four men to flog Louis again, but Louis escaped and went to the colony's fiscal, making visible one of the many ways that a driver's use of coercion to increase productivity could instead slow down production.[21]

Drivers also struggled to keep everyone at work for the entire day, adhering to whatever schedule their enslavers set. Trying to enforce arbitrary yet exacting rules while maintaining some discretion was ultimately impossible, however, and often led to situations in which a seemingly minor infraction on the part of an enslaved laborer escalated into a major crisis involving many workers. A detailed examination into one such incident on the Peru plantation in Trinidad is illustrative. One afternoon, two brothers working in the pasture under the supervision of a driver, Yeyé, announced "it was time to knock off" even though the afternoon bell—which sounded every day at 4:00 P.M. to signal the end of the workday—had not yet rung. The brothers, Dauphin and Elizé, left anyway, even as their father and a former driver, Garçon, tried to talk them out of it. Garçon "knew they were acting wrong and told them so," likely hoping to dissuade them from a risky course of action all but guaranteed to backfire. For Yeyé, things got worse when the other enslaved laborers "refused to work," taking their cue from Dauphin and Elizé, and then left the pasture. When Yeyé told the manager what had happened, the manager saw that it was still several minutes before 4:00 P.M., confirming that everyone had abandoned their work before quitting time. Yeyé accompanied the manager in his search for Dauphin and Elizé and found them at the overseer's house. When the manager asked "whether they were the first to leave the field," they "replied in an insolent Manner 'Oui Monsieur.'" At that point, the manager decided to seek additional help and rode his horse to the local commandant, perhaps because he wanted to subject Dauphin and Elizé to a more severe punishment than he was legally authorized to inflict, or maybe because he feared things would escalate futher without some kind of official backup. He complained to the commandant that Dauphin and Elizé had "set the example to the rest of the Gang to leave off work contrary to orders."[22]

The commandant's investigation underscored the extent to which individual resistance to the labor schedule drivers had to impose could generate bigger problems. Dauphin justified his actions and incited other enslaved people on the estate to resist en masse. He insisted it had indeed been 4:00 P.M. when he left the pasture, as indicated by the bell toll on another plantation, and that he left because "he felt hungry" and "his stomach was not the stomach of the other negroes." He denied having told the others to follow him and became increasingly agitated, "speaking with too much violence" while the commandant "reproved" him for his language. Dauphin "said with a loud voice, that he would die sooner than give up his right." He continued "to behave with increased violence and insolence." More problematic for Yeyé and the manager, Dauphin's "conduct" was "much approved by the Gang," who had "assembled outside the Peru house" to support him. At this point, Yeyé was called upon to help deal with Dauphin and restore order. Before long, "the noise and uproar became so great" that the commandant ordered Yeyé to lock Dauphin in the stocks. Later, Dauphin would receive twenty-five lashes for "gross insubordination" (Elizé "manifested regret" and was "dismissed with a reprimand").[23] For Yeyé and the enslaved laborers he supervised, the message was clear: disobeying a driver's orders was an attack on the entire plantation regime—and would be punished accordingly.

Throughout the workday, drivers aimed to complete whatever quantity of work their enslavers demanded by closely supervising the people below them and cajoling, threatening, or whipping all they determined were not working as hard or as fast as they could. Problems setting the right pace of work were inevitable because the gang system relied on the assumption that everyone in the same gang was physically able to work at the same pace and intensity—an assumption that even planters sometimes admitted was a fantasy. According to Barbadian planter William Dickson, for example, a major disadvantage of gang labor was that an "*equal* task must be performed, in *the same time*, by a number of people who, it is *next to impossible*, should all be *equally strong* and dexterous." And while a driver was sometimes "obliged," Dickson continued, "to set such negroes, as cannot keep up with the rest, to work, in a separate corner, by themselves," drivers "too often first trie[d] the effect of flogging."[24] Henry Whiteley similarly observed drivers in Jamaica "march up to those who ha[d] fallen back in their work, and flog them on to further exertion."[25]

Under pressure to make everyone work in unison, drivers found themselves in the difficult position of having to differentiate between people who deliberately worked at a slower pace and those who could not work any faster due to physical debility or illness. Or, as the abolitionist James Stephen put it, drivers had to contend with the "frequent impossibility of distinguishing between real and pretended incapacity for labour," especially when an enslaved person said he or she was sick.[26] But because drivers would ultimately be held accountable for incomplete work on their watch, they had strong incentives to treat people who claimed to be sick as malingerers and coerce them into working. Doing so, of course, risked punishing someone who was legitimately ill and thus incurring the anger, and possible insubordination, of the very people whose cooperation a driver needed.

Such dynamics were at play one morning on the Mon Repos sugar plantation in Demerara when the driver, L'Amour, was approached by an enslaved man named Joe who said he had a fever. L'Amour told Joe—who had done "very little work" by that point—that "there was nothing the matter with him." He ordered Joe to get back to the trench he was supposed to be digging. Instead, Joe "remained talking upon the dam." L'Amour "begged him" once again to do his work because he "knew he was not sick," but Joe still refused to dig. Eventually, L'Amour had a teenager take Joe to the manager, with instructions to report "that Joe had trifled all the morning away & now pretended to be sick." The manager had the overseer lock Joe in the boiling house's "Brick Cell" until the following morning. After his release, Joe went to the protector to file a complaint against the driver. Strategically, he claimed that the manager was "kind" to him and the others on the estate, "but all this punishment is caused by the Driver L'Amour who tells Manager stories about us."[27]

On the same day that L'Amour confronted Joe, he had already dealt with another challenge when a different man could not finish his work because, the man claimed, the task was unreasonable given the conditions. Allick had been assigned to dig a parapet alongside a trench but only managed to complete half of his task ("3 roods, 2 shovels deep"). He insisted it was not his fault—a justification drivers frequently heard. "The mud was so soft," Allick later explained, "that as fast as I threw it up it fell back into the trench again. I did my best but was not able to do more." L'Amour, however, did not believe him or did not care. Besides Joe, the other field laborers seemed to have no trouble completing their work, so L'Amour apparently blamed Allick rather than the difficulty of the task itself. He locked Allick up in "the dark house" for the night and reported him to the manager, who gave L'Amour orders to flog him the next day before sending him back to work.[28]

Drivers could afford little patience for people who could not keep up, even when it came to women who were pregnant. Take, for instance, the conflict between a driver named José Raymond and an enslaved woman named Anne on Trinidad's La Soledad sugar plantation. Anne was working in the mill when José Raymond came and "told her the work she was doing was not enough." She responded that "she could not do more because she was not well" and was also five months pregnant. José Raymond reacted by beating and kicking her, which caused her "great pain." Was he indifferent to Anne's plight? Did he see her explanation as insolence? Or did he have orders from the manager not to make any accommodations for people who were sick or pregnant? Such behavior on the part of drivers inevitably provoked a response, thereby interrupting the work routine, and when an enslaved mason, Juan Joseph, intervened, telling José Raymond to stop kicking Anne because she was pregnant and "he might hurt her," José Raymond turned on him. He "began to curse" Juan Joseph's "father mother &ca," and when Juan Joseph told him "that he ought not to curse people in that way," José Raymond grabbed him by his shirt collar "and said he was going to beat him." The two had a "scuffle," and after José Raymond "succeeded in throwing [Juan Joseph] down," he went to the manager. The manager backed his driver, blaming Juan Joseph for having "commenced the row" and "abused the driver," and had him flogged. Anne's own appeal to the manager also backfired. He "ordered the Driver to put her in the stocks and gave her three blows with his fist on the head," she said. When Anne and Juan Joseph later went to the protector, their complaints were dismissed a second time, though the protector did warn José Raymond "that he must not take the Law into his own hands, and in future not to slap the women's faces."[29] To judge by these reactions, it appears that José Raymond lost all around: he jeopardized his authority among the enslaved laborers working under him and compromised his status with the protector.

As the previous cases demonstrate, drivers generally tried at first to handle problems that arose during the workday on their own. Savvy drivers knew that it if they reported too many problems to white plantation authorities they would be seen as ineffective. Nevertheless, they often found it necessary to report people who did not complete their work or otherwise challenged them to white authorities.

This was the strategy a female driver named Joan used one Saturday on plantation Prospect in Berbice to deal with a nineteen-year-old woman named Venus, who finished only about a third of the work she had been ordered to do. Everyone else Joan supervised had completed the fourteen beds they had been assigned, but Venus only did five. Why, Joan asked Venus, did you not finish your work? Because I "was not able," Venus replied. Unwilling to accept such a perfunctory excuse, perhaps because of how other people within earshot might interpret it, Joan reported Venus to the manager. He, in turn, ordered Venus to go to the "sick house" until a doctor could examine her. When she resisted being confined there and fought the sick nurse, the manager sent her to town so that she could be locked in the "barracks," or jail, because it was "not safe to keep her on the plantation."[30] Drivers like Joan recognized that reporting troublemakers to higher-ups could both shift the blame for shortfalls away from drivers to the people they supervised and help them reassert their authority by publicly demonstrating their ability to mobilize the disciplinary power of the plantation regime.

Drivers also had to deal with enslaved laborers who tried to leave work early by tricking them into thinking they had finished their task. Late one afternoon on a sugar plantation in Berbice, the driver of the women's gang, Louis, noticed something strange. The women had been cutting sugarcane and stacking it in individual cords so that Louis could monitor each person's progress. At some point, the sticks marking the size of a woman named Margaret's cord had been moved, by which "the measurement was altered," essentially reducing the quantity of cane Margaret needed to cut. Louis's investigation revealed a complicated explanation for the moved sticks that implicated Margaret's husband, Curry. For most of the day, Curry had worked with the men's gang, planting sugarcane in a different location. He managed to finish his task around 4:00 P.M., at which point he decided to "assist his wife, so that she might go home and cook his victuals." Margaret had struggled all day, working more slowly than the other women, and the sun would soon set. Curry carried the canes that Margaret cut and stacked them in her cord, but at some point, Louis realized that he had also moved "the sticks in order to reduce the size of the cord" by two feet.[31]

Louis must have been worried about being punished for not delivering the quantity of cane the manager expected, so he threatened to report Curry to the manager. But "Curry said he did not care a d—n for the manager—That the manager and the drivers were trying to kill him." Of course, Curry was not wrong: work on a Caribbean sugar plantation was indeed, as one historian called it, "killing labor."[32] Nevertheless, Louis and another driver who overhead Curry refused to tolerate what they saw as insolence and reported Curry to the manager, who immediately had him flogged. When Curry appealed to the protector and claimed he had been "unjustly punished," the drivers testified against him. So, too, did the manager, who explained that Curry had been punished for "insolence to superiors" and "cheating" the driver out of the work his wife had been ordered to do. Predictably, the protector dismissed Curry's complaint, thus reinforcing the drivers' authority.[33]

For drivers, getting the day's work done meant not only making sure that everyone under them stuck to the schedule and finished the entire task but also that work on their watch was done correctly. Drivers knew that at some point overseers, managers, or planters themselves would inspect the work, and if it was sloppy, drivers would be held accountable. In this precarious position, drivers therefore had to be exacting in enforcing quality standards. On one Trinidad sugar plantation, a driver named Orion took issue with the work of an enslaved woman, Felicité, during his inspection in the field. Orion pointed out some weeds that had not been cleared—a routine part of the driver's job—and the issue might have ended there, but Felicité "told him it was not in her task." They began to argue, and ultimately Orion "struck her in the face and pushed her down and then put her into the lock up house [for] four days."[34] A driver named Daniel, on plantation Overyssel in Berbice, faced a similar problem when he noticed that the men he had ordered to clean the canal dams had done it "in such a careless manner." Daniel ordered them "to do it over again," but one of the men said "he would not do it over on any account." When he refused again, even after Daniel emphasized the "necessity" of redoing the work, Daniel reported him to the manager for "disobedience and Insolence."[35]

A similar conflict developed on a different Berbice plantation, Utile et Paisible, when the driver, Pitt, "found fault with" an enslaved man named James "for not paying attention to his work." James cut six of the twelve beds of cane he had been assigned that day but left several canes on the beds uncut. So, Pitt ordered James to go back and cut those that remained. James later claimed that he told Pitt he would return and cut them after he finished all twelve beds, but Pitt ordered him to do it "at once," threatening to report him to the manager if he did not, at which point he complied. Pitt, however, said that James refused outright to cut the canes and that even when he cut them himself and tied them in a bundle to help out, James did not obey his order to carry the canes away. James "not only refused," Pitt added, "but became so very abusive, that he reported his conduct to the manager." James was confined overnight and flogged the next morning "for not doing good work & for Insolence to the driver." Afterward, when the manager denied James's request for a pass to go to the protector—telling him to wait until the next day, when he was headed to town himself—James became "very outrageous," according to the manager, and then "ran off." Following the manager's orders, Pitt chased after him, brought him back to the plantation, and locked him in the sick house stocks.[36]

Due in part to the disruptions and slowdowns that their struggles with field laborers created, drivers faced a constant struggle in trying to make plantations productive. With calibrated acts of violence and strategic appeals to white plantation authorities, savvy drivers nevertheless managed to get other enslaved people to do the work their enslavers demanded. In doing so, they reinforced the structures of power and coercion that made plantation production possible. Yet their situation was so volatile that small flames of labor resistance could quickly spread into larger, more dangerous conflagrations.

Managing Insubordination

In some cases, enslaved field laborers openly defied drivers with egregious acts of insubordination. Enslaved people tried to organize collective resistance, insulted drivers with insolent speech, threatened them with violence, and sometimes went so far as to physically attack them. Skilled drivers presumably knew that it was wise to choose their battles and turn a blind eye to certain acts of defiance. Some threats, however, prompted drivers to take decisive action, and those were the kind of conflicts that made it into the archival record.

For drivers faced with blatant insubordination, the stakes were high. If they tolerated people who refused to respect their authority, they would look weak and thus find it next to impossible to get the people they supervised to obey their orders, thus risking their position. At the same time, one of the most effective strategies drivers used to reassert their authority—enlisting the support of white plantation officials—carried its own risks. For plantation managers, a driver who sought help disciplining troublemakers could easily be seen as incompetent. How, then, could drivers respond to insubordination in ways that both reasserted their authority over the people below them and maintained the confidence of the people above them?

One obvious form of insubordination that drivers knew they could not ignore involved field laborers who tried to organize collective resistance. Take, for instance, the case of an enslaved man named Welcome on the coffee plantation Vryberg in Berbice. According to the fiscal's investigation, Welcome—a Berbice-born man in his early thirties—was "a riotous insubordinate character, and was always the head man when anything was going on on the estate." In short, Welcome was exactly the kind of person who created problems for drivers. Most recently, "Welcome was endeavouring to persuade the other negroes that they had too much work given to them" and should push back. If Welcome succeeded, the drivers would have a major crisis on their hands. Dealing with a single troublemaker was one thing; trying to crush a strike or prevent a mass desertion on a plantation with some one hundred and seventy enslaved laborers was a much more difficult and dangerous problem. So, the drivers lost little time in reporting Welcome to the manager.[37]

He took the threat seriously. Perhaps worried about the drivers' ability to deal with Welcome, he took matters into his own hands and summoned Welcome to his door. He demanded to know "what was the matter with" Welcome and why he had supposedly been bad-mouthing him "for the last two or three days" as he tried to rally others. The manager also told Welcome he had heard Welcome was "a bad man." Welcome knew or guessed that the person who reported him was one of the drivers and tried to shift the blame to him. "'Well, master, if the driver don't like me, I cannot help it,'" he said. Welcome also claimed that the workload the drivers assigned was impossible. The drivers "always" gave him "double the work" he was "able to do." Fortunately for the drivers, Welcome gave the manager all the evidence he needed to conclude that the problem was not the drivers or the workload but Welcome's refusal to respect plantation authorities. Welcome declared that he "never saw an estate as bad as this." In response to this "very insolent" remark, the manager authorized the drivers to lock Welcome in the stocks and, the next morning, flog him.[38]

Drivers and white plantation authorities alike were highly sensitive to any perceived threats to their status and authority. They knew that the fragile plantation system relied on making subordinates show respect and deference toward their supposed superiors. And a driver was, as one planter in Martinique called him, other enslaved people's "boss."[39] As a result, when field laborers openly disrespected drivers with what the drivers saw as "insolence," verbal "abuse," or "impudence," drivers were quick to report them to white plantation authorities for exemplary punishments.[40]

Under the driving system, conflicts over work easily blurred into conflicts about authority. Take, for example, the following confrontation between John Baptiste, a driver on the St. Clair plantation in Trinidad, and a fourteen-year-old girl named Pauline. When John Baptiste told Pauline "to get on with her row" one day, she told him "she was getting on fast enough" and then "jawed" him "and called him names." John Baptiste dragged her to the manager for having, as he put it, "cursed him" and given him "hard words." In response, the manager had Pauline locked up for "insolent conduct to the Driver in the field."[41] A driver named Just on plantation Rotterdam in Berbice responded similarly to insolent defiance from a man named Nicil. During work one day, Nicil refused to obey an order from Just and told him, "You must be crazy." Just reported Nicil to the overseer, who went to the field only to find Nicil still "quarreling & using abusive language to the driver." The overseer, in turn, reported Nicil to the manager, who had Nicil locked up overnight. Later, Nicil appealed to the protector of slaves, only to have his complaint dismissed. Even as the protector admitted that Just had issued a problematic order, he was adamant that "nothing could justify [Nicil's] Insolence to the driver." At every level, the power of the plantation system came to the support of a driver faced with egregious insubordination.[42]

Drivers could be reasonably confident that when other slaves challenged them, white authorities would help them reassert their power. One illustration of typical dynamics comes from the Enfield sugar plantation in Berbice, where a driver named Bob enlisted the manager's support in making sure an enslaved woman named Sando was held accountable for "cursing him." One morning, Sando showed up late for work, and Bob sent her to the manager so that she could be punished. To Bob's surprise, a short time later Sando returned to the field. When he asked why she had not been put in the stocks, her explanation was meant to provoke him. She asked: "Bob, do you think the manager would kill me for the sake of you?" Bob refused to tolerate Sando's response and took her back to the manager himself. This time, the manager did order her to the stocks. Sando denied having been "insolent" to Bob, but both the manager and the assistant protector who investigated her complaint believed Bob. Moreover, they agreed that Sando needed to be punished for using "contemptuous expressions" toward the driver.[43]

As drivers knew, they could not do their job if other enslaved people did not respect their authority. So, when enslaved laborers defied them and they turned to white plantation authorities for help, drivers sometimes explicitly referenced their compromised "authority." The driver of plantation Niewen Hoop in Berbice was one of them. In this case, the driver was fed up with a man named Woensdag (Dutch for "Wednesday") who had become a persistent problem for him and the manager-attorney alike. Woensdag was, according to them, a regular deserter and a poor worker—a man whom the manager-attorney described as "healthy and strong" but nevertheless "always backwards in his work." Eventually, Woensdag and the driver got into what seems to have been only the latest of many arguments in the field, and the driver decided that something had to be done. "You are a lazy bugger," he told Woensdag, "& constantly going to the Fiscal to complain and whether you are on, or off the Estate, we don't care."[44] The driver then told the manager-attorney "what had passed in the field," emphasizing the need to hold Woensdag accountable for everyone's sake. Strategically, the driver emphasized that Woensdag posed a threat not only to him but to the plantation's white authorities, too. He reported that when he had ordered Woensdag to do his work, Woensdag had replied: "Neither you nor the overseer nor the manager shall speak to me this way." As the driver saw it, Woensdag was such a "bad character" that it would be better if he were "altogether off the property." He insisted that "if Woensdag was not punished for his conduct ... towards him, his authority in the field would be entirely done away."[45]

If the attorney-manager had any doubt that Woensdag posed a serious threat to order and discipline, Woensdag's subsequent actions confirmed that the driver was right. After being locked in the stocks overnight, Woensdag was to be flogged the next morning, but before the driver could bind him, he escaped to "the bush." A week later, he appeared at the fiscal's office and asked to be sold to another owner. If the fiscal sent him back to the plantation, he threatened that he would simply "go to the bush." Instead of the redress he sought, Woensdag only proved that he was indeed, in the fiscal's view, "a very bad character." He was sentenced to thirty-nine lashes "for making [a] frivolous complaint."[46]

Drivers also faced threats of physical violence. When a young enslaved man on a Martinican sugar plantation threatened a driver three times with a knife, the driver tried to whip him into submission. But after three lashes, the man "seized the whip and cut it in two." When the planter found out about this violent act of defiance, he had the young man given twenty-nine lashes and fitted with an iron collar.[47] A similar case was documented on Trinidad's La Soledad sugar plantation and involved José Raimond, the José Raymond who had earlier had an altercation with the pregnant woman Anne. One afternoon in 1834, when Raimond passed along the manager's orders to the cane-cutting gang he supervised, a man named Isaac told Raimond that "he would see him damned" before obeying his orders. Later, Isaac "would not keep up" with the pace of work set by Raimond, who told him "it was his duty to report him to the manager." Isaac then approached the driver "in a threatening manner," cutlass in hand, and told Raimond "that if he did not take care he would beat him."[48]

Bedoe, a driver on plantation Batseba's Lust in Demerara, faced an even more serious problem with a man named Albinus. One morning, a major dispute erupted between the enslaved people who had lived on the plantation for a long time and new arrivals who had recently been purchased from another estate. For Bedoe, the major problem was that no one would "set into their rows," or do their work. Albinus seemed to be the main instigator. According to another enslaved man, "Albinus refused doing what the driver ordered, cursed and shook his cutlass at the said driver, and said he would make him see something." Undoubtedly worried that Albinus might incite the others to violence, the driver went to the manager and told him that everyone was "disputing and idling away their time" rather than working. The manager went to the field at once, where he found "the whole of the men in an uproar" because of the "bad feeling" between the two groups. Even worse, Albinus was still "flourishing his cutlass," and the manager "feared blows would have ensued" had he not intervened. Yet even as the manager helped the driver solve one problem, getting everyone to disperse and return to work, Albinus remained a threat. He "shook his cutlass again at the driver and menaced him with threats of his vengeance at some future period."[49]

Sometimes enslaved laborers made good on such threats and physically attacked drivers, as illustrated by a violent conflict on a different Demerara plantation between seven enslaved women and a driver. One day the "driver of the women gang," Isaac, saw a woman named Patience weeding where he had not ordered her to work. He called her, but she ignored him. So, Isaac went to her and took away her hoe to try to get her to stop, but, undeterred, she began cutting the grass with a knife. When Isaac took her knife, Patience grabbed him by the waist, ready to fight. Alarmed, another driver and two other enslaved men intervened and carried her to the manager.[50] Unfortunately for Isaac, this sparked another wave of violent protest. The other women "seemed determined not to do their work." And then, when he told a woman named Molly that if he had known the others would refuse to work he would have left them with the manager rather than leading them to the field, Molly grabbed his shirt and "tore it off." In the struggle that followed, Isaac, in turn, "tore her wrapper." Later, the women—all of them mothers of young children—traveled some fourteen miles to the protector of slaves' office to protest what they said was excessive work and complain about drivers who supposedly did whatever they wanted to in the field, even punching them. They had already appealed to the manager, but he gave them "no redress." When the protector came to the estate the following day to investigate, Isaac countered that the problem was not the workload—they could "easily" complete their daily work if they wanted to—but the rebellious women. He also bitterly complained about their insulting speech, telling the protector they were "in the habit of cursing me and my family every day." The manager and resident attorney, unsurprisingly, supported Isaac's testimony, and the protector dismissed the women's complaint as "entirely frivolous and unfounded."[51]

Punishment record books from plantations in Berbice similarly document drivers' vulnerability to a wide range of physical assaults. They also provide further evidence that white plantation authorities inflicted brutal punishments on enslaved laborers who dared to attack drivers. For threatening "to beat the driver," a woman named Fanny was confined for four and a half days. Jane received the same punishment for an unspecified "assault on the driver." For "drawing his knife on the driver and making his escape," a man named Lovelace was flogged. Matilda was punished with two months' solitary confinement for "wounding the driver." And when a woman named Prudence "was very violent and seized the driver"—grabbing him, as the manager phrased it, "I will not say where"— she was confined for a month.[52]

Records from other slave societies offer additional evidence that white plantation authorities took decisive action against people who assaulted drivers. They believed in this advice from one of the first sugar planters in the French Caribbean: enslaved laborers "who disobey" or "rebel against" a driver "must be punished severely, and those who have the audacity to strike him must be punished without mercy."[53] Among the many enslavers who followed such advice was a planter in Martinique, who recorded in his journal how shocked he was when a man named La Prière not only "refused to obey the driver" but even "actually hit him." La Prière had previously worked as a driver himself, so he "should have realized the gravity of such an offense." Indeed, hitting the driver was such a "serious" act of resistance that the planter considered handing La Prière "over to the law" for exemplary punishment before deciding to instead inflict a swift punishment on his own: seventy-five lashes and an iron collar.[54] The seriousness with which white authorities responded to assaults on drivers—their first line of defense—suggest that they saw them as proxy attacks on their own authority with the potential to escalate into larger, more dangerous acts of resistance.

Drivers also faced the existential threat that the people they supervised might kill them. A 1768 "RUNAWAY" notice in Jamaica's *Saint Jago Intelligencer*, for example, referred to a man named Simon who "immediately absconded" from Spring Garden plantation after he "committed a murder upon the Driver."[55] One Louisiana driver died after the people he supervised mixed crushed glass into his food.[56] In Mississippi, two enslaved men ambushed their driver and bludgeoned him to death with axes.[57] In South Carolina, two drivers on the same plantation were murdered by other slaves in separate incidents.[58] The nature of the evidence that survives in most cases, including those above, makes it difficult or impossible to understand the context for such extreme violence. Did other enslaved people attack drivers because they saw them as too supportive of the enslavers who tormented them? Were other, perhaps more personal, motives also involved?

Other evidence shows that enslaved laborers who killed drivers sometimes did so because they saw drivers as unnecessarily severe. In one representative case, a driver on a Cuban sugar plantation faced fatal retribution from an enslaved man he attempted to punish. The story of Francisco's murder was related by his wife, María Guadalupe *mandinga*.[59] According to her, Francisco arrived home late one afternoon complaining about an enslaved man, José del Rosario, who had "sassed him." A short time later, Francisco went to find José and put him in the stocks. But according to another enslaved woman who witnessed the confrontation, José told Francisco he was "not going to the stocks" and pulled out a dagger or knife. When María tried to break up the ensuing struggle, José stabbed

her in the thigh. He then "went on to stab . . . Francisco, leaving him for dead."
José, when interrogated by colonial authorities, first claimed that he killed Francisco because Francisco was going to punish him for no legitimate reason, but
José ultimately admitted that he had he had forgotten to "fetch a bull that had
gotten into the paddock." He also said that he knew in killing Francisco "he had
committed a grievous offense and that therefore he [had to] be punished." Ultimately, José's strategic show of remorse did not save him from being hanged and
then dismembered by Cuban authorities determined to make an example out of
a man who dared to kill a driver.[60]

In other cases, too, drivers were killed by enslaved laborers who decided that
they abused their authority to punish. In Spanish Louisiana, an enslaved African
man named Pedro was accused of fatally poisoning the enslaved "overseer" or
driver Gonzalo, for having supposedly punished him not only when ordered to
do so by his enslaver but also "sometimes through caprice."[61] In Cuba, an enslaved
man named Antonio *carabalí*—fed up after having endured repeated whippings
for what he said were trifling offenses—killed a driver, Fermín *congo*, with a
machete. When the fiscal interrogated Antonio, he pointed out what seemed
to him the absurdity of having killed the driver for fulfilling one of his primary
duties. Don't you know, he asked, that enslavers gave drivers the "power" to "cor-
rect and punish" other enslaved workers?[62] And yet, in the course of doing their
job, drivers faced violent resistance and could even lose their lives.

Their job exposed drivers to pervasive threats from below. Enslaved laborers
defied their orders, actively undermined their authority, physically attacked them,
and even killed them. And yet skilled drivers developed strategies for responding
to such threats, including calculated appeals to white plantation authorities who
could be persuaded to see attacks on drivers as broader, more dangerous threats
against the driving system itself. Resistance to the labor regime thus drew drivers
and white plantation authorities together, revealing their mutual dependence
and shared investment in the authority that came with the rank of driver. In
enlisting the support of their enslavers to crush resistance from other enslaved
laborers, drivers also implicitly reinforced structures of power that were never
designed to help them and ultimately had profoundly negative consequences for
all enslaved people.

Sometimes, however, drivers recognized that no matter what kind of coercion they used, getting the people they supervised to do the work their enslavers demanded would be simply impossible. Some problems ultimately required
more creative—and riskier—solutions.

"We slaves must help one another"

Drivers worked hard to satisfy white plantation authorities, but there were times when they realized that they were doomed to fail. In some cases, the workload itself was excessive; other times, extenuating circumstances were at play. Under such conditions, the typical power dynamics of the driving system shifted. Drivers gave up on trying to meet demands from above and instead allied themselves with the enslaved laborers they supervised, taking part in enslaved people's ongoing struggle to negotiate the terms of their labor and aiming to maintain whatever authority they had among the enslaved.[63] The problem, of course, was that white plantation authorities had no interest in setting "reasonable" workloads or deferring to drivers' judgment. As a result, drivers' attempts to negotiate labor expectations or otherwise stand up for other slaves could lead to volatile confrontations. Faced with such challenges, what options did drivers have?

One strategy drivers used when given an impossible workload was simply to force the people they supervised to work all day without rest. Doing so allowed drivers to avoid direct confrontations with white plantation authorities but came with its own risks. Making people work without breaks was a major violation of custom and, in some places, of law. Enslaved laborers were also quick to assert their right to rest. The following case from a Berbice sugar plantation, Highbury, illustrates how some drivers nevertheless made people work without breaks and, more broadly, underscores the countervailing pressures drivers faced. In this case, an enslaved man named Jan Brock complained to the protector of slaves along with nine other enslaved laborers that they had "too much work." The breaking point came on New Year's Day, when a woman named Samba died and her friends and family were forced to work as Samba was buried by "strange negroes" from another plantation. According to Brock, every day they worked from 6:00 A.M. until 6:00 P.M., without getting the legally required "two hours intermission" or breakfast time (11:00 A.M. to 1:00 P.M.). Strikingly, Brock did not blame the driver, Hendrick, recognizing that Hendrick ignored the 11:00 A.M. bell because he had "orders not to let us quit our work"—orders he was "obliged" to follow.[64]

Two days later, when the protector traveled to Highbury to investigate, Hendrick found himself forced to choose between supporting the other enslaved people on the plantation or defending his enslavers. The overseers and managers insisted that the tasks they assigned were manageable and that the field laborers always had their break, but the complainants "begged to be allowed to introduce other negroes to prove what they had stated." Hendrick—who was about fifty-five years old and had been the plantation's "first driver" for at least a decade—was the first to be questioned.[65] Despite the major risk, he sided with Brock and the others, testifying that the bell was rung every morning at 5:00 A.M., that they were "in the field at sunrise," and that they had to work "though the eleven o'clock" break to make it home by 6:00 P.M. Even then, most people could still not finish their tasks. "Only the best workmen of the estate," he said, could complete their daily task. "If in the morning the manager tells me to commence *such* a field, and it must be done by eleven o'clock, when I see it is not done by that time, I force them to work through eleven o'clock," he explained.[66]

The protector determined "that there existed a misunderstanding" on Highbury and that the enslaved people there could choose to work "by task or otherwise." They responded that "they were willing to do any task work if it was given as on other sugar estates, but that their task work exceeded that of other estates by far, and that if they finished their task one day by four o'clock it was increased next day by the manager to as much as to keep them constantly at work till six o'clock in the evening." The protector "promised" he would ask other sugar planters what was considered a normal task and then "send it to the Manager for his guidance," while also warning the complainants to "behave themselves civilly to their manager, and be obedient to their superiors." Otherwise, he threatened, he would be "obliged to chastise them severely." At the same time, the protector "thought it his duty to remind" the manager "that he had no right to force any more work upon the negroes than was generally performed on other sugar estates."[67] In this case, the driver's gamble paid off: he succeeded in helping the people below him set a limit on the amount of work they could be forced to do and had publicly stood up for them, which must have encouraged them to see him as a leader.

Another strategy drivers used to mitigate impossible workloads was to find their own private workarounds. The simplest way of doing so involved reassigning field laborers from one task to another, as illustrated by the experience of a driver named Hull. One Sunday evening on a Berbice sugar plantation called Enfield, Hull received orders from the manager to have seven men dig portions of a trench in one of the fields while the other laborers cut cane. Each man was supposed to dig a section of trench measuring five roods long and "two shovels deep." Hull, who had previously been a field laborer and had worked on Enfield for more than a decade, quickly saw that this was too much work for seven men. So, he reassigned three men from another gang in an effort to make the workload more reasonable, which likely enhanced his authority among the people below him.[68]

Hull's decision, however, backfired when the plantation manager came to inspect the work several hours later. The manager "found fault with" Hull's modifications and called him a "stupid driver," trying to humiliate him in front of the people whose respect he needed, and then ordered another man to flog him.[69] Hull "begged" that he be spared, "promising" not to modify work arrangements again, but his pleas fell on deaf ears. After Hull's flogging, the manager accompanied Hull to the field, where he threatened to punish the men if they did not finish their day's work. They objected, pointing out that Hull had changed their task when "the sun was high already." The manager beat them and then flogged them the following morning. For Hull, what began as an effort to insulate himself and the people he supervised from the consequences of not finishing the day's work wound up making things worse for them all.[70]

When all else failed, drivers faced with what they saw as an obviously impossible workload were left with the risky option of negotiating with white plantation authorities. Doing so put drivers in the precarious position of openly questioning their enslavers' judgment and managerial skill. Nevertheless, it is likely that drivers were often tactful enough to persuade their enslavers to reduce or modify workloads, striking bargains and making fragile compromises that might diffuse volatile situations.[71] Such cases, of course, never made it into the documentary record. What did were moments when drivers' efforts to negotiate failed.

The experience of Samuel, an African-born driver on a Berbice coffee plantation, illustrates the challenges drivers faced in negotiating workloads and the consequences of failure. As soon as the Christmas holidays were over—one of the few times of year when enslaved people were allowed a brief respite from work to gather with friends and family—it was time to get back to work. But "some of the people were still insobriated," others were no doubt hungover, and many therefore were unable to finish "the large task" they had been given. When their owner gave them a similarly large workload the following day—and expected them to finish the uncompleted work from the day before—Samuel objected. It would be "impossible," he told their owner, to finish so much work in one day. Even Samuel himself, who was "accustomed to the field work, could not accomplish it," and he knew that the others—especially the women—could not either.[72]

Like any driver, Samuel was in a much better position than his owner to know what constituted an impossible task. About forty years old, he had likely worked on plantations in Berbice or elsewhere in the Caribbean for most of his life. His owner, in contrast, had "been but a short time in this colony, and never was on an estate before," according to another enslaved man. As Samuel later told the protector, his owner therefore knew "very little of negro work and treat-ment." Unfortunately for Samuel and the others, the owner did not defer to his expertise. Instead, he "insisted on the performance of the task given." And when the people Samuel supervised failed to complete it, as Samuel predicted, they were all flogged. Shortly afterward, in another desperate move, Samuel joined another man, Esterre, in making a complaint to the protector about their impos-sible workload (as well as their lack of food and clothing "allowances" and the constant floggings they endured). They were "so overwrought by their cruel mas-ter," they said, they were "scarcely able to keep it out" with him.[73]

Drenna, the head driver on the Berbice sugar plantation Friends, described a similar dilemma to the protector. "Sometimes the Manager gives me task work for the people to do," Drenna said, "and if I tell him it is too much for them, he says I am to go in the stocks." The second driver, Matthew, also insisted that the manager assigned "excessive tasks." Things were so bad on Friends that Drenna, Matthew, and another driver, Harry, eventually took the risk of joining more than a dozen people from the plantation when they went to the protector. According to their "spokesman," Bemba, they were not given "the time allowed by Law for food and rest during the day." They were also often forced to "feed the mill" at night after a full day's work—sometimes until daybreak—before being sent back into the field. Predictably, the manager denied that the workload he assigned was excessive, insisted he never prevented anyone from taking their breakfast break, and claimed Drenna had been put in the stocks for "having deceived" him by "passing over slaves who neglected their work." If the last accusation was true, Drenna may well have been trying to quietly protect the people under him from being unfairly punished for not completing impossible tasks. The protector dismissed their complaint and decided to make an example out of Drenna for having encouraged them rather than crushing their collective bargaining efforts. While everyone else was merely "reprimanded," Drenna was given forty lashes.[74]

A final set of challenges drivers faced when their enslavers made egregiously impossible labor demands involved the problem of punishment. Under normal circumstances, white plantation authorities ordered drivers to punish enslaved people who failed to complete their work, and drivers followed orders. But there were times that drivers viewed particular punishments as unjustified or excessive, and in such cases drivers sometimes intervened, openly or clandestinely. Either way, they did so at great personal risk.

Sometimes enslaved laborers about to be punished appealed to drivers for protection, as illustrated by an incident on a Trinidad sugar plantation in 1834. There, an eighteen-year-old woman, Johntongue, was blamed for supposedly having allowed mules into the mill. When the manager ordered her into "the dark hole," she ran to the driver and asked him to intercede. The driver went to the manager and "begged for her," and it seemed to work: the manager "said he forgave" Johntongue, and she returned to her work. But her reprieve was short-lived. Later that day, the manager ordered her into the dark hole again, at which point she apparently decided that the driver could not protect her. She left the plantation and went to the protector, who wrote a letter to the manager, "interceding for the complainant."[75]

Other cases demonstrate that drivers themselves sometimes intervened on their own initiative to mitigate the suffering of the people they supervised. One such instance was observed by Henry Whiteley on New Ground plantation in Jamaica, where a group of people were singled out to be flogged on the overseer's orders for "some deficiency in the performance of the task prescribed to them." When it came time for the sixth "offender" to be flogged, however, soon after she was "laid down and uncovered for the lash," one of the drivers interceded, and "she was reprieved."[76] In another case, a driver on a St. Lucian plantation managed to negotiate a reduced punishment for an enslaved man, Regis. The driver had followed the manager's orders to lock Regis in the *cachot* (dark hole), but when Regis was released the following day—after a painful night with nothing to eat or drink—so that he could be given twenty-five lashes, the driver paused halfway through the flogging and "begged off the other half for him."[77] Such cases rarely include enough context to know exactly why a driver would risk challenging the authority of white plantation officials to punish, but it is likely that drivers recognized that doing so was a powerful way of bolstering their own authority among other slaves.

The fact that drivers themselves were normally in charge of inflicting punishments—especially floggings—offered drivers an additional opportunity to influence the level of violence other enslaved people endured. The nature of whipping itself made it impossible to standardize its severity, and some enslavers worried about the discretion drivers had when it came to punishing other enslaved people.[78] Jamaican planter John Stewart complained that the driver's role in administering punishments allowed him, on one hand, to "maltreat and persecute, in a petty way, the unfriended slave against whom he ha[d] a grudge" and, on the other hand, to "connive at the faults of those whom he wishe[d] to favour." Stewart recognized that the driver knew that he had to "make a show, by way of saving appearances, of equal severity to both"; "but by the dexterous command he ha[d] of the whip, he ha[d] it in his power to inflict either a very slight or a very severe punishment."[79]

For drivers, being able to strategically calibrate the level of violence they used against other enslaved people enhanced their power. Some drivers took pride in their mastery of the whip. A driver in Demerara named Abraham, when called to respond to a complaint from an enslaved carpenter whose body showed "very severe marks of Punishment," boasted about the damage he could do. "I flogged him hard," Abraham said, "the same as I do others." He continued, "I can crack the whip well and make it cut like a knife."[80] What Abraham did not say was that he also had the ability to manage the whip in such a way that it caused minimal physical harm.

Sometimes, drivers' discretionary power to mitigate violence came to light. On a Berbice cotton plantation in 1821, a driver tried to spare several men he had been ordered to flog; he believed they had done nothing wrong. One Sunday morning the driver, an African-born man named Watson who had previously worked as a carpenter, was asked by the manager "if the cotton was dry enough" to gin. Watson said no, but, according to one of the men, the manager said, "Never mind." "I want the cotton ginned," he demanded, "and if they mash the seed I will cut their a––– at flog-time." The men had little choice but to gin the cotton throughout the week. They must have been anxious that their work would not satisfy the sort of manager who insisted that "he did not want forty-nine [pounds], he wanted fifty" pounds, and that "if a single seed was mashed," he did not want the cotton. When the ginned cotton, inevitably, contained mashed seeds, the manager followed through on his threat and ordered Watson to flog the men. But Watson evidently decided that he would flog them as lightly as possible, which became a problem for him when the men went to the fiscal to complain against the manager. After a routine physical examination, the fiscal asked one of them "why the recent punishment did not appear" on his body. He explained that Watson had purposely spared him and the others a more severe punishment. "The driver knows we are in the right," he said, "and therefore does not punish us by cutting us," or whipping strongly enough to lacerate flesh.[81]

A similar incident inadvertently became public when an enslaved cooper named Tommy complained to Berbice's fiscal that his owner had ordered two drivers to give him one hundred lashes—an illegal and potentially lethal flogging. The fiscal became skeptical when he examined Tommy's body and failed to find wounds consistent with such a severe punishment. While the marks of "a few lashes" were visible, Tommy's wounds did not suggest he had "been punished beyond the limits of lashes prescribed by law." When asked to account for this discrepancy, Tommy "said he had been favoured by the drivers, who threw their whips over him" rather cracking them on his body.[82]

The driver of plantation Mes Delices in Demerara was surprisingly candid about his reasons for mitigating the suffering of the people he had to punish. In one incident, the driver, Welcome, had been ordered by the manager to flog a man named Primo. When Primo complained to the protector that he had been flogged "wrongfully," the protector's investigation focused on the details of his punishment. Welcome testified that he tied Primo to three stakes in the ground and flogged him "in the usual manner with the long whip," and that he "gave him *30* lashes," which was double the legal limit at the time and thus a potential problem for the manager. Welcome flogged Primo "hastily" at first, but the "manager said I must take time." Afterward, he washed Primo's "back with rum by manager's orders." Another enslaved man who witnessed the flogging corroborated Welcome's account but noted that Primo "did not bleed very much" and that he could not even "tell if every lash hit him." This disclosure led the protector to ask Welcome if he could "swear that every time" he "cracked the whip it touched Primo." Welcome said no, the whip "did not touch him *every time*." He added: "If I had, he would not have been able to walk."[83]

Welcome also offered a remarkable justification: "We slaves must help one another."[84] Such solidarity between drivers and the enslaved laborers they supervised was, of course, exactly what white plantation authorities tried to prevent, since it posed a direct threat to the driving system upon which plantation production and their own safety depended.

When drivers determined that the workload they had been given was utterly impossible, they faced a crisis. To avoid being punished or even demoted, drivers had to satisfy the labor demands of white plantation authorities. At the same time, they knew there was only so much labor they could squeeze out of the people below them. When drivers realized they could not simply enforce orders from above, the ordinary dynamics of the driving system broke down. Under such circumstances, drivers had to choose from a range of bad options. Renegotiating labor demands or trying to mitigate the violence other enslaved people endured were likely to enhance drivers' authority within the slave community, but they also jeopardized drivers' relationships with the white enslavers upon whom they relied for their position and, sometimes, for protection. Drivers' struggles to resolve such crises in ways that would allow them to maintain their own authority—and the price they paid when they failed—deepen our appreciation of just how impossible the driver's position was.

The challenges drivers faced as labor supervisors and the strategies they used to respond to them are encapsulated in the crisis on the Essendam coffee plantation, which began with Max's defiance in the field that morning in September 1824 and culminated in an uprising that night. The driver, Tobias, had been ordered to increase the workload beyond what was customary. Tobias may have anticipated that some people would object, but he also knew that trying to renegotiate the workload with the manager posed its own risks. So, he tried to carry out the manager's orders only to face an immediate challenge when Max led the rest of the gang in protest.

Later that morning, Tobias managed to get everyone back to work, postponing the moment of reckoning until that evening. Around 5:00 P.M. he blew his horn to signal all the enslaved laborers to bring their customary bundles of grass for the plantation's mules. When everyone assembled along the brick path at the center of the plantation buildings—men on one side, women on the other—Tobias and the manager were ready to respond to the day's unrest. They tried to contain the problem by individualizing it. Tobias told the manager that Max was the "ringleader." The manager ordered Tobias to lock Max in the plantation hospital's "dark hole." But this strategy did not work. As soon as Tobias grabbed Max by his "lap" to lead him to the hospital, "the whole gang men and women encircled the drivers and wished to release Max by force." As with their collective action in the field that morning, their defense of Max made clear that the problem was bigger than one troublemaker—and that they were united.[85]

What followed was a violent melee. As Max "wrestled" with the drivers to free himself, another man "pulled off his shirt," "threw himself in the attitude of boxing," and then "seized hold of one of the drivers" as they tried to drag Max into the hospital. The rest of the gang joined the struggle, pushing, pulling, and "using very abusive and threatening language" as they tried to liberate Max. At the same time, they showed remarkable restraint. There were more than two hundred enslaved laborers on Essendam and, had they chosen to, they could have easily overpowered and killed the drivers, overseers, and manager.[86] And yet, their protest did not become a bloodbath, let alone a full-fledged rebellion.[87]

When the exasperated manager, after finally managing to lock Max up along with another particularly rebellious man, asked the others what they wanted, they were clear. "We will all be locked up," they insisted. The manager told them there was "no room" for all of them. They replied that they would then "all go to Town and bring the Fiscal tomorrow on the Estate." Some sixty or seventy of them left Essendam immediately, but rather than going to the fiscal they went to the plantation's attorney, surprising him at his home around midnight. They complained that "the manager had given them more Work than they were accustomed to"; they skipped over their defiance of the drivers and their efforts to prevent Max from being punished. Meanwhile, the manager went to a militia captain for help. The following day, after a brief investigation of his own, the captain decided that the gang's "outrageous and insubordinate" behavior was serious enough that the fiscal himself needed to get involved.[88]

The fiscal, unsurprisingly, was determined to punish all involved in the "disturbance." "Their conduct," he announced to the entire slave population on Essendam, "was highly censurable in two respects." First, they had defied the driver's orders in the field and consequently failed to perform "a certain quantity of Labour," and, second, they had behaved "in a riotous disorderly and disobedient manner" when Max had been ordered into the hospital. Like Tobias and the manager, the fiscal focused on the leaders of the uprising, beginning with Max. He had "assumed to himself the authority of disputing the orders given to the gang by the Manager and intimated to them through the driver." The fiscal sentenced Max to work in chains for a month. Three other men who, along with Max, had been "the ringleaders of the tumult" at the hospital were also given severe punishments: fourteen nights in solitary confinement for two of them and two months in chains for the other. Tellingly, the fiscal also "recommended" that everyone else also be punished for having supported Max instead of respecting the authority of the drivers and the plantation's white employees. He told the attorney that he should stop distributing "the usual supply of Rum, tobacco and pipes" that served as labor incentives "until they evinced a feeling of regret for their ill conduct."[89]

Ultimately, what seemed, at least initially, like a failure of the driving system was an illustration of how drivers and their enslavers made it work even when it came under serious threat. Drivers like Tobias faced constant challenges getting other enslaved people to satisfy the labor demands of their enslavers. Sometimes they faced outright defiance, including threats to their authority and physical safety. And yet, more often than not, they managed to maintain or reestablish a sense of order, not least because they could count on the support of powerful white authorities who needed their drivers to command respect.

CHAPTER 3

Big Men

When Moravian missionaries arrived on Mesopotamia, a sugar plantation in western Jamaica, they singled out as the key to their success an enslaved man named Matthew. He was the head driver. Matthew stood out because of his openness to Christianity, but the missionaries especially valued his influence among the hundreds of other people enslaved on the plantation. The Moravians' efforts to cultivate a relationship with Matthew paid off. When, a few months after their arrival, one of them became concerned that their initial candidates for baptism were "backsliding," Matthew gathered them in his house one Sunday and encouraged them to get back on track. Several months later, the Moravians made Matthew their official "helper." As one of them noted in his diary, "He organizes the people very well."[1]

Men like Matthew were often recognized as respected leaders within the communities to which they belonged long before they became drivers.[2] As the Jamaican slaveowner Alexander Barclay explained, an enslaved man was often appointed to the position of driver precisely because of "the influence he possesses among the other slaves." That influence, Barclay recognized, was "gained, as in other communities, by meriting their respect."[3] At the same time, becoming a driver—as with other intermediary positions in colonial regimes with stark imbalances of power—offered enslaved men additional opportunities to enhance their power and status.[4]

Focusing on the ways that drivers cultivated authority and exercised leadership—while keeping in mind that few enslaved people in the Caribbean were more than a generation or two removed from their African homelands—suggests that drivers aspired to be what many people in Africa and the diaspora called "Big Men." The concept of the Big Man was based on the widespread African notion—both before and during the era of the transatlantic slave trade—that the primary path toward wealth, power, and status lay not in control of land or other forms of nonhuman capital but in control of people. Enslaved Africans in the Americas came from a wide range of societies that stretched from Senegambia to West Central Africa, each of which had its own distinct social practices and political structures. One thing they had in common, however, was the idea of "wealth-in-people."[5] In contrast to contemporaneous European societies, where wealth was closely tied to the ownership of land and other material goods, the most important and valuable "goods" in Africa were human beings. "Wealth embodied in rights in people," the anthropologist Jane Guyer observed, "lies close to the center of African economic and social history over the past five hundred years: in the slave trades on the one hand and in political and kinship history on the other." Where land was abundant and people were scarce, political mobilization and social relationships often revolved around efforts to acquire, incorporate, and control other people.[6] During the era of the transatlantic slave trade, when many African societies underwent a process of what one scholar has called "gendered Atlanticization," Big Man politics became even more widespread and more important in Atlantic Africa and facilitated some men's pursuit of power.[7]

African leaders historically focused on recruiting, producing, and maintaining other people—as wives, children, clients, slaves, and other sorts of followers. That is, they aspired to be Big Men. In doing so, they faced the constant challenge of attracting followers and preventing them from relocating or forming attachments to other leaders. One way they did so was to provide valuable services, such as protection, and access to desirable, often scarce, material resources.[8] Big Men also took advantage of their external connections, including those with merchants involved in the slave trade, to get "foreign" goods and services from beyond their own communities, which they could then strategically redistribute to attract and retain followers.[9]

Those followers were important for many reasons. They performed different kinds of labor, provided specialized knowledge, enhanced leaders' prestige, and helped recruit and produce additional dependents. Women, as wives and as slaves, were particularly valuable both because they provided their own labor and because they produced children, helping Big Men form extended lineages and kinship networks with large numbers of followers.[10]

On plantations in the Americas, enslaved drivers and other men obviously could not pursue wealth-in-people in the same way that they or their ancestors had in Africa. The cultural and ethnic diversity of the enslaved population gave drivers strong incentives to appeal to the most broadly shared understandings of political power and leadership, rather than try to recreate regionally specific political structures or practices.[11] Drivers' slave status foreclosed the possibility of exercising political power beyond the slave community and placed severe limits on their ability to perform some of the essential functions of African Big Men. They could not wage wars against rivals or, in most cases, enslave other people. They also lacked the authority to control their followers' labor and sexuality and had little power to protect their people from physical violence or sexual abuse, especially at the hands of white people. On the other hand, drivers' pursuit of wealth-in-people was ironically facilitated by the fact that enslaved people in the Americas were effectively trapped with one another on the same plantation—a very different scenario than in most African societies, where low population densities and widely available land generally meant that followers who were unhappy with their leaders could leave in search of new attachments.[12]

While wealth-in-people and Big Man politics, like other African ideas and practices, had to be adapted to the extreme conditions of New World slavery, they can still help us understand drivers' social relationships with other enslaved people. Two aspects of those relationships stand out. First, drivers drew on the unique qualities of their official position, especially their connections to white plantation authorities, to offer valuable resources and services to other enslaved people they hoped to claim as followers—a version of what Africanists call "extraversion."[13] Second, in spite of unfavorable demographic conditions and other obstacles, drivers worked to create large, polygynous families by seeking marital relationships with enslaved women, producing children they could claim as dependents, and building kinship networks.

Accordingly, drivers' social role within the slave community can be understood, at least in part, as a necessarily modified form of a broadly shared African political practice adapted to the challenges of surviving on Caribbean plantations. But the roles of driver and Big Man were both complementary and contradictory. How did drivers manage the constant struggle of balancing their need to satisfy their enslavers' expectations against the responsibilities they had to their followers?

Leaders and Followers

Being a driver did not automatically make someone a Big Man. Some drivers failed to earn much respect from other enslaved people, either because they were seen as too weak or because they abused their authority and came to be more feared and hated than respected. Other drivers, however, successfully cultivated strong social ties with other enslaved people and came to be seen as leaders. How, then, did some drivers leverage the opportunities provided by their official position in the plantation hierarchy—and broadly shared assumptions about the responsibilities of leaders toward their followers—to become Big Men?

Drivers who aspired to be leaders drew on their intermediary status to offer valuable goods and services to other enslaved people. They negotiated with white authorities to get scarce goods, appeared alongside enslaved complainants in court, helped enforce unwritten rules and customary rights, and took responsibility for other enslaved people's interrelated physical and spiritual well-being. Taken together, the strategies drivers used to attract and retain followers suggest that the ways they conceptualized their relationships to other enslaved people were not only shaped by the labor structure of the plantation itself but also inflected with African ideas about leadership.

For drivers and the people below them, securing access to provisions—especially food—was particularly important in moments of crisis, as illustrated by an episode on plantation Mesopotamia involving the head driver, Matthew, whose story began this chapter. In 1760, soon after the massive rebellion that would later become known as Tacky's Revolt erupted, almost all the plantation's white managerial staff left to help fight the rebels. The plantation was left in the hands of a single overseer and Matthew. In addition to trying to keep sugar production up during an island-wide war, Matthew faced a more existential threat: his people were running out of food. Rebels had apparently raided the plantation's provision grounds, and the attorney was refusing Matthew's requests to send emergency supplies of rice and flour.[14] Having exhausted other options, Matthew decided to take advantage of a strong patron-client relationship of his own and appealed to the resident Moravian missionaries. "Several" of the enslaved people on the plantation, he told them, "had not even had a bite to eat."[15]

When enslaved people lacked essentials, drivers were uniquely positioned to negotiate with the white plantation employees or slave owners who could provide them. In one instance, the members of a chronically underfed and poorly clothed woodcutting gang on the Berbice River turned to their driver for help. No clothing had been distributed for years, but the more urgent problem was acute hunger. When the woodcutters returned from the bush to their owner's plantation on Saturday evenings, they spent much of the next day reaping cassava (a staple provision) but were only allowed to take "six cakes" of processed cassava with them into the bush for the following week—a quantity that was "inadequate for their support." They "occasionally" received some salt fish but often went for several months without any. The women and children among them were in an especially precarious position. They received no "allowance" of their own and had to rely on their husbands or other family members to "share their [own] scanty allowance." The woodcutters had managed to avoid outright starvation thanks to nearby Indigenous people who "generally supplied" them with food but who were "now tired of" doing so. It was then that the woodcutters turned to Adam, a fifty-year-old African-born "Bush Driver," for help.[16]

According to Adam, he was "deputed by the gang to represent to their mistress that they were not sufficiently fed and clothed." One Sunday, before he was to take his gang back into the bush, Adam tried to negotiate with her. But "instead of affording redress," she had him locked in the stocks. When two of Adam's supporters "stepped forward" to defend him, "they were both flogged."[17]

Rebuffed by his owner, Adam had to find some other way of securing provisions for his people. One option—going to colonial officials who usually ruled against enslaved complainants—was inherently risky and guaranteed to provoke his owner, the very person in charge of distributing the food they needed. But things were desperate enough that Adam decided to appeal to the colonial legal official known officially as the fiscal and by some enslaved people as the "massa in town."[18] Like other Big Men, Adam knew that even slave owners had to answer to higher authorities.

Adam and eight other men told the fiscal, in great detail, that they had long endured inadequate supplies of clothing and food, that they were frequently subjected to arbitrary and brutal violence, and that their workload was unbearable. Their legal acumen put the owner and the overseer she employed on the spot. After the fiscal examined the owner, the overseer had to answer more than a dozen questions about provisioning and punishment before the Court of Criminal Justice. The fiscal determined that three of the major "grievances" Adam and the others put forward had been "satisfactorily proved": they had been forced, against the law, to work on Sundays, they not been "clothed agreeable to the court's ordinance," and they were "not sufficiently fed." He fined the owner five hundred guilders and the costs of his investigation.[19] Whether this punishment led to any lasting change in provisioning is unclear. But Adam had managed, against all odds, to get a powerful official to intervene on behalf of his people—a striking demonstration of how a savvy, courageous Big Man might leverage his access to external authorities to help his followers.

A similar case came before Berbice's protector of slaves more than a decade later from a remote plantation on the upper Berbice River. The enslaved people there, like many of their peers throughout the Americas, had long struggled to get enough to eat. The little bit of cornmeal the manager gave his driver, Abram, to distribute was supposed to be supplemented by plantains purchased from another plantation, but the punt that delivered them was regularly delayed by up to three days. The consequence, as Abram explained, was that "after finishing the corn" people would "suffer at their work from hunger." Of course, this posed a problem for Abram too, since he would ultimately be blamed for any shortfalls in the output of the people he supervised. So, he asked the manager "to give them something in addition to eat." The manager refused and told Abram they would have to wait for the plantains.[20]

Soon after, two enslaved woodcutters—perhaps encouraged by Abram—traveled downriver to the colony of Berbice's capital, New Amsterdam, and appealed to the protector. They showed him "a small calabash with ground Indian corn," which constituted "their allowance for three days." The manager, responding to the complaint, claimed that the corn in the calabash was merely their breakfast—given each day during the 11:00 A.M. break—and that when the plantains did not arrive before dinnertime, he distributed additional corn. Abram, however, contradicted the manager and supported the laborers he supervised, putting his very position in jeopardy. The two men who appealed to the protector, Abram said, had "spoken the truth." The punt captain also corroborated their account, and in the end the plantation's owner "pledged himself that a better system of management should be introduced." The people he enslaved should "never be without an ample supply of Corn meal, Rice or other provisions"—a tacit acknowledgment that Abram and the others had a legitimate grievance and a customary right to better provisions of food.[21]

Drivers' ability to secure material resources for other enslaved people depended not only on the personalities of their enslavers or the whims of the colonial officials to whom they sometimes appealed but also on their negotiating skills. Those skills, developed through years of practice balancing the competing demands of their enslavers and the enslaved people they supervised, were put to the test during crises.[22] One such crisis developed on a small coffee plantation of about thirty slaves in Berbice where the longtime driver, an African-born man in his late thirties named McRae, faced an increasingly recalcitrant labor force.[23] The current problems had deep roots. For years, the plantation's enslaved men had complained, as one of them told the fiscal five years earlier, that there were "no women on the estate at all."[24] In late 1826, having "no wives on the Estate" became an especially acute problem for the nearly all-male gang when the owner reassigned the sole woman from the role of cook to picking coffee (ordinarily, enslaved men expected their wives to prepare meals and perform other domestic labor, which they saw as women's work).[25]

A man named Brutus was especially vocal in expressing his anger. On one occasion he refused McRae's order to clean the drains that prevented rainwater from flooding the fields, saying "he would not do so unless the Fiscal came on the Estate." Another time, he refused to return a borrowed punt to a neighboring planter. (Part of the problem, as Brutus saw it, was that the plantation's owner was illegitimate because he was not white but of mixed race.)[26]

For McRae, the most pressing problem was that the people under him were not picking enough coffee—and the owner knew it. Comparing notes with three neighboring planters one day, the owner found that his enslaved labor force was picking only a quarter of what other plantations' slaves picked each day. McRae knew that if he could not find a way to get the gang to work harder, he would be punished, perhaps even demoted.

To get things back on track, McRae attempted to negotiate an arrangement with the owner that would get the people below him to do more work while he simultaneously showed them that he was looking out for their interests. One evening, when the owner complained to McRae about the progress of the coffee harvest, McRae said that "all the people" were "very dissatisfied." But there were, he said, some practical things the owner could do to boost morale and increase production. First, he proposed that the owner reassign someone from field labor so that the gang would again have a dedicated cook, saving them from the time and energy that food preparation required. Second, he suggested the owner "promise each negro a dram [of rum] for a full basket of coffee" as an incentive. The owner "immediately consented" to McRae's suggestions. Three days later, everyone also received tobacco and pipes to further "animate them."[27]

The fragile compromise that McRae brokered seemed to have worked—at least at first. McRae had no doubt boosted his owner's confidence in his skill as a labor supervisor and encouraged the enslaved field laborers he oversaw to be grateful that he had got them what they wanted. But, three days later, McRae pushed for another concession. He told the owner, perhaps at the urging of his followers, that it would be good to "give them some additional fish in the field (exclusive of the usual allowance on Sunday) as was done on other Estates."[28]

At that point, the owner lost patience with McRae and decided to negotiate directly with his enslaved labor force. He went into the field and told everyone he was "determined to ask two of [his] neighbors to come and see if they could not pick more coffee." He also announced a new balance of carrots and sticks: anyone who brought a full basket would get rum, anyone who did not would get twenty-five lashes. And if they wanted "good and kind treatment," which he defined as the additional fish McRae had asked for, they would have to bring two baskets of coffee every day. How things turned out for the owner and the enslaved people on the estate is unclear. But for McRae, this must have been an embarrassment. He had tried to perform one of the essential functions of a Big Man, only to fail and be rendered irrelevant by the owner.[29]

Drivers who appropriated scarce resources for their own purposes—instead of sharing them with those in need—risked being seen as illegitimate leaders and could face strong opposition from below. In one incident, a driver named King on a riverside woodcutting estate in Essequibo fell out of favor with the other enslaved people there. Instead of distributing rum and cane syrup that were supposed to be shared among the men he supervised, King took them for himself and gave or traded the rest to nearby Indigenous people. After multiple complaints, the other enslaved people there persuaded the owner—who suspected that King had also been involved in the theft of goods from his own house—to act. He had King whipped severely and threatened to send him to the fiscal for additional punishment.[30]

Other drivers occasionally went to great lengths—and took extraordinary personal risks—to show their followers that they were trying to solve problems on their behalf. One such driver was a man named Primo, who worked on a notoriously brutal plantation in Berbice called Berenstein, which the British government purchased in 1817 to grow provisions for enslaved people working in New Amsterdam. From the beginning, Berenstein was plagued by problems, including its location far up the Berbice River. Some enslaved people were transferred there from New Amsterdam as punishment, and many people considered living so far from town "a remote & disagreeable banishment." Berenstein was also terribly managed, and tensions between the resident managers and the enslaved labor force—as well as conflicts between the managers and their employers—led to a remarkable rate of turnover. By 1820, Berenstein was on its fifth manager in three years. The current manager, J. Deussen, was widely detested. Among other abuses, Deussen forced enslaved people to care for a large quantity of livestock (including some animals he claimed as his personal property) that consumed most of the food grown on the estate, driving the enslaved population to the brink of starvation.[31]

Toward the end of 1820, Primo found himself under intense pressure both from the enslaved people he supervised and from Deussen. In November, an enslaved woman complained to the fiscal about the "extremely severe" manager and the driver who carried out his orders. According to her, Primo, "instigated by Deussen," treated them "very cruelly." There was "general dissatisfaction on the estate," and the only solution, she said, was "the removal of ... manager Deussen and the driver Primo."[32] Even though the fiscal was unlikely to intervene in response to such a complaint, Primo must have known that his situation was precarious. Meanwhile, he himself endured humiliating punishments from Deussen that threatened to undermine his authority in the eyes of the people he supervised. One day in late December, Deussen unfairly blamed Primo for supposedly allowing another enslaved man to escape and then had Primo whipped, tore his clothes, and locked him in the stocks "during the whole of the holidays." Some of the others stood up for Primo and asked Deussen to release him from the stocks. Humiliated and embittered, Primo apparently concluded that his situation was impossible. He decided to make an explicit break with Deussen and publicly cast his lot with the people below him.[33]

Soon after his release from the stocks, Primo led a group of ten enslaved people on the twenty-mile journey from Berenstein to New Amsterdam, arriving at the fiscal's office on December 29. He knew the mechanics of testifying before the fiscal, having been the subject of a complaint himself six weeks earlier and, about a year and a half before that, having appeared as a witness for a different driver in another complaint.[34] This time, he joined the others in urging that Deussen be fired. Primo himself asked that "the manager might be taken away, or that he might be elsewhere employed." Everyone agreed that Deussen was an impossibly demanding, cruel manager who did not allow them enough time to eat or rest and boasted that he could treat them however he wanted. Like many complainants, they stressed that they had exhausted other options. The multiple appeals they had made to Deussen's boss—one man had gone to him four times—had backfired. Far from being chastened, Deussen treated them "worse than before" and claimed he had "full power from the Fiscal to punish them" as he saw fit. Primo and the others emphasized that they had not made the decision to go to the fiscal lightly. As one man put it, "He never complained before" but was "now compelled, hoping that he may get another manager to live with." Several of the complainants issued an explicit ultimatum or threat: if Deussen continued as manager, one man said, "every thing will go on wrong." But if Deussen were "removed," another man testified, everything would "go on well." Another said he would "not return to the estate if the manager be allowed to remain there, preferring punishment in town to ill treatment on the estate."[35]

In taking such a strong stand in support of the people on Berenstein, Primo displayed the kind of leadership expected of a Big Man in a moment of crisis.

In the end, the complaint failed. Three months later Deussen made a point-by-point rebuttal to the charges Primo and the others had levied against him. If anything, Deussen became even more brutal after such blatant resistance, as indicated by continued complaints of horrific abuse. His "reign of terror," as one historian called it, continued until early 1822, when he was finally fired (only to be replaced by a manager who was arguably even more sadistic). Not long after that, the owners abandoned the plantation entirely. Still, Primo had shown everyone on the plantation how far he was willing to stick his neck out for the people below him.[36]

Drivers also attracted and retained followers by taking on the role of judicial authorities who handled interpersonal disputes within the slave community. Even some white observers were aware of this role. In the words of Jamaican slave owner John Stewart, "The head-men [on many plantations] erect themselves into a sort of bench of justice, which sits and decides, privately, and without the knowledge of the whites, on all disputes and complaints of their fellow-slaves." Those found guilty typically had to pay "pecuniary fines."[37] Such judiciaries may have been modeled on West African precedents, where kings or chiefs dispensed justice in consultation with local leaders and elders.[38]

Some white plantation authorities worried that these "courts" exacerbated social tensions—a concern confirmed by enslaved people's complaints about what they saw as unfair sentences—and tried to eradicate them, but they were unsuccessful.[39] Other enslavers actually legitimized such "courts" but made efforts to supervise them and bring them into the open.[40] Enslaved people themselves apparently valued this means of adjudicating disputes and punishing wrongdoers without subjecting their communities to the scrutiny of their enslavers or the colonial judicial system. For drivers, this role allowed them to provide another important service to the people below them, further enhancing their authority.

However common drivers' role in adjudicating conflicts may have been, given the secrecy involved, it was rarely documented. Some of the best evidence for this role comes from investigations into drivers' leadership in diasporic sociopolitical communities, or "nations," which were organized in part to punish crimes within the slave community, and from cases where enslaved people publicly objected to a driver's actions and complained to people outside the community—that is, white plantation authorities or colonial officials.[41]

Given the extreme poverty in which most enslaved people lived and the material inequalities between people with different occupational roles or social ties, drivers were probably called upon routinely to respond to accusations of theft.[42] After a turkey and ten chickens went missing one night on a Trinidadian plantation, an enslaved man named Jean Charles was suspected of having stolen them. The manager did not find sufficient proof to have Jean Charles punished, but the driver, Peter, and the watchman on duty the night the animals were stolen took matters into their own hands. Without consulting the manager, they went to Jean Charles's house, convinced that he "was a notorious robber." Failing to find the turkey or chickens, they took several items of clothing, a blanket, bowls, glasses, and fowls as collateral. Jean Charles, however, left the plantation and made a complaint to the protector of slaves, which is the only reason this episode came to light.[43]

Another incident, on a different plantation in Trinidad, involved a series of thefts from enslaved people's provision grounds. According to the watchman, who was supposed to stay up all night to prevent thefts and other problems while everyone else tried to get some sleep, "some yams were stolen" one night, and "the Driver wanted the Manager to make [the watchman] pay for them." Presumably, the owner of the stolen yams had notified the driver, who promised to make the watchman compensate him for his loss. The manager agreed with the driver and told the watchman that if he did not pay for the yams, "he would flog him." The watchman, thinking this was unfair, fled and appealed to the protector. He complained that "whenever any provisions [were] stolen out of the negro grounds" the driver expected him "to pay for them." The protector, however, agreed with the manager and the driver, telling the watchman that "as he was [the] guard, he was responsible for the grounds under his charge."[44]

For drivers, responding to such thefts was a way of protecting enslaved people's customary right to the crops they cultivated on their own time as well as a means of resolving disputes that might otherwise escalate as the aggrieved party retaliated. Doing so thus reinforced drivers' authority in the slave community beyond the scope of their work as labor supervisors.

The relentless illnesses that plagued Caribbean plantations presented drivers with other opportunities to provide an essential service to their communities. Like some leaders in Africa, drivers sometimes took responsibility for the physical and spiritual health of their people.[45] When enslaved people fell sick under mysterious circumstances or death rates soared to new highs, they felt especially vulnerable. Their enslavers generally responded either with indifference or with medical treatments that were ineffective, at best.[46] Under such circumstances, enslaved people often turned to spiritual healing, including a range of rituals and practices known across the British Caribbean by the catchall term "obeah."[47]

Drivers were uniquely positioned to facilitate the practice of obeah. By the late eighteenth century it was illegal throughout the British Caribbean, and its practitioners had to operate without being noticed by or reported to white plantation authorities. Obeah practitioners generally expected to be paid for their services. And, especially in divination rituals designed to identify the person or thing responsible for harming others, they expected the entire slave community to participate. Given their position in the plantation hierarchy and the widespread respect other enslaved people afforded them, drivers were the best people to solicit help from obeah practitioners (who were often outsiders), collect funds to pay them, encourage or force other enslaved people to join in the necessary rituals, and make sure everyone kept quiet.

As a result, in obeah cases that came to the attention of colonial authorities, drivers often played a central role. Two especially well documented cases involving the use of a collective divination ritual known as the Minje Mama or Water Mama dance in early nineteenth-century Berbice suggest a common pattern to drivers' involvement in it.[48] In both cases, an unusually high incidence of sickness and death raised suspicions that someone was using malevolent spiritual powers or poison. White plantation authorities were oblivious to or incapable of handling the problem, so the drivers took matters into their own hands. They asked well-known obeah practitioners who lived nearby for help. When the obeah practitioners arrived, the drivers consulted with them about the situation privately in their homes before gathering everyone to explain how obeah would help, as one driver put it, "bring things on the estate to order."[49] The drivers made sure that all the enslaved workers helped pay the requisite fee and that they all participated in the rituals, which lasted for hours and took place over several days. They also tried to make sure that the dozens—or hundreds—of participants and witnesses kept quiet. And when problems arose, drivers took charge of managing the fallout. For drivers, helping other enslaved people access the spiritual healing knowledge and practices they needed to sustain life was yet another way they established themselves as leaders within the slave community.

Overall, the kind of drivers who became or remained Big Men stand out in part for their willingness to take major personal risks on behalf of the people they supervised. To be sure, many drivers had a range of other attributes that also encouraged other enslaved people to see them as Big Men, from physically intimidating size and stature to charisma and oratorical skill. But the most successful drivers also recognized that they had much to gain by deliberately working to secure the loyalty, goodwill, or dependence of the people they supervised and lived among. Nevertheless, juggling their official role as planter-appointed enforcer of labor discipline with their unofficial role as community leader among the enslaved exposed them to dangerous risks.

Marriage and Kinship

In Africa and the African diaspora, one of the most obvious marks of a Big Man was a large family that included multiple wives and many children. African men recognized that one of the most effective ways to establish a large following was to seek out relationships with multiple women, including female slaves and wives. African men valued women both for the labor they performed and for their reproductive capacity, which allowed would-be Big Men to produce additional dependents in the form of children. As a result, polygyny was widely practiced throughout West and Central Africa, where it fed intense competition between men who pursued wealth-in-people. It prevented some men from becoming husbands and fathers at all while providing Big Men opportunities to produce large families and extended kinship networks that tied them to their many followers.[50]

In Caribbean plantation societies, too, polygyny was a key strategy Big Men used to amass followers. As enslaved men themselves, drivers and others who pursued wealth-in-people could not enslave women—but they could and did marry them. Even then, the extreme conditions of New World slavery challenged drivers' efforts to establish marriages and build families. Many colonies did not even legally recognize enslaved people's marriages or kinship ties, leaving enslaved families vulnerable to the whims of their enslavers, who routinely split husbands and wives—and separated parents from children—via the slave trade. Rampant disease and high death rates also created chaotic conditions that made it hard for enslaved people to reproduce and raise children. For enslaved men, high male-to-female ratios posed an additional challenge. By the eighteenth century, on most plantations in the Caribbean and other slave societies with African majorities, there were many more men than women, which exacerbated male rivalries over sexual claims to women.[51] And even when men managed to establish sexual or intimate relationships with women or became fathers, their slave status made it extraordinarily difficult to provide for their kin and protect them from harm.

Nevertheless, there is plenty of evidence that enslaved men aspired to marry and have children—and even exert a degree of patriarchal authority.[52] Even clearer is that drivers were much more successful at becoming husbands and fathers than most enslaved men.[53]

On two especially well documented plantations in late eighteenth-century Barbados, for example, only about 15 percent of male field laborers had wives, whereas nearly half of all drivers did. At the same time, compared to field laborers, drivers had about three times as many children.[54] Tellingly, enslaved men with other high-ranking occupations, such as tradesmen, were also more likely to be married and have children.[55] What such men had in common were positions that gave them both high social status within the slave community and better access to material resources.[56]

The same dynamics that made it difficult for enslaved men to establish marriages with enslaved women made it especially difficult for them to practice polygyny. One problem was demographic: where women outnumbered men, some men never managed to find a wife at all and very few men could hope to claim multiple wives. Another problem was that white authorities—especially those who were Christian—generally saw polygyny as an illegitimate practice to be discouraged, if not outright prohibited. Drivers, however, again distinguished themselves from other enslaved men by their unusual success in maintaining polygynous relationships.[57] Indeed, in some colonies the only enslaved men with multiple wives were drivers.[58]

Strikingly, enslavers themselves not only recognized that some drivers had multiple wives but sometimes even formally recorded in official records those relationships and the children drivers had with multiple women. Take, for instance, the kinship ties occasionally recorded on slave registers in the early nineteenth-century British Caribbean—a time and place where colonial authorities and missionaries alike put intense pressure on enslaved people to embrace monogamy and the nuclear family. On one plantation in Berbice, a forty-six-year-old, African-born head driver, Alexander, had eight children with his wife, Juno, six children with Nelly, and several grandchildren.[59] Another driver on the same plantation, also born in Africa, similarly had two children each with two different women, both identified as his "wife," four children with another woman, and many grandchildren.[60]

Slave registers from St. Lucia, which recorded enslaved people's family connections in more detail than many other West Indian colonies, are even more revealing. On one plantation, a driver named Alex, who had been born in Grenada and was in his early fifties, was listed as the husband of a thirty-seven-year-old woman named Catine, a field laborer. But Alex also had a sexual relationship with another African woman, Celeste, a sixty-four-year-old also listed as a driver. Together they had two adult children: Philip, a twenty-six-year-old "House Servant," and Eleonor, a twenty-four-year-old field laborer.[61] On another plantation, a forty-eight-year-old driver named Timothy Ewing, born in St. Vincent, was listed as the husband of Mary Ewing, a forty-three-year-old "Mandingo" washer, and also as the husband of Delea Ewing, a thirty-three-year-old "Congo" field laborer, with whom he had an adult daughter, Sally. In addition, with a third enslaved woman—a forty-year-old Igbo hospital nurse named Jenny Ash—Timothy had an eighteen-year-old son, Dick.[62]

That slave owners recorded these polygynous marriages and kinship ties indicates that even they recognized that drivers maintained long-term relationships with multiple women and extended family lineages. In short, enslavers acknowledged that some drivers succeeded in accruing wealth-in-people. In other slave societies, even when such relationships were not formally acknowledged by enslavers, they were probably commonplace, both because drivers wanted polygynous marriages and because they had a better chance of establishing them than other enslaved men.

Other kinds of evidence confirm that drivers often had remarkably large families. In late eighteenth-century Saint-Domingue, a driver on a large sugar plantation reportedly fathered more than sixty children.[63] In 1824, a forty-seven-year-old Creole head driver in Berbice—despite the colony's exceptionally high male-to-female ratio—had more than seventy children and grandchildren.[64] Several decades earlier, according to a planter with holdings in St. Vincent and Grenada, one of his drivers had a family that consisted of more than forty people. He also reportedly possessed property valued at more than £200, which hints at the connections between a driver's social status, relative material wealth, and ability to create large families.[65]

What, if anything, made the prospect of marrying a driver appealing to enslaved women? For starters, drivers had greater access to material resources, including food, clothing, and shelter, that they could share with their wives and other family members.[66] Such arrangements echoed African practices, where Big Men used their access to scarce resources to attract and retain followers. For enslaved women, who often received smaller "allowances" of essential provisions from their enslavers than enslaved men, marrying drivers thus offered important tangible benefits. On one South Carolina plantation, for example, a driver's wife had "plenty of provisions," cultivated several acres of rice and sugar with her husband, and raised "a yard of poultry."[67] Enslavers who made provisions for drivers in their wills sometimes included drivers' wives, too, as in the case of a Demerara planter who left a bequest of fifteen joes (Guyanese currency named after the Portuguese gold Johannes coin) to his driver, Henry, "and the same sum to his wife Isabella."[68]

The link between drivers' special access to provisions and ability to marry multiple women and maintain large families drew the attention of some white observers. One English visitor to Barbados in 1825 took note of a driver who had a much "larger and smarter" home than other enslaved people. He had a house with "two large four post beds, looking glasses and framed pictures" as well as wine to offer the visitor. Reportedly, the driver had also "begotten twelve children or more."[69] A century and a half earlier, the prominent Barbados planter Henry Drax made an even more explicit connection in his detailed written instructions about the management of his plantation (discussed in chapter 1). Drax recommended that his resident manager make special accommodations for the enslaved man named Moncky Nocco who served as "head overseer," or driver. In a revealing acknowledgment by a planter of a driver's polygynous family and his obligations as a husband and father, Drax specified that in addition to Moncky Nocco's "own diet in the house," he should receive ten additional pounds of "fish or flesh," which he was free, wrote Drax, "to dispose of as he shall think fit to his mother, wives, and family."[70] For women like Moncky Nocco's wives, such material advantages likely improved their odds of survival.

Being part of a driver's family also offered enslaved women and children important intangible benefits. Scattered evidence suggests that in some cases drivers were able to pass on their occupational advantages to their children, especially when they were married to women with high-status occupations of their own, as in the case of Alex and Celeste, mentioned above.[71] One Jamaican family's genealogy—traceable over four generations—is illustrative. In 1786, an African-born driver named Qua and his Jamaican-born wife, Betty, entered the archival record when they were purchased by the owner of Mesopotamia (the same plantation where Moravian missionaries cultivated a relationship with the head driver, Matthew). At the time, Qua and Betty were in their mid-forties and had seven children (ranging in age from seven to twenty-two years) who were bought along with them. On Mesopotamia, they both held high-ranking jobs. Qua continued to work as a driver, a position he held before being sold, for the rest of his life (he died in 1789 at the age of forty-nine). Betty worked as a children's nurse for more than two decades. Their two oldest sons, Charles and Chelsea, managed to escape fieldwork for the rest of their lives. Charles was a carpenter for most of his twenties and thirties before serving as a "house servant" for perhaps a year before becoming afflicted with rheumatism and listed as an "invalid." His younger brother, Chelsea, worked for a decade as a domestic before a three-year stint as a cooper and, finally, when he was thirty years old, a driver—a position he would hold for the next twenty-three years.[72]

Taken together, the material and social advantages of being married to a driver clearly mattered to enslaved women. When their husbands were demoted, drivers' wives protested fiercely, at great risk to themselves and their families, and sometimes tried to get their husbands reinstated.[73]

If drivers had qualities that made them attractive potential partners, they also had coercive power. As several historians have observed, drivers were more likely than other enslaved men to be accused of using threats and violence to pressure women into sex and marriage—and of outright sexual assault.[74] Usually, such incidents did not make it into the archival record, and when they did, the perspectives of the women involved are obscured. An imaginative account, not bound by the constraints of the archive, about drivers' sexual predation and the ways that enslaved women responded appears in Marlon James's *Book of Night Women* (2009), a novel set on a Jamaican sugar plantation at the turn of the nineteenth century. In an emblematic and disturbing scene at the end of the opening chapter, the fifteen-year-old protagonist, Lilith, is nearly raped by a young enslaved driver. After fighting back with a pot of scalding tea and then hacking him to death with his own cutlass, Lilith struggles to manage her trauma, despite having repeated nightmares and flashbacks. She finds a measure of protection thanks to other women even as she faces the retribution of the other drivers on the estate, who at one point attempt to kill her. As James emphasizes, such incidents were part of a broader culture in which drivers physically and sexually abused enslaved women without the interference of white plantation authorities, who themselves subjected enslaved women to similar abuse. For enslaved women and girls like Lilith, predatory drivers provoked fear and hatred in equal measure.[75]

A rare, detailed historical account of a driver's sexual coercion can be reconstructed from a series of incidents documented by a plantation attorney in early nineteenth-century Jamaica. In this case, a driver named Napier was accused by an enslaved woman, Johannah, of using obeah against her and her children in an effort to force her into a sexual relationship. Johannah was already married to an enslaved carpenter on another plantation, and they had several children together. But when Napier began to make "addresses" to her, she must have taken him seriously. She was no doubt aware that the previous year Napier had broken up a marriage between another enslaved couple after threatening to use obeah against them. Still, Johannah refused to leave her husband. She rebuffed Napier's "courtship," but her husband eventually left her, perhaps because he was afraid of what Napier might do to him if he stood in the way. Even then Johannah continued to resist Napier's efforts to make her "his own." So, Napier ordered Johannah not to be with anyone else. He also made an explicit threat: "If she would not have him," he told her, "he would do her bad."[76]

Johannah recognized this for what it was—a threat to use obeah against her if she refused to marry him—and went to the head driver, who outranked Napier, for protection. He "reprimanded" Napier and threatened to bring him to the attorney if he continued to harass Johannah.[77] Several months later, when two of Johannah's children died in short succession and the third became "very ill," she concluded that Napier had made good on his threat. With the support of her mother, Johannah "went to Napier to beg for the child's life." Napier acknowledged responsibility but refused to relent. Soon after, Johannah's family told the attorney about Napier's pursuit of her and recourse to obeah, and he punished Napier severely—not for sexual coercion but for having used obeah.[78] Drivers like Napier, who would have seen women as the most valuable kind of followers, knew that they could not pursue many of the methods they or their ancestors could in Africa, such as warfare or enslavement, for getting female followers. Some of them apparently tried instead to coerce women into marital relationships, abusing their power and jeopardizing their status among the enslaved.

Polygyny itself could also create tensions between drivers and their wives, especially when a wife objected to her husband's efforts to establish another relationship with a new woman. In one 1799 case from a sugar plantation on Danish St. Croix—adjudicated by colonial legal authorities—an enslaved field laborer named Sally became distraught when she learned that her common-law husband of the past five years, an African-born man named Leander, "had taken another wife" on a different estate. Sally was unwilling to accept a polygynous relationship—or tolerate what she saw as her husband's "infidelity." Jealous and angry, she tried various tactics to break up the other relationship without directly confronting Leander, at least initially. First, Sally fought the other wife, even though she "was bigger and stronger." When that failed, Sally mixed "some marl" into Leander's water, presumably hoping that the concoction would work as a sort of love potion, binding Leander to her and keeping him away from the other woman. Finally, late one night, while Leander slept, Sally set fire to his house, hoping it would "terrify him and deter him from the other wife." After the fire, Leander and Sally supposedly "lived happily together" for some time, but when Sally learned that he once again "went astray and remained unfaithful," she became so enraged that she set fire to a cane field and confessed to Leander everything she had done to break up his other marriage.[79]

In court, Sally was charged with attempted murder, while Leander—who interpreted the water mixed with marl as an attempt to poison him—minimized the importance of his relationship with Sally and defended his right to maintain multiple wives. He "had taken" Sally as his wife for the sake of "convenience," he said, and his other marriage had also begun "a long time ago," facts that he apparently hoped would make both relationships seem equally legitimate. Remarkably, white authorities seemingly accepted Leander's polygynous marriage, referring to Sally as his "co-wife." They also sentenced Sally to be executed by decapitation (though her sentence was ultimately reduced to criminal transportation).[80]

Drivers' efforts to establish relationships with enslaved women also made other enslaved men resentful and sometimes provoked violent confrontations. Many enslaved men—especially those in lower-status positions such as field laborers—resented drivers and other high-status men for enticing "their" wives away from them and for what they viewed as monopolizing scarce women. According to the missionary John Wray, who lived for many years in Berbice and Demerara during the early nineteenth century, enslaved men lamented that it was "too much the practice for the Drivers[,] Head people, house boys, & white People to get the women from their husbands, because they can give them a few fine Clothes more than the others."[81] Similar tensions on an Essequibo woodcutting estate—where the driver and "head man," King, apparently asserted exclusive sexual control of the only woman on the estate—may have led enslaved men there to retaliate by telling the owner that King had embezzled rum and cane syrup meant for them, for which King was severely punished.[82]

White plantation authorities feared that such conflicts over the sexual possession of women could be dangerously destabilizing. Consequently, as one French Caribbean planter explained, no matter how much "talent" a driver had, white authorities should not hesitate to demote him if he committed the "unforgivable" crime of targeting another man's wife. When a driver displayed "such a dangerous abuse of authority," he needed to be given a punishment in front of the entire gang "of the greatest severity."[83]

In line with such thinking, white authorities on one Essequibo plantation took the extraordinary step of selling a driver named Bacchus after a series of conflicts that culminated in 1831. Bacchus claimed a woman named Lydia as his wife despite her marriage to another man, Jonas, with whom she had two children. According to the plantation's attorney, Bacchus "took" Lydia and forced her to live with and have sex with him. Bacchus himself openly admitted that he had made Lydia his wife "by force." The two "cohabited" for several years and had two children, but their relationship "caused a great deal of commotion upon the estate between" Bacchus and Jonas; they "were always quarreling." Things eventually became so bad that the attorney sold Bacchus "to prevent further disputes," which led Bacchus to complain to the protector of slaves about being separated from Lydia. For her part, Lydia reportedly "made no complaint about Bacchus being sold," but since authorities did not solicit her testimony, we can only guess about her thoughts and feelings.[84] What is clear from the crisis that Bacchus provoked is that drivers' efforts to claim women as their own sometimes undermined their larger pursuit of wealth-in-people by turning potential follow-ers into enemies.

Drivers themselves faced similar threats from white plantation authorities who asserted their prerogative to have sex with drivers' wives. Such incidents con-fronted drivers with the limits of their authority, knowing that white men would not be prosecuted for raping enslaved women and that they were all but pow-erless to protect their wives or assert their sexual claims.[85] Despite the obvious risks, drivers sometimes stood up to white plantation authorities who sexually abused the drivers' wives. A driver on Egypt, a Jamaican sugar plantation man-aged by the infamous overseer and diarist Thomas Thistlewood, found himself in the fraught position of trying to prevent a white man from sexually exploiting his wife. Thistlewood's nephew, John, apparently expected a driver named John-nie to interfere with the nephew's sexual predation, so he locked Johnnie in the boiling house the first time he raped Johnnie's wife, Little Mimber. For the next two months, the nephew repeatedly raped her. Eventually, Johnnie complained to Thistlewood that the nephew was, as Thistlewood phrased it, "taking" his wife. Thistlewood reprimanded his nephew at least five times, he noted in his diary—not for rape but for targeting a married woman attached to a driver. But the abuse continued. Eventually, Johnnie may have decided to get retribution. Nearly two months after the nephew raped Little Mimber for the first time, he was found dead in a river under mysterious circumstances. To Thistlewood's cha-grin, the enslaved people on Egypt celebrated.[86]

Perhaps the most dramatic account of a driver's efforts to protect his wife from sexual abuse—or reassert his exclusive claim to her—comes from a coffee plantation in mid-eighteenth-century Suriname. The plantation's owner, Amand Thoma, forced himself on multiple enslaved women on the estate, shifting between them in what may have been an effort to mitigate their husbands' rage. One of them was Eva. She was an Indigenous woman and one of several wives claimed by Coridon, a driver. When it became obvious that Eva was pregnant—at the time no one knew whether the father was Coridon or Thoma—Coridon could not control his jealousy. One night, he went to Thoma's room and killed him in what turned out to be the beginning of an armed uprising and mass deser-tion. During the brutal reprisals that followed, Coridon was tortured and then killed, his body ripped apart by four horses.[87]

As fathers, drivers also faced the horror of watching white men sexually abuse their daughters. In one instance, the head driver on Mesopotamia, Mat-thew, was forced to stand by helplessly as a series of white plantation employees sexually exploited his teenage daughter, Hannah, who worked as a house servant.

Three days after the death of Hannah's second mixed-race child in March 1761, Matthew was anguished but powerless. He told the resident missionaries—the only white people around he could potentially see as allies—what he could never have said directly to his daughter's rapist: that "the whites" on the plantation "were none other than heathens who were completely without God in the world and lived based on their carnal desires." The missionaries recorded Matthew's complaint but took no action; indeed, they blamed him for what they saw as his daughter's sexual immorality.[88]

Drivers tried to protect their immediate family members from other threats, too. Some drivers did so, where possible, by appealing to legal authorities for help, as illustrated by the efforts of an African-born driver named Samuel on a small Berbice coffee estate to fulfill his patriarchal obligation to rescue his family from a desperate situation. In January 1821, Samuel told the fiscal that he and the five other enslaved people he supervised were "so overwrought by their cruel master"—an inexperienced planter who had purchased Samuel just over a year and a half earlier—that they were "scarcely able to keep it out" with him. Their owner knew "very little of negro work and treatment," assigning impossible tasks and then punishing people, especially women like his wife, when they did not finish them. They also received inadequate provisions: "nothing but a small piece of pork, a little fish, two pipes, and some tobacco; nothing else no clothes or anything more." Samuel knew, he said, that he and his family "would be able to please a reasonable master." So, casting himself in the role of a Big Man responsible for his immediate family, Samuel asked "that he, with his wife and brother, might be sold." While the fiscal had no authority to order a slave owner to sell anyone, Samuel eventually got what he wanted: in September his owner sold him and everyone else on the estate.[89]

Drivers also fought—sometimes successfully—to keep their families intact despite the pervasive threat of separation by sale. In one instance, the manager of several cotton plantations in Berbice wrote to the absentee owner who employed him that he had recently purchased several new people, including an "exceedingly good" driver who "was not willing to separate from" his wife and three young children.[90] That the manager was willing to respect the driver's kinship ties in order to obtain a skilled, experienced driver suggests that at least some drivers leveraged planters' reliance on their expertise and skill for their own benefit.[91]

Despite their best efforts, drivers were severely constrained when it came to protecting their families from harm, as underscored by the fact that they were often forced to use physical violence themselves against their own family members. The archives of Atlantic slavery are full of accounts in which drivers had to whip, beat, or otherwise torture their children, siblings, parents, and wives.[92] Enslaved laborers knew that drivers were not ultimately, or at least solely, responsible for most of the violence they inflicted. Still, such acts must have strained drivers' relationships with their families and the wider communities in which they lived.[93]

Drivers' efforts to protect their kin, provide for their dependents, and especially to establish large, polygynous families suggest that African ideas about wealth-in-people and kinship persisted in American slave societies. In seeking the social roles of husband and father, drivers also resisted the pervasive threats slavery posed of natal alienation and social death.[94] Under the logic of *partus sequitur ventrem* (offspring follows the womb), the legal doctrine that a child's legal status followed that of the mother, rather than the father, enslaved people's paternity was often obscured or erased outright.[95] Yet surviving records reveal that drivers saw the link between a father and his children (and the connection between a husband and his wife) as socially meaningful and that they managed to get other people, including their enslavers, to recognize the legitimacy of such ties.

Even so, the kinds of Big Man politics practiced in West and West-Central Africa could not simply be maintained or recreated wholesale under the violent, exploitative conditions enslaved people endured in the plantation-based slave societies of the Americas. Even when drivers managed to build large families or amass many followers, whatever wealth-in-people they possessed was overshadowed by the brutal logic of racial capitalism, where enslaved people were legally and financially treated as laborers and property.

Nothing better illustrates the unresolvable tension between a driver's official role as enforcer of plantation discipline and unofficial role as Big Man than an incident on the Salt Spring sugar estate in Jamaica toward the end of 1831. One Friday morning, about a week before Christmas, the overseer flogged an enslaved woman for stealing sugarcane and then ordered the head driver to flog her a second time. The driver was the woman's husband. And he refused. In taking such a bold stand, he explicitly put his duty toward family above his obligation as driver. Even more remarkable was the reaction of the other drivers, who also refused to whip the woman, in a courageous display of personal loyalty to the head driver.[96]

The panicked overseer, anxious to regain control, went to nearby Montego Bay for help and returned to the estate with two magistrates. There they were met by "the whole body of slaves," men and women, who had united in open defiance. Backing the drivers, the other enslaved people brandished their cutlasses, took possession of the magistrates' mules and pistols, beat the magistrates, and even threatened to throw the overseer into a vat of boiling cane juice. Rumors of a general strike had been circulating in the region for some time, and before the Salt Spring people forced the magistrates back to town, they declared that after New Year's Day they would no longer work for their enslavers. Fifty militia members were dispatched to the estate to restore order, but when they arrived on Salt Spring they found the estate deserted; everyone had fled to the hills. A week and a half later, enslaved laborers across Jamaica launched what became the largest slave rebellion in the Caribbean since the Haitian Revolution.[97]

Some drivers clearly achieved a certain esteem and legitimacy that transcended their official role as planter-appointed labor supervisors. But there were sharp limits to how much drivers could do when it came to providing resources, protection, and leadership for their followers and families without jeopardizing their relationships with enslavers, who could demote them—or worse. The most successful drivers presumably managed to walk the knife's edge of convincing white plantation authorities they had a driver who was working people as hard as possible while also making other enslaved laborers feel as though they had a protector or leader and not just a taskmaster. Often, however, the competing demands enslaved laborers and enslavers made on drivers exposed the irreconcilable gap between being at once a driver, on the one hand, and a Big Man, on the other. While some version of wealth-in-people and Big Man politics endured in American plantation societies, at least as ideas or frameworks, the severe constraints drivers and other enslaved people faced limited their practical implications.

CHAPTER 4

Unbounded Authority

When absentee owner Thomas Winter arrived to take up residence on his Berbice River coffee plantation, Deutichem, in early 1829, he unwittingly set off a
crisis that had been building for a decade. What began, early one Sunday morning, as a gathering of the plantation's enslaved labor force to welcome Winter
would soon devolve into a violent power struggle between the resident manager
and a former driver that threw the plantation into chaos.[1]

At the center of this conflict was an enslaved African man named January, who had once been the plantation's head driver. According to January,
their day of rest started peacefully as almost all the nearly three hundred slaves
on the plantation assembled before Winter's front door "to wish him good
morning." January, who was not among them, watched from a distance as "they
stood in a row and said Good morning Master! & cheered." Although January was piqued that they had not waited for him, he went to join them. And
even though the current drivers were present, January took it upon himself to
represent everyone. He went through the crowd, entered the house, wished
Winter "Good morning," and said, "We are glad to know we have a Master."
Playing the role of a Big Man, he asked Winter if they might "be allowed to
drink a dram at the door to welcome" him. Winter agreed to this customary
entitlement and sent his personal servant to get "rum for the people" from the
resident manager, Mr. Boas.[2]

The gathering at Winter's door took Boas by surprise. He was at his own
house at the time and thought it was odd to see "the whole gang" assembled
in front of the owner's house, especially when he heard what he described as
"a hussa from upwards of 200 negroes," but he overlooked it. Boas went about
his business, leaving the plantation on the back of a mule to run an errand.
Soon, however, Boas's wife "ran after him" and told him that the gang had not

simply assembled to ingratiate themselves with Winter or get some rum. "Don't you see," she asked, "the Gang are gone up to their Master's door to complain against you."[3]

As Boas rushed to confront the assembly, he was intercepted by the man Winter had sent to get the rum. By the time Boas approached Winter's house, he had come to see the gathering as a challenge to his authority. "I said," he later recalled, "if these people wanted a dram I think they might as well have come to me for it." Having lived on the plantation for more than a decade and having worked his way up from the position of overseer, Boas was evidently anxious about his status. According to January, Boas "cried out 'you dogs, who gave you permission,'" and then ordered the drivers to make everyone "shut their mouths" before they could answer. Even then, Boas later recalled, one man offered an explanation for having gone to Winter directly instead of him: January had told them "not to do so."[4]

Enraged by this symbolic disregard for his authority, Boas pushed his way "through the crowd" and walked up the steps to stand next to Winter and address everyone. Switching from Creole to English for the benefit of his newly arrived employer, Boas began by berating his drivers. They had met with him less than fifteen minutes earlier at his house to receive their instructions for the next day's work—and their own customary drams of rum—and Boas was troubled by what he saw as some sort of conspiracy. "You know I have lived so long with you," he said, "what is the reason of your going up in a body in this manner without giving me notice of your intentions." He told the drivers he would withhold their rum for a week as punishment. Turning to the others, Boas told them they were "not to blame, it is the Drivers' fault," and complained that it was "a pretty thing for the Manager to be sitting in his house and hear 200 people huzzaing (it being no holiday) without his having the least notice." Boas then "directed the negroes to get a dram," flailing to assert some measure of authority even though Winter had already approved the distribution of rum.[5]

Then Boas turned his attention to January, convinced that he was the actual ringleader. What business did you have, Boas asked January, "to prevent the Drivers and the people from going to my house when they were actually doing so . . . ?" "You January," Boas demanded, why are "you concerned in this, you are not a Driver."[6]

In fact, January had not been a driver for nearly ten years. But he continued to exert remarkable power—enough to overrule the current drivers, undermine the manager, and, ultimately, provoke a violent confrontation and crisis of authority that would continue for more than a week.

For white plantation authorities, there was always a risk that demoting a driver would be the spark that would ignite the combustible plantation system. Having invested someone with authority as a driver and having worked to get everyone else to respect him, they now had to reverse course and convert that person back into an ordinary enslaved laborer—or at least try to do so. Plantation managers therefore avoided gratuitous demotions, knowing how destabilizing it was to demote a driver and appoint a new one.[7] In some cases, the driver being demoted was not seen as an effective leader anyway. But things were more volatile in situations like January's. In such cases, white authorities were confronted with the fact that a driver had earned authority over time through his leadership within the slave community, as we saw in the previous chapter. And sometimes they learned the hard way that a driver's authority could be impossible to strip away.

Reconstructing the long history of January's case, juxtaposed with other cases involving demoted drivers, offers an opportunity to explore these often tense transitions of power and the nature of drivers' authority. Given that white authorities were reluctant to face the risks of demoting a driver, under what circumstances did drivers lose their position? What options did such drivers have for protesting their demotion or getting back at those responsible for their downfall? And how can we explain circumstances like the 1829 crisis provoked by January, where a long-demoted driver could still count on the loyalty of his many followers?

Paths to Demotion

January's demotion—and its decade-long aftermath—was unusual, both because it was so well documented and because January lost his position for reasons very different from those most drivers lost theirs. In general, planters and managers were reluctant to demote drivers because they knew all too well that punishing a Big Man was fraught with danger. As slave owner Thomas Roughley cautioned in his *Jamaica Planter's Guide* (1823), "It gives a great deal of vexation to an overseer when he changes his head driver. Caprice should never have any hand in such a transaction."[8] So, drivers were typically demoted only when it became obvious to white plantation authorities that they were unable or unwilling to perform their basic duties—and especially when drivers were disruptive.

There were many reasons white plantation authorities came to see drivers as ineffective, including excessive drinking that interfered with their work. The owner of a Trinidad sugar plantation decided to "break," or fire, his driver for being a habitual drunk, even after he had been warned "that he as a Driver was setting a very bad example to the rest of the Gang." For this driver, as for others, part of the problem with being drunk was that it lowered inhibitions and could lead to what enslavers saw as insolent outbursts. In this case, the driver was, in the owner's eyes, "not only drunk but excessively insolent."[9] A driver on a different Trinidad plantation was similarly fired for what the manager saw as drunken insubordination. Ever since the manager had taken over the plantation, the driver had "been very frequently intoxicated." Worse, from the manager's point of view, whenever the driver was drunk, he acted "very violently." Even then, the manager hesitated to demote him but reached his breaking point when he found the driver so drunk while supervising field laborers that he could not even keep his balance. Confronted by the manager, the driver hurled at him "all the curses generally used by Slaves" and called him "a damned infernal liar," a "scoundrel and a vagabond," and a "villain." Even more shockingly, the driver threatened to blackmail the manager. He said that if the manager punished him, he would go to the plantation owner and tell him about "the tricks" the manager was playing in order "to have him discharged."[10]

Drivers could also be demoted for apparent negligence. In one case from Berbice, a forty-year-old man named Jupiter who had worked as a driver for at least thirteen years—a long tenure, which suggests he maintained his enslavers' confidence—eventually gave the plantation manager the impression that he was no longer cut out for the job. After a period of what the manager described as "repeated neglect & evident incapability," the straw that broke the camel's back came one morning when Jupiter failed to get the people he supervised to their work early enough. In response, the manager flogged Jupiter, locked him in the plantation hospital, and ultimately "broke" him as a driver.[11]

Drivers who did not use as much violence as their enslavers expected against other enslaved people or were not exacting enough in supervising fieldwork could also find themselves demoted for being too soft. Such was the case with a demoted driver in Nevis who told magistrates that he and the manager "never agreed together" because the driver "did not beat the negroes for every fault."[12] A female driver on a Jamaican sugar estate named Mary Tait was similarly fired "from her Office" for what the plantation's attorney described as "winking at the Idleness of those under her charge and for not paying attention to the children and reporting the dirt eaters to the Overseer and the Head Man."[13]

In extraordinary cases, drivers themselves recognized that they were not capable of doing such a difficult, dangerous job and actually asked to be given a different one. A driver in Martinique named Césaire reportedly asked the owner of the sugar plantation where he worked "to relieve him of his command, saying he was not well and did not feel talented enough to be driver." The owner had not been "displeased with him" but nevertheless "accepted his resignation" as "driver of the work gang" and reassigned him to supervise work "in the woods or in the sugar buildings."[14] In Grenada, a head driver named Mitchel similarly admitted that he struggled to get the people he supervised to follow his orders. The underlying problem, as even Mitchel's sister later admitted, was that his fellow slaves deeply "dislike[d] him" and apparently did not respect him either. Mitchel tried to terrorize them into compliance, but that only prompted more defiance. People regularly complained to the manager that Mitchel was "ill-treating them" and deserted the plantation. The manager, who must have known that a widely unpopular driver was also likely to be counterproductive, granted Mitchel's request to be reassigned to his old role as a cooper. That Mitchel had an alternative to field labor helps explain why he could welcome demotion. At the same time, Mitchel recognized that the way he had treated people while he was a driver had damaged whatever standing in the community he may have had previously. "Don't you think," he asked his brother, "the negroes hate me?"[15] Mitchel's experience is a stark reminder that being able to command the respect of other slaves—or being seen as a Big Man—was an essential quality of a successful driver.

Drivers who were openly insubordinate were also very likely to be demoted, as demonstrated by an incident involving a driver named Fielding on a large Berbice coffee plantation. After the manager ordered an enslaved woman to be confined in "the black hole," Fielding released her so that she could seek the attorney's "pardon." The enraged manager confronted Fielding and ordered him to the stocks. Fielding denied having released her, "resisted being put in the stocks," and "became very violent." Fielding then appealed to the fiscal, claiming he had been punished unjustly, but the fiscal was characteristically unsympathetic. He agreed with the attorney that an exemplary punishment was necessary to "quell the insubordinate conduct of this man to prevent others from following his evil & dangerous example." Fielding was taken back to the plantation, where he was flogged in front of the entire slave population, locked in the black hole for four weeks, and demoted as a driver.[16]

For white plantation authorities, even worse than such acts of insubordination were drivers who actively conspired with other people to sabotage plantation production—precisely the opposite of what they expected drivers to do. One driver on a Trinidad sugar plantation, for instance, was demoted when the

manager concluded that his "Gang did not perform enough work." The underlying problem, however, was that the driver and the people under him were
apparently colluding to reduce sugar production. The manager suspected that
the reason his output declined by a third was that "some understanding existed
between" the driver and "the People."[17]

The wide range of ways that a determined driver could sabotage production—and thus get himself demoted—is illustrated by an especially well documented case from Orangestein, a sugar plantation with about one hundred
enslaved people on the Essequibo River in what is now Guyana. Over the course
of several months in 1830, the plantation's head driver, Manuel, came under
suspicion for actively working to undermine his owner's authority, disrupt production, and foment resistance. At one point, while his owner was ill and presumably unable to supervise Manuel closely, Manuel allowed his gang "to idle
for 2 weeks," getting only half as much work done as the owner thought they
should have. Even worse, as Manuel's owner saw it, Manuel used his influence
over the other slaves—which the owner admitted was "more extensive" than his
own—to encourage "disobedience of Orders, dilatoriness of work, and to every
thing injurious and ruinous to the interest of the Property." On one occasion, for
example, Manuel conspired "with the Punt Driver to retard the work & caus[ed]
the Gang to idle," for which the owner had him flogged. Manuel's most recent
punishment—thirty lashes inflicted by the driver of a neighboring plantation—
was for having allegedly allowed freshly cut sugarcane to remain in the field so
long that it "soured" before it could be milled. Manuel also found himself blamed
for encouraging people to run away. His owner believed that every person who
deserted—many of them "without the smallest cause"—had been "instigated to
it by Manuel," who also "received & entertained them in his house at night."[18]

In addition, Manuel undermined his owner's efforts to track production.
The owner had ordered Manuel "hundreds of times" to report on the day's work,
"as every other Driver d[id]," but Manuel refused, "from insolence & determined disobedience." On the rare occasions Manuel did make his daily report,
"he told barefaced falsehoods," exaggerating the amount of work done to protect
himself and the people below him. For this deception, the owner had Manuel
tied up to the rail of the stairs leading to the owner's house, trying to humiliate
Manuel into compliance.[19]

By early October, Manuel knew he was poised to be demoted. As a man in
his early fifties, he must have also known that demotion to field labor on a sugar
estate was akin to a death sentence. So, he decided to take a major risk and traveled
nearly twenty miles to Georgetown, Demerara, where he appealed to the colony's

protector of slaves. Manuel's gambit backfired. The witnesses he called upon to substantiate his claim of having been punished without cause instead supported his owner's narrative: Manuel was actively undermining his enslavers. So serious was the threat posed by Manuel's "really ruinous conduct," his owner concluded, that he needed to not only demote him but also "remove him from the Estate where his harmful influence [was] attended with such prejudicial effect."[20]

Compared to other demoted drivers, January was different. There is no indication that he was unable or unwilling to get the people he supervised to do their work. Neither his enslavers nor his fellow slaves described him—during his long tenure as driver—as an alcoholic, insolent, or insubordinate, much less a saboteur. These differences, and the unusual circumstances of his demotion, would ultimately have important consequences for January, for the other enslaved people on his plantation, and especially for the white authorities who struggled to control him.

January's Demotion

January's demotion in June 1819 stemmed from his efforts to address a mysterious and deadly epidemic that was wreaking havoc on plantation Deutichem. Desperate to find a solution to a problem no one else seemed able to solve, January turned to a practitioner of obeah, the criminalized Afro-Caribbean spiritual practice.[21] In doing so, he provoked a series of investigations—each of which produced different records—by white authorities on and off the plantation who saw obeah as a multipronged threat. Plantation managers thought obeah was disruptive to plantation discipline and led to violent, sometimes fatal, power struggles, so as soon as Boas heard that people on Deutichem had turned to obeah, he initiated an investigation that implicated January. Colonial officials, meanwhile, were determined to uphold the legal prohibition on obeah—on the grounds that it promoted "the total subversion of all subordination and ultimate destruction of the inhabitants of this colony"—and prosecuted several people, including January, in the Court of Criminal Justice.[22] And the Christian missionary John Wray, who saw obeah as African superstition that stood in the way of his efforts to convert the enslaved, followed the investigation and trial closely, interviewing a key participant from jail before the trial and reporting what he heard in a long letter to the abolitionist William Wilberforce.[23]

Ironically, January turned to obeah not to sabotage production but effectively to stabilize it by preserving the lives of the enslaved laborers who made it possible. Focusing on the events that resulted in January's unusual demotion deepens our understanding of the extent to which some drivers saw themselves—and came to be seen by others—as community leaders. January must have been well aware that the practice of obeah was illegal, so his decision to take the major risk of using it was a sign of the extraordinary lengths to which he went to look out for the welfare of the people below him—to be what they would have seen as a proper Big Man.

Everyone was accustomed to sickness, suffering, and death in Berbice, which was, even by the horrific standards of Caribbean slave societies, especially deadly. But in the spring of 1819, things seemed worse than normal. Children in particular were getting sick and dying more often than before.[24] And no one seemed to know why. White plantation authorities throughout the colony generally focused on the obvious symptoms of sickness, when they paid attention at all, and subjected enslaved people to medical treatments that rarely made things better and often made them worse.[25] Nothing white management did gave the enslaved people on Deutichem any confidence that they understood the underlying cause of the epidemic—or had an effective plan to combat it.

Eventually, many enslaved people began to suspect that the epidemic was the result of someone deliberately harming others with poison or obeah. If that was the case, the only solution was to find a spiritual healer who could discern the underlying problem and then solve it.

This placed January in a difficult situation. Any divination or healing rituals would have to be performed clandestinely, and secrets were hard to keep on a plantation with more than three hundred enslaved people.[26] There were also inherent risks to obeah rituals themselves, which were unpredictable and sometimes physically dangerous. And there was no guarantee that they would work. What's more, obeah was a capital crime, and pretty much anything January did to combat the epidemic on his own would look to the plantation's white employees like an affront to their authority—an implicit assertion that January knew how to run the plantation better than they did.

Nevertheless, January ultimately decided that things were bad enough for him to risk going ahead with consulting an obeah practitioner. Fortunately, he knew of someone who might be able to help: a half-blind enslaved Central African man named Hans.[27] January knew that Hans had successfully solved similar problems on other plantations. In one case, Hans had stemmed a tide of miscarriages by treating pregnant women, and in another he had identified the men behind two poisonings.[28]

When approached by January, Hans was reluctant to get involved. Only after January asked him six times did he agree to travel to Deutichem and help.

In advance of Hans's arrival late on the night of Saturday, June 12, January organized the others. According to a woman named Venus who would soon play a key role in the identification of the suspected poisoner, January ordered "that nobody was to quit the estate; every body [had to] come to his house."[29]

When Hans arrived, January noticed that one man was conspicuously absent: the head carpenter, Frederick. January went to Frederick's house, woke him up, and told him to join the group.

Once everyone had assembled, January initiated the proceedings with an oath.[30] He poured some rum into a ram's horn, took a drink, and announced "that he wished to have the bad people off the estate, and everybody [had to] listen well." He told them that Hans would help them "put every thing to rights." Hans began to sing "his country song" and conducted a series of rituals that lasted all night. Around sunrise, before everyone dispersed to complete their normal Sunday morning tasks, Hans announced that he would need to be paid for his services—as was customary with obeah practitioners—when they reconvened. As Hans put it, since "he had come to set things right on the estate, every body, big and little, [had to] contribute a bit," or coin.[31]

Hans's payment sparked a revealing dispute about the power dynamics and complex hierarchies within the slave community, where drivers were not the only Big Men. January began taking up the collection, but Hans interrupted and told Frederick to do so instead. "You must collect this money," he ordered. Frederick objected, on the grounds that January was the head driver and the one who had brought Hans to the plantation. Frederick, however, occupied an unusual position on the plantation, which may explain both why Hans considered him "the head man of the estate" and why Frederick was reluctant to get involved.[32]

Frederick was among the oldest and most materially well-off people in the Deutichem slave community. The previous owner had left him a monthly bequest of one joe as a reward for his supposed loyalty. Frederick carefully saved his money and eventually accumulated enough to purchase his own slave. His age (about forty-six years) and status as head carpenter also commanded respect; some people knew him as "uncle Frederick."[33] At the same time, some evidence suggests that other enslaved people were jealous of him. According to the missionary John Wray, long before 1819 they "had frequently blamed Fredrick as a poisoner." Despite his understandable reticence, Frederick ultimately agreed to collect the money for Hans.[34]

By about 11:00 A.M., Hans was ready to begin the next phase of his work: the Minje Mama dance. This collective divination ritual, with variations throughout the Black Atlantic world and performed in moments of crisis, would allow Hans to "pull off all the poison that was in the ground." He sacrificed a chicken, placed its feathers in the children's hair, and washed everyone with a mix of water, grass, and "wild canes." He then had everyone form a circle, singing, clapping, and dancing on one foot, until several of them fell into a trance, possessed by spirits who might reveal the identity of the poisoner. Before long, Venus fell into an especially deep trance, "burst into Hysterical laughter," and denounced Frederick as "the bad man on the estate." She ran out of the circle, said "'come, and I show you where the poison is hid,'" and led a large group to Frederick's house.[35]

Frederick, in a show of confidence that he was not the poisoner, allowed Venus and the others to ransack his house. They overturned water casks, broke apart the kitchen and fowl house, and even pulled up the floorboards to dig into the earth below, but the poison was nowhere to be found. Venus apparently panicked and said she had made a mistake, that she had meant to accuse another carpenter. She wanted to go back to Hans, who had stayed at January's, to get her "eyes property washed." But Frederick insisted that they complete their search, presumably so that he could be exonerated. When Venus and the others left to consult Hans, Frederick decided that enough was enough.[36]

Frederick went to the plantation's overseer, Boas. He, in turn, reported what he learned to the plantation's attorney, who confronted January and the other drivers.

January insisted he had done nothing wrong. He explained that they had asked Hans for help, that Hans was a good man, and that the only purpose of the Minje Mama dance was "to find out the cause of these sudden deaths."[37] In short, January asserted that he had done what was necessary to take care of his people.

January's explanation fell on deaf ears. The attorney locked January and the other drivers in the stocks and alerted colonial officials so that the fiscal could initiate a formal investigation.

Meanwhile, Hans was determined to finish his work. After evading capture by hiding out on the plantation, he resumed the divination process on Monday night. With a few other men, he returned to Frederick's house after dark to uncover the "bad thing." Hans knew it was there "from the smell he had of it" and, after a complicated ritual, produced a "pot of obeah."[38] This, he said, was "the bad thing which had destroyed the Children but it would do so no longer."[39]

The fiscal's investigation was quick and ruthless. Hans was soon apprehended, and he, Venus, and several others were convicted and given brutal sentences.

Figure 4. In this vivid painting, a driver presides over a spiritual ritual, likely
one associated with the Afro-Surinamese practice of *winti*. Like obeah,
it often involved trance-induced spirit possession. Dutch painter Dirk
Valkenburg worked as a bookkeeper and artist on sugar plantations in early
eighteenth-century Suriname. Dirk Valkenburg, *Slavendans*, oil on canvas,
22.8 × 18.3 in., ca. 1707. Statens Museum for Kunst, Copenhagen, Denmark.

January was singled out as especially culpable because he was a driver. According to the fiscal, "the offence ... would be rightly censured & severely punished if committed by any individual." But it was "far more deserving of the utmost rigour of the law when committed by the Head driver of an Estate, in whom great trust & Confidence [was] placed." January was sentenced to a series of painful, humiliating punishments. He was publicly flogged under the gallows and branded. Then he was taken back to the plantation, where he was forced to work with a heavy chain locked to his leg for the next year. Of course, January also lost his position as head driver and was demoted to the status of an ordinary laborer.[40]

The events that culminated in January's demotion ultimately led enslavers and enslaved laborers to see him in contradictory ways. While no one doubted the extent of January's authority, whites saw him as a man who had abused that authority to induce others to participate in a criminal conspiracy. He was therefore, in their eyes, guilty of the most egregious abuse of power—the epitome of a driver who betrayed their trust. In contrast, other enslaved people likely saw January as the exact opposite: a courageous leader, a true Big Man, who had taken great risks to heal and protect them when no one else would. For them, January was anything but a bad driver. What's more, the authority that he earned by sticking his neck out for others would turn out to be remarkably enduring. Even the plantation's owner, who described January some ten years later as a "disgraced Driver," recognized that January still "held an unbounded authority over the gang of slaves."[41] In retrospect, everyone could see that the unusual circumstances surrounding January's demotion had sown the seeds of the conflict that would erupt a decade later.

Blowback

For a time after his demotion, January took out his anger through small acts of retribution. As Boas put it, "[January] conducted himself when ever an opportunity occurred of treating me with the utmost disrespect." The "many instances" of January's "disrespectful conduct" included deliberate efforts to undermine Boas's authority. When January addressed Boas, he made a point of dropping the "Mr." He also directed others to follow suit. As Boas learned from one of the current drivers, January had told others "not to call [him] 'Mr.' but plainly 'Boas.'"[42] With the political skill that characterized the most adept drivers, January managed to make his bitter grudge against Boas clear without going far enough to provoke white plantation authorities to punish him. He may well have guessed that Boas felt pressure to overlook his behavior out of a sense that cracking down on a widely respected Big Man would backfire.

For most other drivers who lost their position, the consequences of demotion were quite different. To be sure, like January, they often found demotion devastating. It came with a series of social and material losses. No longer would they enjoy the status that came with the position of driver or the special access they had previously received to scarce material resources like clothing and food. For most, demotion also meant the end of being exempted from exhausting, dangerous fieldwork. But many demoted drivers, unlike January, lacked strong enough social connections within the slave community to mobilize followers and thus had little effective recourse. Such demoted drivers, no matter how embittered, posed little permanent threat to the plantation regime. Exploring the various ways that demoted drivers reacted nevertheless reveals both the deep investment drivers had in their position and the wider consequences of demotion, not only for drivers themselves but also for other people on the plantations where they lived.

For some drivers, the humiliation of losing their position provoked intense despair. According to the son of one planter, being "cast out of that favored circle . . . was a disgrace almost more to be dreaded than death."[43] Some demoted drivers in fact saw no alternative other than suicide. When Philip, an African man on a Berbice sugar plantation who worked as a "Driver to the Creoles," or children, was demoted, he was hopeless. As his wife put it, "His heart was turned." Philip was, she clarified, "ashamed of being put into the field after so long [being] a Headman." The day after the manager demoted him for chronic drunkenness and negligence—and then humiliated him with a public flogging—Philip ran to the Canje River that bordered the plantation. When he jumped in, the overseer feared Philip was trying to escape and sent others to capture him. But Philip had other plans. Soon he was too far away, and "before they could reach him he disappeared" and drowned himself, leaving behind a wife and several young children.[44] Philip may have been driven to suicide out of a sense that as an ordinary laborer rather than a Big Man, he would find it impossible to protect and provide for his family in the way that he had hoped.

The emotional unraveling of another demoted driver, Joseph, was documented by Moravian missionaries on plantation Mesopotamia in Jamaica. By the late 1770s, Joseph had been a driver for at least two decades and for several years had been head driver. Like Matthew, whose experience is recounted in the previous chapter, Joseph became one of the Moravians' earliest converts and a leader in their spiritual community. In 1778, he came into conflict with a new overseer. As the sympathetic missionaries noted, the overseer was "very sharp, & wanted [Joseph] to whip the Negroes more than he liked, & more than he could for Conscience sake." A year later, Joseph was "put down" from head driver to second driver. Soon thereafter he lost his position as a driver entirely and "was put to Rat catching." For being an ineffective rat catcher, he "got severe Punishment, which he took too much to heart." After his being a Big Man for decades, these humiliations were too much to bear. Joseph began drinking heavily and struggled with his Christian faith. The missionaries lamented that he "almost lost his Confidence to our Saviour," and he even showed up drunk to a burial service. Joseph was, the missionaries observed, "cast down with grief" and "seemingly heart broke over his hard treatment." A short time later, he died.[45]

Other drivers tried to leverage personal relationships with white people in positions of power to protest their demotion or regain their position. One such case involved an enslaved woman named Asia, who worked as driver of the "feeble gang" on a large Demerara plantation for some thirty years until the manager demoted her around May 1821. By October, Asia's predicament was dire. In her mid-fifties, she was unable to endure the rigors of field labor and, after just a few weeks, fell ill. According to the missionary John Smith, who lived on the same plantation, Asia "told the manager her strength was not equal to the work, and she could not do it." He responded by locking her in the stocks, on and off, for several months. One afternoon, after the manager "used her very ill by kicking and thumping her," Asia appealed to Smith's wife, asking her "to use some means to endeavour to get her out of the stocks" and, presumably, get her position back. Mrs. Smith recognized that fieldwork was "doubtless too laborious for such an old woman" and told the manager "that if he intended to continue such severe treatment to the old woman," she would appeal to the plantation's attorney. When the manager responded that he intended to lock Asia in the stocks until she "would promise" to work in the field as he demanded, Mrs. Smith made good on her threat and wrote to the attorney. Several days later, when he visited the plantation, he instructed that Asia be released from the stocks and, after regaining her strength, be given "some light work." There is no indication, however, that she ever regained her position as driver.[46]

A case from a remote plantation on the upper Berbice River illustrates how drivers sometimes appealed to colonial authorities in the wake of their demotions. Willem was a driver who experienced a change of fortune over the course of several years.[47] At least some of the other enslaved people on the plantation thought he was harsh and callous, as evidenced by a complaint from one man who told the fiscal that Willem was "so severe" that "the people [were] scarcely able to keep it out with him." Willem often told them he did "not care whether the people hang[ed] or drown[ed] themselves, or whether they r[an] away in the bush."[48] Willem's manager, however, considered him an effective driver—perhaps precisely because he was "so severe"—and even described him as "a great favorite."[49]

Over time, however, the manager soured on Willem, beginning with a drowning accident that claimed the lives of three of the "best people" on the plantation, which the manager blamed on Willem. Things really took a turn for the worse when Willem went to the fiscal—presumably to complain against the manager, though his complaint was not recorded—only to be dismissed and then "exemplarily punished." As a result, Willem retaliated against the manager. He allegedly neglected his own work and encouraged other enslaved people to do the same. He also became distressed that the manager no longer called him "a favorite," he said, but considered him "worthless," "good for nothing," and a "bad negro." The manager concluded that Willem was "endeavoring to ruin" him, so he "broke," or demoted, Willem.[50]

Finding it impossible to "agree with" his manager and the other enslaved people on the plantation in the wake of his demotion, Willem appealed to the fiscal. He did not complain that his manager had broken the law or otherwise abused him. Willem "ultimately admitted" that "his only Cause of complaint was a desire to be sold" or "hired out" because "his Master no longer liked him." His situation was so bad that he would "rather work in chains than on [his] master's place."[51]

For Willem, appealing to the fiscal only made things worse. The fiscal said nothing about the emotional dynamics in the case, ignoring Willem's despair. More relevant to the fiscal was that he had no "authority to compel a proprietor to dispose of [that is, sell] a slave merely to satisfy the wish of such a slave." Moreover, Willem had broken the implicit rules that governed relationships between enslaved people and their enslavers.[52] Willem's "master" was "bound to treat him with kindness & care" and "supply him with plenty of good food & necessary comforts." Willem, in turn, "was bound to perform his duty diligently & faithfully." Instead, Willem's "conduct" both as a driver and afterward was "very reprehensible." So, too, was the act of making a supposedly groundless complaint that deprived his enslaver of "much time & labour." The fiscal ordered Willem to be given forty-eight lashes and then sent back to the plantation, where Willem continued to face the humiliation of working alongside those he had formerly supervised—and the risks that came with working under a manager who hated him.[53]

Other demoted drivers who went to colonial authorities recognized that they had virtually no chance of regaining their position, no matter what they did, and instead seem to have been motivated by a desire to get some sort of retribution against their enslavers. In such cases, demoted drivers did not complain about demotion per se or ask to be reinstated but instead alleged that their enslavers had broken the law.

Take, for instance, a complaint from a man named Gabriel who lost his position as "chief driver" on a St. Lucian sugar plantation. Soon after his demotion, Gabriel joined another enslaved man in making a complaint against the manager. Gabriel told the protector of slaves that the manager had "taken away the Command from him," but he also alleged that the manager subjected him to an excessive, potentially illegal punishment. He had been confined in the cachot, or black hole, from Saturday afternoon until Tuesday morning and during his confinement was not provided with sufficient food. Gabriel also alleged that he had not received the required weekly allowance of "salt meat" but only one and a half pounds. The protector ignored the issue of Gabriel's demotion, which was not his prerogative, and focused on the details of his punishment. The manager and other witnesses said that Gabriel had lied about not receiving enough food—and Gabriel eventually admitted that he had refused the food offered because "he had food of his own." The manager also explained that Gabriel had been "deprived of his command" for doing his work poorly and for being "impertinent to him," especially when he sent "a chair to the field [so] that Gabriel might be more at his ease." The protector dismissed Gabriel's complaint and sentenced him to an additional punishment: thirty lashes and an entire month of confinement.[54]

For white plantation authorities, firing ineffective drivers without broad support from below was, most of the time, only temporarily disruptive. Even when such demoted drivers were bold enough to protest their demotion or retaliate, their resistance could usually be thwarted. In time, they might even learn to live with their new role, calculating that the risks of continued defiance were too great.

January's experience once again stands out. His decade-long antagonism toward Boas made clear that the wound inflicted in 1819 had never healed. Everyone, including Boas, knew that January continued to see him as "the cause of his being flogged under the gallows" and then demoted—and that January was determined to get his revenge by getting Boas fired, or worse. But it was not until 1829 that things reached a boiling point.[55]

January grew bolder in his opposition to Boas in the days ahead of the new owner's arrival. One night, when he was "quite drunk" and his inhibitions were lowered, January went so far as to taunt Boas at his own house. January told Boas that he "was not cunning enough for him." Then he made the most thinly veiled of threats. Pointing to the "Burial Ground," he asked Boas whether he didn't think he would be "laid there." Turning to two other white plantation employees who were with Boas, January answered his own question. Yes, he said, that is where Boas will go.[56]

Crisis

When the large group of enslaved people on plantation Deutichem assembled at the house of the newly arrived owner, Thomas Winter, that Sunday morning in March 1829, Winter was probably the only one who failed to realize that the roots of the ensuing confrontation between Boas and January stretched back a decade. Speaking in English, rather than Creole, so that Winter could understand, Boas accused January of having organized the gathering for nefarious purposes. January replied that his involvement was benign. He told Boas that he was not the instigator but the last one to join the group, that they had only gone for rum, and that there was "no harm" in having done so. Boas continued to insist that January was trying to undermine his authority. As tempers flared, Boas and January switched back into Creole, and it became clear that Boas was right to expect the worst. At one point, January explicitly challenged Boas's authority. Isn't Winter, he asked, our actual "master"? Boas weakly retorted that January was a "rascal" and tried to shut him up.[57]

Instead, January pressed the issue. He asked Boas: "Do I belong to you? Is the rum yours? or are you able to buy me?" In front of Winter and everyone else, January continued to make other comments that Boas knew were "intended of course to lessen [him] in their opinion."[58]

For Boas, things went from bad to worse when he ordered the current drivers to take January to the hospital and confine him in the stocks. January refused to leave. He would not go, he insisted. "No man," he added, would "hurt" him. And when the drivers tried to drag him away from Winter's house, "he began to fight."[59]

Boas panicked. Determined to assert his power, he insisted he would do whatever it took to get January under control. "If you will not go with two men," Boas told him, "I will put four, and if they are not sufficient I will put six, for you must, and shall go in confinement."[60]

Winter, shocked by such blatant defiance and no doubt concerned by his manager's inability to restore order, decided to intervene himself. "Take that man away," he ordered the drivers. But Winter and Boas would both soon realize that no matter how much of a threat January's resistance posed, their problem was much bigger.[61]

January, unlike many demoted drivers, had clearly succeeded in attracting followers during his tenure as driver and, remarkably, maintained many of them for some ten years after his demotion. To be sure, his enslavers had stripped him of his official title and rank, or his ascribed status, but they could not take away his achieved status. There is no evidence that they succeeded in getting anyone to see January as they did, as "a disgraced driver." Instead, January was a Big Man who could call upon his many supporters to help him strike back at the people he blamed for his downfall, with explosive consequences for the white plantation regime.

A series of conflicts in 1832 on a sugar plantation in Trinidad illustrates just how much trouble a demoted driver with allies, or followers, willing to take up his fight could cause. Goyo had an especially difficult job as driver because he worked for a particularly brutal manager, Thomas Fletcher, who routinely violated customary and statutory rules about labor and punishment. During crop season, everyone Goyo supervised had to wake up as early as "first cock crow" and begin work before sunrise. They were not allowed breaks to eat and sometimes had to work until 10:00 P.M. They also had no time to cultivate their provision grounds, which had been overtaken by "bush," and were often forced to work on Sundays. Fletcher, who actually thought they were not working hard enough, was also "always beating & illtreating them." Faced with such a desperate situation, Goyo eventually decided to help the people he supervised make their work less onerous. Predictably, white authorities on the estate noticed that Goyo was not driving the gang hard enough or, as the overseer put it, that "instead of forwarding the work" Goyo "did every thing to prevent them pushing on." For instance, Goyo "often" told "the able people not to go before the weak ones," in order to set a slower collective pace of labor. When Goyo was demoted, he responded by redoubling his efforts to sabotage production. The overseer concluded, "[There is] a Combination against Mr. Fletcher instigated by Goyo more particularly since he has been broke from being the Driver."[62]

Having stood up for the people below him, Goyo continued to enjoy widespread support among the plantation's slave community. If anything, his demotion only drew him and the other enslaved people on the estate closer together in their campaign of resistance, which became obvious in late April when ten people—nearly a fifth of the plantation's slave population—made a joint complaint to the protector of slaves.[63] Among the complainants, who were apparently instigated by Goyo, were Goyo's wife, sister, and nephew. And in early May,

Goyo himself left the plantation and traveled to the protector's office to support
the complainants. Goyo and the others alleged that Fletcher had committed several acts of egregious and illegal abuse. Goyo did not mention his demotion,
but it was clear he had a personal stake in seeing Fletcher punished. He told the
protector that Fletcher had once beaten three women, including his wife, with a
stick. Goyo must have known that by 1832 it was no longer legal to flog or beat
enslaved women in Trinidad and that such an offense could get the manager into
trouble. The protector found the charges—especially the beating of the three
women as well as an incident one night in which Fletcher allegedly broke the
current driver's nose with the butt of a pistol—serious enough to forward the
complaints to the attorney general. Fletcher avoided criminal charges due to a
supposed lack of evidence, but the collective complaint shows that a demoted
driver who could mobilize support from kin and community had the potential
to cause major problems for white plantation authorities.[64]

Additional evidence from other slave societies confirms that popular ex-
drivers could rally support from their fellow slaves and even encourage them to
commit bold acts of violent retribution. One day on a sugar plantation in the
Danish colony of St. Croix, some thirty enslaved people responded to the demotion of a driver by deserting and, that night, setting the cane fields on fire.[65] On
a Cuban sugar plantation, the demotion of a driver for supposedly disrespecting
the manager led to a violent confrontation with plantation officials and the newly
appointed driver. Having been forced to gather to witness their former driver,
José, be punished with twenty-five lashes and then locked to a ball and chain, the
other enslaved people on the plantation protested by striking. Desperate to reestablish control, the manager handed a whip to the new driver, Cristóbal *carabalí*,
and ordered him to terrorize the others into submission. Cristóbal tried but
wound up provoking fiercer resistance still from people who refused to respect
his authority. They began taunting him, asking sarcastically, "Are you perchance
our new [manager]?" And "by the time he had cracked his whip three or four
times," according to one witness, "the slaves beg[an] stoning Cristóbal," who "had
to run for his life."[66]

Among the most formidable allies some demoted drivers had were their
wives. These women were deeply invested in their husbands' status and were
sometimes willing to use their own considerable authority to fight back. One
demoted driver's wife, Caroline, organized a tenacious campaign of resistance
on a Berbice plantation in 1830. When the plantation was reorganized under a
new manager, Caroline's husband, a forty-nine-year-old African-born man, lost
his position as driver.[67] In response, Caroline collaborated with other women

to sabotage production. This became obvious to the manager one day when he found "two women doing the work of one" and tried to modify working arrangements, which prompted Caroline to declare that "the task was too great" and then refuse "to do any thing at all." Faced with such open defiance, the manager called Caroline a "d—— B——h."[68]

Even then, Caroline refused to back down. Instead, she escalated the conflict by looking the manager in the eye, which provoked him to threaten to "confine" and "cool" her. What, Caroline challenged, "are people not to look any more?" The manager ultimately had her locked in the "dark house" and, later, the public stocks. Caroline appealed to the protector, adamant that she had been punished without cause. As the manager saw it, the problem was not simply Caroline's defiance but her role in organizing "a combination among the gang" not to finish their work. Even after the protector dismissed Caroline's complaint, the manager found that confining "the greater part of" them in the public stocks night after night had not broken Caroline's determination.[69]

Instead, Caroline continued to instigate others to challenge the manager's authority, as shown by a second complaint to the protector just six days later. This time, fifteen women and girls, including Caroline's ten-year-old daughter, asked the protector to intervene. Alarmed by such a large group and by multiple complaints from the same plantation in the space of a week, the protector went to the plantation to investigate. There, the manager insisted that there was a "conspiracy among the women, not to finish their work." The overseer concurred that Caroline had been "the instigator of the rest."[70]

Just a year later in the same colony, the reorganization of another plantation under new owners led to a similar conflict when the common-law husband of a woman named Barentje was demoted from his position as driver and Barentje declared war on the plantation's white management.[71] In the wake of her husband's demotion, according to one of the new owners, Barentje was "disaffected to all order and propriety, openly declaring lately in the field that she would not work well, nor finish the task given her unless the Manager was removed, and that she would not be quiet or obedient."[72] Simmering tensions exploded one day in early 1831 when the owner decided to crack down on the customary practice of "walking at night," or leaving the plantation to visit friends and family. Barentje had been purchased a few years earlier from "a Dutch Estate," where, the owner knew, enslaved people "were much given to this custom." But he was determined to put an end to it. He repeatedly warned everyone not to leave. So, when Barentje and her husband left the plantation one night, they wound up in serious trouble. The current drivers reported her and several others who had gone "walking" and, when they returned, locked them all up. After several hours, the owner released them with what he described as a gentle rebuke—as well as a threat that future transgressions would be severely punished. Everyone "departed thankfully," except for Barentje. Infuriated that she had been ratted out, Barentje "immediately turned upon and began to abuse the Drivers."[73]

Barentje's defiance ultimately forced the owner to recognize that he was losing control of his enslaved labor force—and all because he could not control one enslaved woman. In an extraordinary move that must have been humiliating, he went to the fiscal to plead for help. The most recent confrontation, he emphasized, was part of a larger and more disturbing pattern. At root, his problem was, he said, that Barentje had "acquired such an ascendancy over the other Women that they do not finish a very reasonable task of work through fear of this woman." So, he asked the fiscal to punish her in order "to preserve some share of discipline . . . and prevent this woman from breaking through all restraint."[74] Women like Barentje and Caroline were evidently powerful authority figures in their own right, who could draw upon their social connections to wreak havoc on the plantation regime when their husbands were demoted.

These were exactly the kinds of crises that January threatened to provoke on plantation Deutichem. When, in front of the entire gang, Boas ordered the drivers to seize January and lock him up, the plantation dissolved into chaos. According to Boas, "the moment" the drivers managed to drag January away, everyone erupted in protest. The "whole gang" told Boas that if he was going to lock January up, he would have to lock all of them up. Boas told them the hospital would not hold them all, but if they insisted, he would confine "as many as the Hospital will contain." "No!" they responded, "January must be released."[75]

Even though Winter was a newcomer, he tried to use his authority as the plantation's owner "to reason with the people." "You begged for a dram," he said, "and it has been given to you—the man January has behaved ill and is punished—what have you to do with that? go home quietly." But they refused to disperse. For more than two hours, they continued to protest—a remarkable demonstration of just how far they were willing to go to stand up for a man they continued to recognize as their leader. Seeing that Winter was getting nowhere and anxious to demonstrate his managerial competence, Boas suggested that Winter had to "be a good deal fatigued" and might want to return to his house "and repose on the sofa."[76]

Winter retreated, but everyone followed him into the house. It was an egregious disregard of the owner's status and a courageous show of solidarity. Once inside, they continued to insist "that January [had to] be released" and that Boas "had no right to confine him." Winter told them he had "authorized" January's confinement, as if they cared. As Boas saw it, the world had turned upside down. Everyone was disobeying him and Winter, and even the drivers concluded that they "could do nothing and went away to their houses."[77]

Boas ordered the drivers back, stressing that Winter was "very much dissatisfied with their conduct," and insisted he would "not be forced to release January." Finally, after hours of turmoil, the drivers and "a few well disposed slaves" managed to get January's followers to disperse. Even then, the crisis of authority on the plantation was far from over.[78]

While Boas left to get help from a civil magistrate, two of January's supporters tried to appeal to white authorities on a neighboring plantation.[79] The plantation's owner saw them "come over running like madmen," but when he learned what they wanted, he "laughed at them" and sent them back with a letter for Winter.[80]

By this point, January's defiance and his widespread support was undermining whatever confidence Winter had in Boas's capacity to manage the plantation. Confronting Boas, Winter demanded to know what Boas had done to prompt this latest act of resistance. Boas essentially threw up his hands. "You have seen what has occurred to day," he replied. He did, however, promise to deal with the two troublemakers in the morning.[81]

Boas's interrogation of the two men the next morning revealed just how much discord January had sown. Strategically, one of the men apologized and said that he had only gone to complain because one of the drivers had "put him up to it." The other man remained defiant. He admitted their goal was the same as January's: to get rid of Boas. He pointed out that the longtime attorney—who had planned to transfer January to another plantation—had already left. So now, he told Boas he had to "go also." When Boas threatened to lock him up, he "pointed to his throat" and said, "You may cut this, but you shall not confine me." He also issued a threat: "I will plague you til you are forced to leave the estate."[82]

Boas's efforts to punish January and his followers had indeed jeopardized his own position on the plantation. In an attempt to salvage whatever was left of his reputation, Boas asked the civil magistrate he had summoned for help "to write down the old story" of Hans, the Minje Mama dance, and January's demotion ten years earlier. To keep his position, Boas needed to make it clear that the problem was not his incompetent management but January's influence and the uprising he had sparked. Boas suggested to Winter that there was a permanent solution to their problem: January could be removed from the plantation entirely.[83]

Winter agreed. As he later told the fiscal, it was critically "important to remove this slave who possessed such unbounded authority over the others."[84]

For several days, January languished as a prisoner on Deutichem, alternating between fits of rage and last-ditch efforts to change his fate. At one point, when his wife brought him something to eat, "he took it & dashed it away." Repeatedly, he asked Boas if they were really going to send him to a plantation on the remote Corentyne Coast (on the colony's border with Suriname) and, as if he did not know, why he was to suffer such punishment.[85]

For January, being uprooted from his community was understandably terrifying. He was close to fifty years old and had lived on Deutichem for many years, perhaps most of his life.[86] Over the course of years, perhaps decades, he had cultivated relationships there and earned a reputation as a respected Big Man. It must have been horrifying to imagine having to start all over on a plantation where he would be an outsider and utterly alone—even his wife refused to go with him.[87] Leaving Deutichem thus brought January face to face with the threat of social death.[88]

Boas taunted January, telling him that he had already been symbolically erased. "I have," he said, "taken your name off the list as being attached to Deutichem." In desperation, January made a fruitless appeal to Winter and then asked Boas for a pass so that he could go downriver to see the fiscal in New Amsterdam, the colony's capital. Unsurprisingly, Boas refused and ordered January to board the schooner that would take him to the Corentyne Coast.[89]

When the schooner passed through New Amsterdam, January, in a final act of defiance, fled and made his way to the fiscal's office. Even though January did not have a pass, the fiscal heard his lengthy complaint, committing some version of his story to the written record. The fiscal then summoned Boas, Winter, and other witnesses, who gave their own detailed accounts of what they had seen, heard, and done. Like almost all aggrieved drivers who appealed to colonial authorities, January did not get what he wanted; the fiscal refused to intervene and sentenced January to fifteen lashes.[90]

The problem of January's "unbounded authority" exposes a tension at the heart of the driving system. White plantation authorities relied on strong drivers to run their plantations and keep them safe. They knew that to get other enslaved laborers to follow orders, drivers had to project authority and command respect. That was why they appointed people to the position of driver who were already recognized as leaders—and why they went to great lengths to make everyone treat drivers as authority figures.

When planters or plantation managers concluded that drivers were ineffective or disruptive, however, they did not hesitate to demote them. Demoted drivers found their loss of status and the related material advantages devastating, but they often lacked the political capital to mount effective resistance. If anything, the feeble and counterproductive ways in which some demoted drivers lashed out essentially confirmed that they were not capable leaders.

Ironically, the demoted drivers who posed the greatest threat to white plantation authorities were those who had become too powerful. Such drivers had succeeded all too well in one of the driver's primary goals: earning the respect of other enslaved people and convincing them of their authority. When drivers like January—who had established themselves as strong leaders far beyond the scope of their official role and consequently commanded fierce loyalty—were demoted, they could not be easily controlled. Instead, such drivers could draw on their strong social ties to mobilize allies against the very plantation regime they had once made function. Sometimes, drivers conspired to overthrow their enslavers entirely.

CHAPTER 5

Rebellion

Sometime around Christmas in 1813, Alexander grew suspicious. The head driver on Bath, one of many cotton plantations spread across Berbice's west coast, he heard rumors that other enslaved Africans had been secretly gathering—at night—for the past several weeks or months. Alexander also heard that those gatherings had been organized so that enslaved people could appoint leaders to preside at the "festivals & funerals" of the different "nations" to which they belonged. Such assemblies, where people came together, away from the prying eyes of white authorities, to eat and drink, socialize, dance, bury their dead, and pledge support for one another, were relatively common in Caribbean slave societies. But the most recent gatherings were "private." Alexander had not been invited, and he began to wonder if the organizers had more "sinister motives."[1]

Alexander decided to investigate. Concluding that he would be unwelcome, he sent a spy. He asked Bacchus, another enslaved African man on Bath, to attend future meetings and "enter into the spirit of it." If the organizers asked Bacchus to swear an oath of secrecy, for instance, he was to take it "so as to deceive the party plotting." Then, he was to report to Alexander "all that would pass."[2]

What Alexander learned from his informant was alarming. Supposedly, plans were under way for a major uprising. Several plantations along the west coast—which stretched some twenty-five miles from Berbice's border with Demerara to the mouth of the Berbice River—were involved. Among the leaders, or "officers," were several drivers, including three men from the same plantation where Alexander lived. Alexander also heard that Africans of many "nations," including Coromantees (from the Gold Coast), Cangas (from the western Windward Coast), and Congos (from West Central Africa), were involved.[3] They were united by a common goal: "the overthrow of the Whites & the establishment of the authority of the blacks."[4]

Alexander's inquiries would turn out to be only the beginning of a much larger investigation. Starting in February of the following year and continuing for several months, colonial authorities interrogated more than one hundred people from dozens of plantations, including some twenty drivers. Almost all of those interrogated were men—reflecting the gendered assumptions of colonial officials, the decisions enslaved men made when it came to rebel organizing, the demographic dominance of enslaved men in the colony, and, perhaps, the strategic silence of enslaved women.[5] Some witnesses were interrogated at Government House in New Amsterdam, the colony's ramshackle capital and only urban center, and others were questioned in hastily assembled "courts" on various plantations. Government officials and individual slave owners alike pressured suspected ringleaders, participants, and bystanders to tell them what they had done, seen, and heard. The questions enslaved witnesses were asked and the answers they gave—or refused to give—were carefully recorded by colonial authorities. Surviving testimony spans some six hundred handwritten pages.[6] Why, investigators wanted to know, had African "nations" assembled and appointed officers? Was there really a rebel plot, and, if so, how far did it stretch?

The mountain of evidence generated during the investigation into this little-studied uprising offers an opportunity to build on the rich tradition of scholarship about the organization, leadership, and politics of Caribbean slave revolts by focusing on the drivers at their center. Historians have long recognized that rebellions across the Caribbean—and in other Atlantic slave societies—were often organized and led by drivers.[7] Enslaved drivers played prominent roles in rebellions, both in slave societies like nineteenth-century Barbados, where most enslaved people had been born in the Americas, and in places like eighteenth-century Jamaica, where Africans predominated. We also know that rebellions from Antigua (1736) to Cuba (1825) were frequently organized by the leaders of different "national" or "ethnic" groups and that rebels' previous experiences in Africa—particularly as veterans of war—shaped their military strategies and political visions.[8]

The 1813–14 uprising also highlights the multiple, contradictory, and pivotal roles of drivers in rebellion. Many African-born drivers were leaders in the national groups that were at the center of the planned rebellion, which they saw as an opportunity to construct a new political order that would serve their own interests. Other drivers, meanwhile, tried not to get involved while keeping quiet. And some drivers actively betrayed the rebellion.

Exploring the 1813–14 uprising thus offers an opportunity to ask a new series of questions about what drivers meant for rebellion and what rebellion meant for drivers. What role did drivers' leadership in African national groups play in forming—or undermining—the kind of solidarities and political communities that were necessary to organize a successful rebellion? What motivated drivers like Alexander, when confronted with a rebellion in the making, to make the excruciating decision to support, avoid, or oppose the rebel cause? When drivers did organize and lead a rebellion, how did their previous experiences, memories, and investment in hierarchical political structures shape their politics and plans for the future?

To Make the Country Good

Whatever Alexander heard about the secret meetings that took place in late 1813, only fragments of the many rumors spreading across the colony reached him. Subsequent investigations would eventually reveal dozens of accounts about the origins of the 1813–14 rebel plot. The accounts, often confusing and incomplete, overlapped, intersected, and contradicted one another. Nevertheless, from those accounts one can piece together three major narratives, all of which centered on the activities of different "nations" and their leaders.

For drivers, national associations presented both challenges and opportunities. On the one hand, since nations were not limited to individual plantations and membership in them was defined by ethnic identity rather than geographic proximity, drivers had no inherent political authority over these alternative sociopolitical communities.[9] On the other hand, national associations offered African-born drivers an opportunity to extend the geographic reach of their authority, seeking followers beyond their own plantations. Some drivers also used nations to claim an additional basis of political authority by seeking or accepting appointments as kings, governors, or other officers.[10] Doing so, however, inevitably brought them into conflict with other Big Men.

National associations, in one form or another, were common in slave societies throughout the Americas and the result of an ongoing process of ethnogenesis or group-identity construction. During the era of the transatlantic slave trade, displaced Africans from the same broad region—who sometimes spoke similar languages and shared cultural similarities—created new identities as members of the same diasporic "nation," such as the Coromantee (Akan people from the Gold Coast). In most cases, such people would not have considered themselves members of the same polity or ethnicity in Africa, where they had more localized identities, but in the Americas these broader "national" identities became socially, culturally, and politically meaningful.[11]

In the Caribbean, as elsewhere, national associations played a wide range of day-to-day functions as burial groups, mutual aid societies, organizers of social gatherings, and spaces for shared spiritual practices. At the same time, as political communities, nations were commonly associated with organized, collective resistance. Enslavers suspected that national assemblies—which provided enslaved people from different locations opportunities to communicate and coordinate—were a major locus of rebel organizing.[12] The Jamaican planter-politician Edward Long, for instance, worried about the nighttime funeral gatherings, commonly called "plays," that Coromantees and other nations organized.[13] Their assemblies needed to be surveilled with "particular attention," he recommended in his widely read *History of Jamaica* (1774), because they had "always been" a "rendezvous for hatching plots." Long was not mistaken: just over a decade earlier, Coromantees had organized what became known as Tacky's Revolt, the largest rebellion to date in the island's history. To prevent future rebellions, Long stressed that enslavers needed to "break that spirit of confederacy, which keeps these Negroes [Coromantees] too closely associated with one another."[14] For drivers, then, there was always the inherent risk that participating in national associations, even when they had no insurrectionary plans, would lead their enslavers to see them as rebels.[15]

In Berbice in 1813, many people said, the planned rebellion that was commonly known at the time as simply "this story" began on a plantation called Washington, one of the largest plantations on Berbice's far west coast, with enslaved people who identified as Congos.[16] The first organizer, they said, was a man named Congo Sam. He was a relative newcomer on Washington but had previously worked nearby, on a plantation in eastern Demerara. There, Congo Sam had been what one man called "a Big Man," and, although he was just a field laborer in Berbice, at least some of the two hundred and forty or so slaves on his new plantation began to recognize him as a "head man at Washington."[17]

Sometime in late 1813, it seems, Congo Sam began telling other people on Washington that they should reinvigorate Berbice's national associations. He told them how, on the plantation where he used to live (the Grove), the Congo nation had a king, a governor, and even a fiscal (the same title colonial authorities gave their highest judicial officer). As a result, "the story was good." But on Berbice's west coast, as Congo Sam saw it, things were disorganized.[18] So, Congo Sam proposed that they implement the same sort of "law" there— namely, that they appoint officers for different nations who would, among other things, care for the sick, organize funerals and festivals, and adjudicate disputes involving theft.[19]

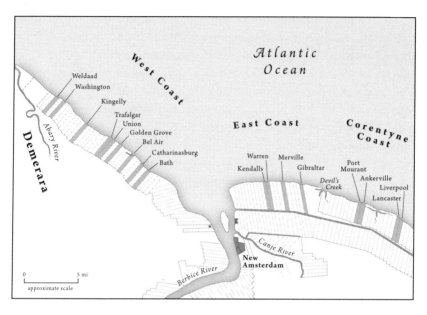

Map 2. Berbice's Atlantic Coast, 1814

The illicit nature of such nations, their association with rebellion, and the resulting secrecy with which enslaved people organized along national lines makes it difficult to gauge the extent to which national associations operated in the region before 1813, but scattered references offer some revealing clues. In 1808, enslaved men in Demerara who identified as Congos and were arrested on suspicion of having planned a rebellion told authorities that a few years earlier, "it had been customary for several years" for "every nation" to choose "*Headmen* or *Kings*, under whom were several other subaltern officers of the same nation." They also said "that the duties of these Kings [were] to take care of the sick among those of their respective nations by purchasing rice, sugar &c for them; to take care, at the burials of their dead, that the corpses were properly enclosed in a cloth, and the customary rites and dances duly observed." Back then, the "District of the Congos" had "extended from Elizabeth Hall to Lusignan," an area that comprised eleven plantations. But at some point, a "quarrel" between members of the Congo nation and their king about his ability to provide burial funds led to the dissolution of the Congo nation, which had since "been without a King or headman." From that point on, there had been no more "assemblies" or "*Companies*," and instead "those of the nation on each estate [had] taken care of the internment of their own dead."[20]

To rectify a similar problem in Berbice in 1813, or "make the country good," as some witnesses put it, Congo Sam enlisted established leaders with different kinds of authority.[21] He appointed Monday, the existing "head man for Washington Congos," as governor and Romeo, a Congo and the plantation's second driver, as fiscal. Congo Sam also included a key leader with ties to a very different region in Africa: the plantation's head driver, Pompey, who was "head man of the Mandingos" (Mandinka speakers from Senegambia). Congo Sam made Pompey king or, as one man identified him, "King—father—at top."[22] Together, the three leaders began recruiting other men on Washington and nearby plantations, using their personal connections and charisma to persuade—and coerce—others to join the nation.

A few weeks before Christmas, Pompey organized a series of nightly meetings, or suppers, at his house, where large numbers of Mandingos gathered along with other people likely to have roots in Senegambia—Bambaras and Fullahs.[23] Like many other men with leadership roles in African nations, Pompey did not include women. His own daughter, Margaret, "was sent out of the way" when they met, like the other women, who "were all excluded from the supper."[24] Once the men had assembled, Pompey began by appointing several "officers," including king, governor, fiscal, lawyer, captain, and *schoute* (sheriff).[25] Pompey was cagey, however, about the purpose of these appointments. At the first meeting, one man related, Pompey did not say anything at all about the officers' responsibilities—"it was within Pompey's breast."[26]

At a subsequent meeting, Pompey was apparently more explicit and more forceful. He focused on a few people he identified for leadership roles and proposed, as one man put it, that they "imitate the good example of the Congos in appointing persons to take care of the sick & their dead & that each should contribute towards relief of the sick."[27] Other participants said much the same—that the officers were "to take care of the sick and bury the dead," and "that as no new negroes come to the Country," referring to the end of the slave trade to Berbice seven years earlier, "they are obliged to work so much the more" and so "they must take care of themselves & do that story."[28]

When they were interrogated months later, several witnesses claimed that Pompey had forced them to participate. A field laborer from Washington named Hercules said that he rebuffed Pompey's offer to appoint him governor because "his house was too near Buckra house," meaning the manager's house, but, according to other witnesses, he ultimately took the role of king or "headman."[29] Greenock, a Fullah from plantation Weldaad and a *logie* (warehouse) driver, said he was "confined with tooth ache" and declined Pompey's invitation to join the meeting until he was "sent for a second time."[30] Even then, Greenock did not go willingly. Pompey had another man tie Greenock and bring him because "he was a big man [and] did not attend the meeting," or, as Greenock claimed, because he had refused to accept the appointment of fiscal.[31] (Another Mandingo man who refused to attend also said he was tied to a table by Pompey and two other men.)[32] Once there, Greenock "approved of the plan" but objected to asking others to contribute money, only to be "overruled" by Pompey, who said that everyone "should give only one or two bits," or coins, "as their circumstances" permitted.[33] Greenock ultimately agreed to be fiscal, he said, and told the others that if they "brought him money he would take care of it & bring it to Pompey."[34]

As Congo Sam explained, in addition to taking care of the sick and organizing funerals, one of the key functions of national associations was to investigate and punish crimes—especially thefts—committed by other slaves. In the Congo nation, if anyone "offended against his countryman," the governor, Monday, would "inquire into it & make the offender pay." A primary reason "this story was made," Congo Sam insisted, was "to prevent stealing." It was Monday's responsibility to "interfere" when any disputes arose and "decide who is right & who is wrong." Enslaved people were to handle these disputes on their own and "not to trouble the whites with these things."[35] Washington's second driver, Romeo, explained his role as fiscal in similar terms: "If any thing was stolen," he "would take the things out of [the suspected thief's] house and flog him to tell," or confess. If the thief did not return the stolen item or "had nothing to pay" as compensation to the victim, Romeo would "punish" the thief with "a good licking," or flogging. If Romeo himself were found guilty, the victim could go to the governor, who would take something from Romeo.[36]

Under Pompey, the Mandingos and Fullahs planned to establish a similar system for responding to thefts. Greenock said that as fiscal he would be the one to whom victims would turn and that he would "take effects" from the suspected thief "to make good what was stolen."[37] If Greenock himself were found guilty of stealing, Pompey said, the victim could appeal to the governor, and "if not brought to issue" the matter could be "laid before the king [Pompey]" himself, who would make Greenock "pay or go & fetch wood" as punishment.[38]

Around the same time that Congo Sam began organizing people on Washington, others were assembling on plantations Union and Trafalgar, in the heart of the west coast. On these neighboring plantations, jointly owned by Scotsman James Fraser and comprising more than two hundred slaves, Coromantees began meeting and appointing officers. The instigator, or "the cause of all this trouble," as one man put it, was purportedly a Coromantee man (though identified by

some as a Cape Lahoo) named Archy.[39] Enslaved for an unknown period of time
in Berbice, at some point—perhaps several times—Archy traveled to Britain
with Fraser. Soon after Archy returned to Berbice, likely in 1812, he reassembled
the area's Coromantee nation.[40] With the help of another Coromantee, named
Agar—who may have been recognized as the Coromantee king during Archy's
absence—Archy began by calling Coromantees to a meeting held at the house
of Union's "chief driver," Thomas. At that first meeting, Archy told the Coromantees that "he was the head man of them" and proposed that they appoint
several other leaders to serve under him. Holding the meeting at Thomas's was a
strategic show of respect as well as a means of getting Africans of other nations to
follow the Coromantees' lead, since Thomas was not a Coromantee but a Viah.[41]

Then, a few weeks before Christmas, Archy reached out to a longtime Coromantee leader on a nearby plantation to the east: the head driver of Golden
Grove, Quashie.[42] Quashie (a variation of Kwasi, an Akan day name for a male
born on a Sunday) was well known to people on the Fraser plantations, especially
Trafalgar, where one of his wives lived and where he visited regularly.[43] Exactly
what arrangement Archy proposed to Quashie is unclear—in the investigation
that followed, no one wanted to admit to having been the leader of an African nation implicated in a rebel plot. Archy said that other men on the Fraser
plantations asked him to be "Head Man of the Coromantees" and that when he
refused, Quashie continued in his role as "head of the nation."[44] Quashie and
other witnesses, however, placed the blame squarely on Archy. According to a
field laborer on Golden Grove, "Archy called our driver," Quashie, and made him
"king."[45] Quashie later claimed that when Archy told him he "was to be Governor of the Coromantyn," he initially accepted but at some point afterward "gave
it over to Archy." According to Quashie, Archy thus became the Coromantee
governor, and Agar took the title of king.[46] Whatever sort of relationship existed
between Archy and Quashie, both would play key roles in the reinvigoration of
a Coromantee nation that spanned multiple plantations.

Several Coromantees explained that they appointed officers for the same
reasons the Congos and Mandingos did: to take care of the sick, bury their dead,
and punish thieves.[47] Quashie's primary duty as the Coromantee governor or
"chief," he said, "was to mind the negroes when they were sick & bury them
properly when dead."[48] Another witness similarly said the officers had been
appointed "to make play at," or conduct, "the burials of the negroes."[49] Archy
said that the two unnamed men who supposedly wanted to make him "Head
Man of the Coromantees" expected him "to preside over them," providing soup
and poultry to the those who fell ill and more generally making sure "that the

sick were property attended to." The Coromantee fiscal's job, Archy said, "was to attend & take care of the sick of the several nations."[50] According to Quashie, the Coromantee nation also handled accusations of theft. "If any robberies [were] committed" by "officers" or other slaves, Quashie said, victims would not complain to white authorities but to the Coromantee governor, Archy, and he "would make the thief pay."[51]

Under Thomas—the head driver of Union and, according to some people, the "king of the Viahs"—there was an even more elaborate system of punishing crimes that reified socioeconomic distinctions among the enslaved. According to one witness, the fines for "common negroes," or "soldiers," were different from those for "officers." They "made a regulation in the event of their quarreling," he said, that "common negroes" who "troubled" one another would have to pay a six-guilder fine. If the fiscal "trouble[d] a common man," he would pay two guilders; a general would pay five bits, and the governor would pay three guilders.[52] Such differentiation suggests that hierarchy, rather than egalitarianism, was central to the politics of national associations in Berbice.

Around the same time, similar developments emerged on the other side of the Berbice River. Along the east coast and farther east along what was known as the Corentyne Coast, everything started with Caesar, the head driver on plantation Lancaster. Caesar had lived in Berbice since at least 1801, but sometime in 1812 other Congos along the Corentyne Coast started to recognize him as their king, or "Yanga."[53] Caesar later openly admitted to being king, insisting that the Congo nation he ruled existed "only to attend the sick and to play," or preside at funerals. Toward the end of 1813, Caesar and other Congos were in the habit of dancing "every Saturday night" on a different Corentyne Coast plantation, Ankerville. A turning point came when a Congo man named Dick died.[54]

When Dick's "countrymen assembled to bury him," Caesar brought rum to share, fulfilling his customary obligation as a Big Man, and proposed that they (re)establish a more formal Congo nation. Various leaders, Caesar explained, should be appointed to collect contributions for burials from other Congos. According to one man, "Caesar said that when a Congo die[d], all of them had to join and contribute."[55]

To extend the geographic reach of his authority, Caesar and his delegates traveled to several plantations on the Corentyne and east coasts. Caesar's commissary (described as his "aid de camp"), a man named Apollo from plantation Liverpool, made several trips to plantation Kendalls on the east coast, where he had previously been enslaved. Brandishing "a stick" Caesar had given him to show his "countrymen that he was a head man," Apollo explained Caesar's goals. Apollo was particularly keen to enlist the support of a man named John, who was evidently an important Congo leader in the region. If any Congos died on Kendalls, Apollo said, John should "send and give notice" so that Caesar and his officers could "play" there. In addition, Caesar hoped to unify the Congos. As Apollo put it, they should do what Caesar had done "in the Courantine" and "make up all their differences and make head men."[56] Caesar would soon "come & settle the Kings business in their quarter."[57] John may have been hesitant, but he eventually played a key role both in the Congo nation itself and in getting Africans who identified as members of other nations to organize their own parallel groups.

As often on other plantations, a key turning point on Kendalls emerged during a funeral. After the death of a child, John criticized the Coromantees there "for not having chiefs" and urged them to form their own national association. According to one woman, John said "the Congos had Kings, governors, and fiscals up the Corentyne & that the Coromantees [had to] do the same [t]here." Clearly, members of different nations in Berbice communicated with and sometimes emulated one another. Some people on Kendalls were opposed—one man said, "This story must not come here," and another was cautioned by his wife "not to have any hand in this story."[58] But John carried on with his plan and enlisted the support of a man named Michael who identified as a Chamba (a group with origins in the Bight of Benin). Together, they reached out to a man on a nearby plantation named Sibly who was an emerging "big man" or "head man" among the Chambas.[59]

The Chamba nation in eastern Berbice had also recently coalesced in the wake of a funeral gathering. According to several witnesses, during a funeral dance on plantation Port Mourant that was "properly conducted," people proposed that the Chambas appoint a "head man" so that they could "continue this good custom."[60] To fulfill this role, they turned to Sibly, head driver on plantation Warren. Another Chamba leader named Con, who was also a driver (on plantation Hampshire), asked Sibly via a messenger if he would help the Chambas do "as the Congos were doing"—namely, make "arrangements for assisting each other" by "collect[ing] contributions for the burial."[61] Sibly ignored Con's overtures until the funeral on Kendalls—which he attended and to which he contributed "fowls, bitts, & hogs"—when he faced renewed pressure from Michael and others to accept the appointment. Sibly ultimately agreed to be the Chambas' king, so long as he and Con would share responsibility. If "Con had a dance and funeral, he would contribute what he could, provided Con did the same."[62]

For the Chambas, who were evidently numerous in eastern Berbice, a major dispute emerged about the ethnic purity of their nation—specifically, whether they should incorporate the region's Coromantees, who came from an entirely

different region with no ties to the Chambas. Sibly favored including the Coromantees, since "there were not many of them," and told Con "he had better
take the Coromantees all with him." As a head driver, Sibly no doubt had experience getting enslaved people from different backgrounds to cooperate. But
"Con said he would not have the Coromantees," and they would have to handle
their funerals on their own. "If Coromantees were to come into this story," Con
insisted, Sibly would have to "come up himself & settle it."[63]

Meanwhile, the Congos grappled with even larger divisions, as Caesar
fought to crush rivals and extend his authority across the entire region, forcing
others to choose sides. On the east coast, a major challenge to Caesar's authority
came from a man named Jem, on plantation Merville. Several others, including
John on Kendalls, wanted to make Jem king of the east coast Congos.[64] It was
rumored that John proposed that just as "the Buckras," or whites, "had made a
division between the Corantine [Corentyne] and the East Coast, it was necessary to have a king" in each region.[65] Even on the east coast, however, some Congos saw Caesar, rather than Jem, as their king, which fed bitter internal rivalries.

When Caesar tried to assert his authority after a burial on Gibraltar, a plantation on the east coast owned by Caesar's former owner, Jem challenged Caesar's
authority. At a gathering of Congos at Christmas, hosted by a woman named
Susannah after her husband's death, Caesar took charge. He told everyone that
those who wanted to see the man's grave "[had to] come in about 3 weeks & bring
rum to throw upon it." But Jem "told Caesar he had no authority to give orders
in that quarter." "You have your side," Jem said, and "we will carry it over here."[66]
To directly challenge a head driver and recognized king—a man who expected
deference and obedience—was a bold and risky move. John, who continued to
back Jem's claim to the kingship, tried to negotiate a power-sharing agreement,
proposing that Jem serve as "governor of the Lower Coast," or east coast. But
Caesar openly questioned whether Jem was really "able to carry through on this
coast." In what some witnesses described as a "toast," Caesar sang "in Congo
language" that a leader needed to have "a strong hand and a heavy heart" as well
as "good sense." Jem insisted, "I can take it and am as good a playman as you are
and can carry it on as well as you, Caesar." But Caesar thought Jem was "an unfit
person to hold the post of king"; he merely "pretended" to possess the necessary
qualities.[67]

The argument about "the king business" went unresolved at Christmas because
Susannah, in an impressive show of her own authority, kicked everyone out of her
house and then "drove them away."[68] But Susannah kept quiet about what she had
seen and heard and, a week later, hosted what by all accounts was a much larger

Figure 5. Attendants carried Caesar, the rebel leader and king of the Congo
nation in Berbice, in a hammock to the New Year's dance on plantation
Gibraltar. This was an important sign of his rank, as suggested by this image
depicting similar practices in Central Africa. Hammocks, originally from
the Americas, were introduced to Africa during the era of the transatlantic
slave trade and were sometimes used as markers of elite status. *Maniere di
Viaggiare* (Ways of Traveling), hand-colored aquatint in Giulio Ferrario, *Il
costume antico e moderno o storia del governo, della milizia, della religione,
delle arti scienze ed usanze di tutti i popoli antichi e moderni . . .* , vol. 3, *Africa*,
2nd rev. ed. (Florence: V. Batelli, 1823–25), facing p. 356. Courtesy of the
Hargrett Rare Book and Manuscript Library, University of Georgia.

gathering at New Year's. There, Caesar returned and showed everyone that he
was determined to, as he put it, "be King of the whole coast from Corantine to
Canje"—that is, from the eastern border of the colony to New Amsterdam, where
the Canje and Berbice Rivers meet. Caesar "would not allow any other" king.[69]

As "many people of all nations" gathered on Gibraltar for a "great dance,"
Caesar made a grand entrance.[70] Carried by four "attendants" in a hammock
to show everyone just how powerful he was, Caesar arrived "a little before day
light," followed by at least a hundred supporters who had joined him during the
march from his home plantation.[71] His following was obvious and undeniable.

On Gibraltar, Caesar received a king's welcome. As Jem bitterly recalled,
people "began to cry out the King is come," and virtually everyone abandoned
the "rings" where they had been dancing to greet Caesar. "All the Big Men,"

other witnesses said, immediately "went to meet" Caesar, shaking hands and paying their respects.[72]

Participating in national organizing was inherently risky for drivers—even when nations focused on seemingly benign activities like organizing burials—in part because it forced them to collaborate with other powerful figures with different kinds of authority and social connections. On the plantations where they lived, drivers were used to being on top. Diasporic nations, however, had their own leaders—Big Men who did not automatically cede power to drivers. As a result, drivers who sought national leadership roles often had to compete for followers and sometimes found their status openly called into question. For everyone involved, the stakes became exponentially higher when people began talking about rebellion.

A Rising Would Take Place

West of the Berbice River, the period between Christmas and New Year's was also a major period of transformation for national groups. As enslaved people took advantage of the rare opportunities that the holidays allowed them to visit friends and family on different plantations, gatherings became larger and more frequent. At some of them, drivers and other national leaders began to talk about not just managing burials, punishing thieves, or helping the sick but also about more revolutionary plans. Later, reports would emerge that on various plantations people were "in the habit of marching & practicing military evolutions," or drills, "always at midnight and armed with cutlasses." Rumors also circulated about people displaying flags, making incendiary speeches, and dressing in royal garb—Archy purportedly wore a sash and cockade on at least one occasion—and about "gangs exercising with wooden swords."[73]

Like Alexander, many people began to suspect that the national groups that had coalesced earlier that year were planning a rebellion. For drivers, such talk forced them to make excruciating decisions. If they were to lead, or even join, the rebel cause, how could they figure out whom to trust, how to keep their plans secret, and how to motivate their followers to risk their lives? Those who aimed to keep their distance from what seemed to many like a suicidal plan, meanwhile, had to find some way of dodging an impending war whose combatants would not respect neutrality.[74] Finally, drivers who determined that they had more to lose than to gain in a war against slavery had to decide when and how to stop the coming rebellion.

National organizing always evoked the specter of rebellion, including those that had been brutally suppressed. Especially fresh in 1813–14 were memories of what everyone referred to simply as "the Demerary story." This was shorthand for a series of rebellions and rebel plots in neighboring Demerara over the previous few decades in which both drivers and national organizations had been implicated. In 1789, seven drivers from four plantations on Demerara's west coast launched a bloody rebellion, only to be overpowered and then hunted down. In the wake of the failed rebellion, "thousands" of enslaved people were forced to witness two days of public torture and executions, as some three dozen convicted rebels were flogged, hanged, and broken on the wheel.[75]

In 1804, colonial authorities responded with alarm to reports that enslaved Africans from multiple plantations on the Demerara River were gathering, or forming a "combination," which "seemed of a very dangerous nature." They had purportedly appointed national leaders "for the purpose of exercising themselves in the handling of arms." Those involved identified as members of multiple nations, including Congo, Igbo, and Coromantee. Dismissing participants' claims that the only purpose of such organizing was to arrange care for the sick and organize burials, authorities arrested and interrogated about a dozen men, including two drivers. Six of them were ultimately deported and sold into slavery elsewhere.[76]

An investigation in 1808 about yet another rebel plot illustrates how enslaved people kept alive memories of previous rebel organizing. In May, a panicked plantation manager told Demerara's governor that he had learned of the plot thanks to Francina, an enslaved woman he owned. According to her, the would-be rebels—which included several drivers and her own father, Valentine—planned to rise on Whitsunday, kill their enslavers, and divide the colony's plantations among themselves. Officials arrested and interrogated the suspected ringleaders, or "Chiefs of the intended revolt," but found no evidence to support Francina's claims. They did, however, uncover evidence that enslaved people remembered, quite accurately, what happened in previously discovered rebellions, particularly the one four years earlier. Valentine admitted that he had "often" talked to his daughter "on the Subject of what he called 'die houw worte,'" meaning the circumstances which took place three or four years [before], when Maurice of [plantation] Success"—one of the alleged ringleaders of the 1804 plot—"and other Negroes were sent out of the colony."[77]

For many enslaved people, such recent reminders that rebellions were hard to keep secret and would be brutally suppressed were reason enough to keep their distance from national organizing in 1813. One man said he "did not like the Demerary story and therefore would have nothing to do with" national groups. He also warned the head driver where he lived that if white people heard that slaves were being appointed as national leaders, they would "say negroes go to rise."[78] A Congo leader on the Corentyne Coast remembered "that story brought a Hell of a trouble in Demerara."[79] Susannah also "remembered the Demerara business beginning the same way" and the "trouble & banishment" that it led to. That was why, when the men who gathered at her house at Christmas began to discuss "the king business," she broke up the meeting and told them "she would not allow them to bring such matters into her house as she knew it would bring trouble."[80]

For drivers, the stakes of being connected to anything that resembled "the Demerary story" were especially high. In some cases, drivers warned enslaved people on the plantations where they lived not to take part. On plantation Britannia, when a driver heard from another enslaved man about meetings organized by the head driver of another plantation, he "cautioned him to have no hand in" subsequent assemblies.[81] A driver on one Corentyne Coast plantation refused to accept an appointment as fiscal from Caesar because he personally knew two men who had been punished for having been connected "with a business of the same kind some time ago in Demerara." So determined was he to avoid getting involved that he threatened Caesar that if he "ever gave him that name again, he would challenge [Caesar] to single combat."[82]

Drivers' concerns were well founded. In some cases, would-be rebels who hoped to recruit drivers explicitly referenced the crushed rebellions in Demerara. On the west coast, when four men from plantation Washington told Joseph, the head driver on plantation Hope, that they wanted to make him a king in the Mandingo nation, they "spoke about the Demerary business." Joseph replied that he wanted "nothing to do" with that "trouble." He knew "White man would not like it" and "would think the negroes would want to take the colony from them."[83]

Such hesitation—from the very people with the leadership skills and authority to organize a rebel coalition and lead a war—proved to be a major obstacle for Congo Sam and other Big Men from Washington as they sought to extend their network and recruit other leaders. Even drivers who initially seemed receptive sometimes turned out to be anything but, as illustrated by efforts to recruit Romeo, the head driver of plantation Kingelly. Romeo agreed to host a large dinner for Congo Sam and other "head men" from Washington and neighboring plantations. A couple weeks into the new year, Romeo provided a supper of hog and fowl to delegates from several nearby plantations.

After supper, "they all formed themselves into a Rank," witnesses recalled, except for the Washington leaders, "who paraded before them." Once all the "gentle-men" had gathered around "the principal table" and "began to talk about this business," the Washington Congos told the Kingelly driver that they "intended to make him King of the Congos."[84] They offered him gifts—silver coins, paper money, and rum—to persuade him to accept, but he had no interest in doing so. Congo Sam and others, however, pressed him so hard that they provoked "a great disturbance," which "nearly ended in blows." Finally, Congo Sam struck his breast and announced that he would be king himself. Even as Romeo "drove them away saying he wanted nothing to do with this story" and to keep it on "their own estates," Congo Sam told everyone "to sup with him at Washington the following Saturday, when they would arrange matters properly."[85]

Other drivers, meanwhile, welcomed talk of rebellion and even became eager rebel leaders. Among them were two of Alexander's fellow drivers on plantation Bath, which had emerged as a central site of rebel organizing around Christmas.

One driver, known by the Akan day name Quamina but identified as a "Cape Lahoo" (from the eastern Windward Coast), was recruited by one of the major organizers from plantation Washington.[86] Washington's second driver, a Congo named Romeo, asked Quamina, "Have you, in your quarter, begun to make the same Law that we have in this neighborhood?" Romeo clarified that the "law" meant "making Kings, Governors, &c &c.," and that the purpose of such appointments was to organize people on different estates for war. "We mean," he told Quamina, "to take the country to ourselves & drive White man." Quamina was receptive but told Romeo he needed to relay the message "to the Big Man" on Bath, a Canga driver named John.[87]

As it turned out, John had already been approached by another national leader, on plantation Golden Grove. Sometime before Christmas, Quashie, the head driver on Golden Grove and a major Coromantee leader, asked John to help him get "rid of the manager" on his plantation. Quashie sought John's help because he was known as a "wizard," or practitioner of obeah. Between Christ-mas and into the new year, he sent a series of messengers to John, including a woman named Queen, who was John's "country woman." She offered to give John "some hogs" if he provided something to make their manager "so sick that he would be obliged to quit the place," or die. After initially refusing to help, John sent a stick with some sort of material stuffed inside to Quashie, who then placed it along "the side dam" where the manager would, they hoped, trip on it and suffer the consequences.[88]

Back on Bath, the process of organizing for rebellion had accelerated after the death of John's child (unnamed in the records that survive) at Christmas. At the child's funeral, John and his fellow Cangas decided that they needed to follow other nations and appoint officers.[89] Even though they were from different parts of the Windward Coast, John worked closely with Quamina and with another driver and fellow Canga, Jean Baart (or John Bart), to organize a series of meetings over the following days and weeks so that they could "make this Law."[90]

However vague their intentions were at first, John and Quamina soon revealed their plans—and made it clear that everyone would have to choose whether to cooperate with them or face the consequences. At one meeting, Quamina reportedly said that since they "were ill treated by the whites . . . it would be good to fight them."[91] They would also hold anyone who did not join them accountable. When one man refused to attend a meeting, telling Quamina "that he was tired after Bacra work all day" and had no interest in whatever they were going to talk about, Quamina "said very well daddy you who mind Bacra will, when story comes on the [plantation], with Bacra suffer."[92] Drivers like Quamina were, of course, accustomed to threatening others to get their way.

If there was any doubt what that "story" would entail, Quamina and John clarified it at a later meeting. "Country people," John said, "if you all join in this business we shall get better by doing the same story also done in Demerara."[93] John would be governor and Quamina would be fiscal. John declared, "[We will] take the Country to ourselves & become our own Masters." With that, according to Jean Baart, "all the negroes assented with a nod, saying it was good." Baart himself, however, had supposedly "entered into this business under the impression that the appointments of chiefs & governors was only to provide at festivals." Once he learned that "a rising would take place," he "drew back."[94]

To put their plan into action, John, Quamina, and the other rebels on Bath looked to an elderly man from plantation Bel Air, a short distance to the west, named Banaba (or Namouay).[95] He was the head carpenter on Bel Air and, like John, a Canga. Banaba was, John and others on Bath had decided, to be their king. But when John told Banaba that they had appointed him, he was reluctant to accept. He was "too old" and, perhaps more important, "if such story reached the white people, they would think something bad."[96]

Banaba may have hesitated for the same reason John and others saw him as a natural choice for king: he had survived the largest rebellion in the colony's history, in 1763, when rebels took control of most of colony for more than a year.[97] At the time, Banaba would have been a boy or young teenager, so he may not have fought in the rebellion himself.[98] But, fifty years later, he was widely known throughout the west coast, in Quamina's words, as an "old fight man in former times."[99] Among Banaba's memories of the 1763 rebellion was the time he had been forced to watch Dutch authorities drag dozens of convicted rebels into a clearing behind the burned sugar mill on plantation Dageraad for public execution. There, enslaved victims were hanged, broken alive on the wheel, and burned at the stake.[100] Such memories must have weighed heavily, but Banaba ultimately accepted the appointment. He may have concluded that at his advanced age he had little to lose if they failed. He was, he said, "an old man," and one way or another "it was likely he should soon die."[101] And he almost certainly knew, as enslaved people throughout the Americas did, that while the 1763 had failed, rebels in Haiti had succeeded just ten years earlier, offering a dramatic example that a war against slavery could be won.[102]

Once Banaba took on the role of king, he began coordinating with national leaders on Bath as well as other plantations. They forged plans for war during a series of clandestine nighttime meetings—some on Bel Air, some on other plantations—and by early February 1814, they were all but ready to fight. Officers had been appointed on more than half a dozen plantations across the west coast. Several Big Men had pledged their support. The dry season was approaching, and it would soon be easier to move over land. And white authorities apparently had no idea what the people they enslaved were planning.

To launch the rebellion, Banaba needed just one more thing: a jug of rum. Presumably, he planned to hold a loyalty-oath ceremony, where rebel leaders would bind themselves and their followers together and accept that breaking the oath would result in death.[103] "As soon as the Rum came from Demerary," Quamina said, "Banaba would settle that story."[104]

Unfortunately, it took too long for the rum to arrive.[105] On Monday, February 14, as Banaba and the others waited for the boat from Demerara that would deliver their rum, Alexander blew the whistle. He told white authorities on Bath what he had learned about the planned revolt and about the meetings that had taken place over the previous weeks. Around the same time, drivers on two other west coast plantations—one of which was owned by the same men who owned Bath—did the same.

Like the many drivers who had kept their distance from national groups—especially once it became clear that plans for rebellion were under way—Alexander and the others apparently calculated that a rebellion was not in their best interest. Exactly why is unclear, but they must have weighed many factors. They may have suspected that the rebels, especially the field laborers who would serve as "soldiers," saw them not as potential leaders of a new political order but as defenders of the status quo and thus targets to be eliminated. They may have also known that in other revolts, from the 1763 Berbice rebellion to the Haitian Revolution, drivers had been killed—sometimes beheaded—by rebels.[106] Their status as Big Men did not necessarily qualify them to lead others toward freedom.

Deeply personal motivations may have also played a role in drivers' decisions to betray the rebel plot. In Alexander's case, informing on his fellow driver Quamina, in particular, may have been easier given the personal animosity between the two men, which apparently stemmed in part from an incident in which Quamina flogged one of Alexander's children.[107] Alexander and others also had to consider the consequences of a protracted war for their large families. By 1814, Alexander had eight children with his wife, Juno, six children with a woman named Nelly, and several grandchildren. Jean Baart similarly had two children each with two different women—both identified as his "wife"—four children with another woman, and many grandchildren.[108] What might happen, they must have worried, to their many family members if war broke out? As they may have known, during the last major rebellion—in 1763—many noncombatant refugees, especially women, had starved or been re-enslaved by rebel forces. Others had been marked as traitors and tortured or killed.[109] Perhaps the slim chance of victory was not worth the terrifying risks.

Overall, evidence suggests that in 1814 most drivers in Berbice—like most enslaved people generally—concluded that they had as much to lose as to gain by supporting the rebellion. Some historians' emphasis on the exceptional drivers who led rebellions in other times and places sometimes makes it hard to recognize that most drivers, most of the time, were not rebels.[110]

Whatever factors influenced his decision, Alexander's disclosure marked the beginning of the rebellion's unraveling. The next day, the co-owner of Bath—who was also a member of the colonial government—rushed to alert other officials. In New Amsterdam, the governor convened "an Extraordinary meeting of the Court of Police & Criminal Justice." They discussed a report from the manager of Bath, including summaries of what Alexander and the others had said about the "meditated rebellion of the negroes & a massacre of the Whites."[111] Then they raced to develop a plan to save the colony—and their own lives.

For most enslaved people on Berbice's west coast, the morning of Thursday, February 17, started out like any other day. Few would have known that just three days earlier, Alexander and a handful of other men had told their enslavers about a rebel plot that had managed to remain secret for months. And no one could have known that, overnight, the colony's fiscal, militia officers, and sixty soldiers ("all that could be spared" from the garrison) had sailed to the west coast in an effort to ambush the rebels before they could attack. So, as the sun rose and enslaved people turned out for work, there was little time to flee into the inland savanna, much less coordinate any sort of armed response. Before long, nearly forty men had been arrested. Dozens of them were loaded onto a ship called the *Planter*, taken back to New Amsterdam, and imprisoned. The following day, colonial authorities launched a "full & careful examination" of the rebel plot.[112]

"To take possession themselves"

As the investigation expanded in scope over the next several months, more than one hundred enslaved people—from the west coast and later from the east and Corentyne Coasts—were interrogated. They were cross-examined, confronted with the testimony of other prisoners, pressured to "confess," and, in some cases, offered pardons or reduced sentences in exchange for information. For everyone, the stakes were literally life and death. They knew that if they were implicated in the rebellion, they were likely to be gruesomely tortured or even executed.

What witnesses revealed—and chose not to reveal—reflected their varying degrees of involvement and their calculated decisions about how they might best protect themselves and those they cared about. Some witnesses said they knew nothing about any rebel plot—entirely plausible for some and obviously untrue for others. Others admitted that nations had been organized, night meetings had taken place, and officers had been appointed, but they insisted that those activities had nothing to do with rebellion. Others still said that there had been plenty of talk of rebellion but that they had kept their distance. And some witnesses admitted—a few from the very beginning, others in last-minute confessions in jail or on the gallows—that they had played key roles in organizing a very real rebellion.[113]

In their relentless effort to find sufficient evidence that they had identified the ringleaders and knew whom to punish, colonial authorities did not produce a single, coherent narrative of the rebellion's making or aims. Many of the questions they asked, moreover, reflected their own fears rather than actual developments. Early rumors that the rebel plot stretched across the entire colony and even into Demerara, or that rebels planned to rape white women, were never substantiated, even when prisoners were explicitly asked about such things.[114] Authorities similarly failed to find any evidence that rebels had coordinated with

Berbice's Maroons—a persistent fear for a government embroiled in seemingly endless "Bush Expeditions" to eradicate elusive Maroon encampments in the coastal hinterland.[115]

Authorities did, however, document tantalizing glimpses of enslaved people's contested rebel politics.

The investigation ultimately revealed that the rebellion's leaders—drivers and other Big Men—had a distinct political vision. That vision was informed by their collective memory of previous struggles against white enslavers as well as their own position at the top of the slave community's hierarchy. As in other driver-led rebellions, the drivers who planned to rebel in 1814 aimed to spark a revolution that would serve their interests, rather than those of ordinary enslaved people.[116] Having necessarily recruited and retained followers in order to do their day-to-day job, such drivers seemingly abandoned or betrayed them.

An especially revealing moment in the investigation came during one of several examinations of a man named Liverpool, who testified that he had heard stories about the nearly successful rebellion of 1763—the largest slave revolt in the Caribbean before the Haitian Revolution. Liverpool told the court that John, one of the drivers on Bath who helped plan the 1814 rebellion, told him "how the revolt was carried on [t]here formerly." John, in turn, had learned about the 1763 rebellion from "an Old Man" on Bel Air. No doubt, this was Banaba. As Liverpool testified, he had heard that in 1763 "the blacks got possession of the Country, & that they kept it till they began to quarrel amongst themselves when the Whites took again possession." During the rebellion, "the Congos fought against the Coromantees, the Mandingos against others," and "then when the whites came they caught them one [by] one & destroyed them."[117]

The basic contours of this account correspond to what historians know about the 1763 rebellion: after taking control of plantations throughout the colony, rebels split into factions as competing leaders advocated different strategies and political visions. At one point, the rebellion's original leader—a Coromantee who negotiated with Dutch authorities and proposed that they divide the colony in two—was overthrown by a rival coalition of Coromantees and "Gangoe" (likely Canga or Congo) leaders. Such infighting, which escalated into a sort of civil war, ultimately made it easier for the Dutch soldiers and their Indigenous allies to crush the rebellion and regain control of the colony.[118]

By 1813, there were only a handful of elders like Banaba who could personally remember the 1763 rebellion. By then, almost every enslaved adult in Berbice had been born elsewhere—most of them in Africa—and arrived decades after the rebellion.[119] And yet, the events of 1763 and its aftermath remained alive in enslaved people's collective memory for generations thanks to the efforts of survivors like Banaba, who taught newcomers the local history of resistance to slavery.

Such insurgent memories became a key part of enslaved people's political imagination, shaping the ways that they understood their situation as well as the strategies they developed to survive, resist, and rebel.[120] For many people, the rebellion that almost happened in 1814 was not a spontaneous outburst of rage, nor was it sparked by any single grievance or immediate development. Indeed, several witnesses described it as the latest battle in an ongoing war against slavery or, in their words, as the "renewal" of earlier battles that stretched back more than half a century.[121] The 1814 rebellion thus formed part of what political theorist Cedric Robinson described as the "Black Radical Tradition," or "an accretion, over generations, of collective intelligence gathered from struggle."[122]

The memory of the 1763 rebellion that enslaved people kept alive emphasized three basic lessons. First, rebelling carried major risks. Those who rebelled in 1763—along with many bystanders—suffered horrific violence at the hands of white authorities. Second, the 1763 rebellion had nearly succeeded. For more than a year, the rebels controlled most of the colony and held their Dutch enemies at bay. And, third, that rebellion ultimately failed not because the rebels lacked martial skill or courage but because of internal divisions.

In 1813–14, such divisions were, ironically, an inherent byproduct of the strategy that would-be rebel leaders used to mobilize other enslaved people. Leaders knew, it seems, that it would take deliberate effort to combine a variety of national groups whose members were spread across different plantations with their own leaders and hierarchies into a cohesive rebel coalition. From the beginning, many leaders worked not only to organize their own people but also to get Africans from different regions, and on different plantations, to do the same. Before long, Africans from more than half a dozen distinct national groups were communicating and cooperating.

At the same time, some leaders advocated for a level of flexibility in regulating membership in the nations they led, allowing Africans of other nations to participate in their activities. Sibly—the driver who was also the head man of the Chamba nation on the Corentyne Coast—wanted to include the small number of Coromantees there in the Chamba nation. Pompey, the driver who served as king of the Mandingo nation on the west coast, included people identified as Fullahs and Bambaras in his meetings. On Bath, Cangas and Cape La Hoos were included in the same gatherings.

Meanwhile, other leaders talked explicitly about the need for pan-African solidarity. One witness recalled that when three Big Men from Washington—

including the second driver, Romeo, who had been appointed the Congo nation's fiscal—recruited him, they told him they aimed "to form one *Great Engine*" and do away with "all distinction" between different nations.[123]

Rebel leaders were united by a widely shared goal, as horrified colonial officials confirmed during their investigation: to kill the colony's white inhabitants. Repeatedly, witnesses described what white authorities, still shaken by the success of the Haitian Revolution barely a decade earlier, viewed as a race war. Witnesses described plans that involved not targeted violence against especially hated enslavers but rather the wholesale slaughter of white residents. They planned, as the rebel leader Thomas put it, to "march straight to Town and fight with the white people."[124] On Washington, "Pompey's mind was bent on war."[125] On Bath, Quamina and John told their followers that the rebel plot "was not confined" to Bath and neighboring plantations and that "they were to fight & kill the whites."[126]

Other witnesses explained that their goal was to do what rebels in Demerara had tried to do a few years earlier, aware that the "Demerary story" was a common reference point (especially for Berbice's governor, who had been governor of Demerara during the 1808 conspiracy and, in November of 1813, just after he arrived in Berbice, received news from the acting governor of Demerara-Essequibo of an alleged rebel plot there).[127] As one rebel put it, "White men oppress them," so they wanted to "renew now" the "same fight they had with the White men in Demerara."[128]

After killing the colony's whites, what did the rebels plan to do? Some authorities assumed they planned to destroy plantations and abolish slavery. Officials asked Jean Baart, one of the drivers on Bath and among the first witnesses to offer detailed information about the rebel plot, if the rebels planned "to burn the estates"—a common tactic for rebels across the Atlantic world. Baart's answer must have shocked his captors. "No," he said, they "intended only to take possession themselves."[129]

Other witnesses confirmed that rebel leaders planned to take over, rather than destroy, the colony's plantation system. Alexander said the rebels' goal was nothing less than "the overthrow of the whites & the establishment of the authority of the blacks."[130] Quamina similarly said that after the rebels had defeated "Buckra," Banaba and John were "to take the Country."[131] An enslaved carpenter admitted that they had organized and appointed kings, governors, fiscals, and other officers "for the purpose of commanding the Estates."[132]

And, as white authorities were terrified to learn, some leaders had already made plans for dividing up plantation property and government buildings.

According to Bacchus, also enslaved on Bath, at one meeting on the plantation the driver John announced that after the rebellion, he would get the plantation's two logies (warehouses), while his fellow driver, Quamina, would get the "sick house" and the cotton gin.[133] And after white authorities were dead, according to Thomas, the head driver from Union, "old Banaba" would appropriate the governor's official residence for himself and "live in Government House."[134]

Rebel leaders did not, however, seek a complete inversion of social hierarchies. The drivers and other Big Men who organized the rebellion assumed that in the new society they created they would naturally be on top. In the lead-up to war, rebel leaders had drawn explicit distinctions between leaders and followers, elites and commoners. Much like under the driving system, they would be "officers," while everyone else—the "field people" or "low class of negroes"—would be "soldiers."[135] Repeatedly, leaders insisted that all "soldiers" were "to obey the Officers."[136] As Congo Sam explained, "The common negroes were to be soldiers," and "any order given by the officers to the soldiers must be obeyed."[137]

By all accounts, the men who planned the rebellion had no intention of sharing power with women. They had not included enslaved women in their meetings or appointed them as officers. Even the wives, sisters, and daughters of the major leaders do not appear to have had any formal role in the rebellion itself or in laying plans for the future. Some enslaved women may have chosen to distance themselves, too, seeing little to gain and much to lose in a Big Men's rebellion that was likely to perpetuate, rather than challenge, existing gender hierarchies.[138]

Ultimately, it seems that rebel leaders envisioned that many of the social hierarchies of colonial slave society would continue after the rebellion—as would slavery. Rather than either abolish the plantation system and the coerced labor that made it possible or flee into the bush and establish an autonomous Maroon community, drivers and their allies would simply take over the existing plantation infrastructure. In this respect, their goals were strikingly similar to those of many leaders of the 1763 rebellion, where drivers had also played key roles.[139] No doubt some people in Berbice had heard that when the rebels took control fifty years earlier, they had forced enslaved people to continue working on the plantations they controlled. Some would have also known about the foiled rebel plot of 1804 in Demerara, where two of the main organizers—one who identified as a Coromantee and the other as an Igbo—both claimed their own slaves.[140] By 1813, enslaved Berbicians had also all but certainly heard about the Haitian Revolution, where newly freed Haitians sought liberty and autonomy as peasant farmers, only to be forced back into plantation labor by elites who were determined to resume the export-oriented sugar economy.[141]

In the end, the kind of political vision at the center of the rebellion clearly appealed to some drivers and other Big Men but must have had little appeal to most ordinary enslaved people.[142]

Nearly two hundred years after the failed 1814 rebellion, a remarkable artifact turned up for sale in a London auction house: a silver medal originally given to Alexander, the driver on Bath, for "his Faithful Services to the Colony Berbice" in disclosing the rebel plot.[143] A similar medal—presented to an enslaved man named February who was a field laborer on a neighboring plantation, Catharinasburg, owned by the same men as Bath—was auctioned by Sotheby's in 1903.[144] In all, six such medals were awarded in August 1814 by Berbice's colonial government to the "trusty Individuals" who had suppressed the rebellion. Those six men, four of whom lived on Bath and two of whom worked as drivers, also received other tangible "rewards," including sizable cash payments and, in Alexander's case, a silver-headed cane.[145] In addition to honoring Alexander and the others for their "fidelity," those rewards were intended to promote "similar good conduct at any future period in other negroes."[146]

To receive his medal, Alexander traveled from Bath to New Amsterdam for a solemn official ceremony. As members of the colonial government looked on,

Figure 6. For his "Faithful Services," Berbice's colonial government awarded Alexander this engraved silver medal. One side reads: "From the Honble Court of Policy of the Colony Berbice To The Negroe Alexander of Pln No 17 West sea Coast as an Acknowledgement of his Faithful Services to the Colony Berbice Anno 1814." 3.15 in., 3.3 oz. Lot No 1499 X, July 13, 2011. Photograph courtesy of Noonans.

the governor presented Alexander the cane and medal as rewards for his "meri-
torious conduct." Alexander thanked the officials and pledged his "Fidelity."[147]
There, surrounded by grateful white authorities who credited him with having
saved their lives, the medal may have reassured Alexander that he had made the
right decision. Betraying the rebel plot allowed him to keep his coveted role as
head driver and gave his enslavers strong incentives to see him as someone they
could trust and, presumably, someone who deserved special accommodations.

Back on plantation Bath, however, the medal's meaning was more ambigu-
ous. Did Alexander wear it proudly, seeing it as an additional mark of his special
status as head driver and a Big Man? Perhaps he also thought it might intimidate
the people he supervised, or at least encourage them to follow his orders, since it
was a tangible sign that he was willing to enlist the crushing power of the plantation regime against his adversaries. Or maybe Alexander stashed the medal away,
out of sight, because he knew that for many people it was a bitter reminder that
he had betrayed a rebellion that might have liberated them.

Whatever meanings Alexander and other enslaved people attached to the
medals and other conspicuous rewards distributed to those who had disclosed
the rebels' plans, they were part of colonial officials' broader effort to construct
a reassuring narrative about the events of 1813–14. From the beginning of their
investigation, white authorities tried to see the rebel plot as a temporary aberra-
tion, the result of some discrete event or individual outrage. They sought answers
that would make the threat seem containable. Instead, witnesses told them what
they did not want to hear. As one man put it, the rebels' motivation stemmed
"not from bad treatment"—though there was plenty of that—but from "their
own heart[s]."[148] The planned rebellion of 1814 was nothing more and nothing
less than what historian Vincent Brown has described as "the natural consequence of slavery itself," the latest battle in a perpetual war.[149]

And yet, officials ignored their own evidence and embraced a different narrative. They told themselves that the foiled rebellion was not a sign of discontent
among the enslaved as a whole but rather the work of "a few unworthy miscre-
ants." They found it especially irrational that drivers and other enslaved men
with high-ranking positions had decided to rebel—despite widespread knowledge that drivers throughout the Atlantic world had joined and led rebellions
for centuries.[150] As whites saw it, drivers had received "the kindest treatment
and attention" and still, for some reason, organized against their enslavers and
"misguided" others into following them. And while the would-be rebels nearly
exposed the colony "to a repetition of those horrors rendered at St. Domingo
[Saint-Domingue]"—by then notorious among whites as "a scene of blood and

devastation"—they had been thwarted by people like Alexander. "A few of the more worthy part of the black population," as the fiscal described them, had been motivated by "sentiments of fidelity and affection to their masters" to betray the rebellion.[151] Colonial authorities thus reassured themselves that there was no systemic problem, no ongoing threat—that the plantation economy remained secure and that the driving system worked.[152]

Authorities' fears, however, were belied by the extraordinary effort, mere months earlier, they had put into making an example of the many people implicated so as to deter others from similar acts of rebellion. Beginning in April, when the trials of the rebels from the west coast concluded, colonial officials launched a carefully calibrated campaign of terror. Eleven of the people they convicted would never even be allowed to return to the plantations to which they belonged, where they had friends and kin. Instead, after being whipped and branded before onlookers in the center of New Amsterdam, they were "banished," or sold into slavery elsewhere.[153] The nearly thirty men who did return to their plantations brought with them visible reminders of the violence colonial authorities had subjected them to—nursing fresh wounds from severe floggings and lugging heavy iron chains they would not be released from for half a year.[154]

The starkest reminders of the colonial government's response to the foiled rebellion, however, were the severed heads of the ringleaders. Banaba and five drivers—Quashie from Golden Grove, Thomas from Union, Pompey from Washington, and Quamina and John from Bath—were convicted of "treason" and publicly executed by hanging. After their lifeless bodies swung from the gallows for an hour, they were cut down and then decapitated. Next, the corpses were taken to Crab Island, in the middle of the Berbice River where it empties into the Atlantic, and buried beyond the reach of those who mourned them. The rebels' heads, however, were taken back to the plantations where they had lived until they were captured two months earlier. There they were impaled on poles as "an awful example" of what happened to rebels, left to "remain until destroyed by Birds of Prey."[155]

Ironically, authorities' own investigation had revealed that such efforts to terrorize enslaved people into submission were doomed to fail. So, too, were their efforts to control enslaved people's political imagination. That many enslaved people remembered all too well the failed rebellion of 1763, the more recent Demerara plots, and the brutal oppression that followed every war against slavery and nevertheless decided to rebel in 1814 suggests that the lessons they drew from previous struggles were different from the ones their enslavers hoped to convey.

The investigation into the 1813–14 rebel conspiracy also shows us what the enslaved knew all too well: just how hard it was to organize a successful war against slavery. In Berbice and in slave societies throughout the Americas, rebellions failed for many reasons. Among them, as the evidence from Berbice illustrates, was the fact that enslaved people were often divided on crucial questions of organization, leadership, and political goals.

Would-be rebels everywhere faced the challenge of organizing large numbers of people spread across large territories. One of the most effective ways of doing so was to leverage existing national associations—or create new ones—in order to gather and strategize at national assemblies. The inherent risk of creating political communities based on distinct national identities, however, was that it reified ethnic and political divisions when broad solidarity was needed. Power struggles within individual nations created further internal fissures that made rebellions even harder to organize.

Successful rebellions also needed capable leaders. Among the most qualified were African-born drivers, who had precisely the kind of social authority and leadership skills to mobilize and command masses. Most drivers, however, tended to be deeply invested in their own position and status and, as a result, were often lukewarm or hostile to the prospect of a destabilizing rebellion. They stood to lose more than most enslaved people if a rebellion failed, which helps explain why most drivers either dodged rebellions or, like Alexander, undermined them. While drivers were ideally positioned to lead wars against the plantation regime, those who did so were exceptional.

To generate and maintain broad support, rebel leaders also needed a compelling political vision. Everyone could agree that overthrowing white enslavers and colonial authorities was a worthy goal, but when it came questions about how society should be organized, enslaved people were as deeply divided as all potential revolutionaries. One problem when drivers and other Big Men led rebellions was that their political goals reflected their own desire to remain in positions of power rather than the concerns and aims of ordinary enslaved people. Drivers certainly wanted freedom for themselves but not necessarily an end to plantation production, social hierarchies, or even coerced labor. Anyone who sought a truly radical, liberating revolution would have to look to other leaders.

Conclusion

At the heart of the driving system was the essential horror of modern capitalism. In the early 1780s—nearly ninety years before Karl Marx published *Das Kapital* (1867)—a head driver on a Jamaican sugar plantation, Francisco, explained the system's brutal dynamics. The field laborers Francisco supervised already worked "harder than any other Negroes, on any Estates round about." But the overseer "wanted more work of him & the Negroes than he was able to make them do, & more indeed than was right, & more than they were able to do." So, Francisco learned that when the overseer was watching, he had to "swear & tear" at his fellow slaves in a futile effort to extract more work from them than was possible.[1]

What do we gain by putting the driving system at the center of Atlantic slavery's history? In addition to a better understanding of how the plantation system worked on the ground and how people dealt with extreme forms of exploitation and oppression, *The Driver's Story* helps us see more clearly how the institution of slavery endured for so long despite enslaved people's repeated efforts to destroy it. If slavery was a never-ending state of war—and the stories told here suggest that it was—why did enslaved people find victory elusive?[2]

Prevailing approaches to the study of Atlantic slavery have offered incomplete answers. Part of the problem is that scholarship has generally been bifurcated. As the historian Vincent Brown observed, "trends in the study of slavery, as with the study of dominance more generally, often divide between works that emphasize the overwhelming power of the institution and scholarship that focuses on the resistant efforts of the enslaved."[3] Scholars writing in both traditions have given us a sophisticated understanding of the many ways enslavers flexed their power and the many ways enslaved people subverted their enslavers' control and fought for freedom. Nonetheless, the durability of the plantation regime calls for more explanation. With the critical exception of the Haitian Revolution, enslaved people's tenacious efforts to overthrow their enslavers were unsuccessful.

Focusing on drivers and the driving system offers one path forward—and an opportunity to integrate the methods and findings of the two dominant approaches to the study of slavery. Drivers stood at the epicenter of the daily war between enslavers and enslaved. They had to strike an impossible balance between the insatiable labor demands of their enslavers and the constant resistance of other enslaved people. Understanding the driver's world, then, helps us better understand how strategies of coercion and strategies of subversion developed in response to one another, and, ultimately, why the balance of power tilted toward enslavers.[4] It also lets us see how these power dynamics, too easily reduced to abstractions, played out in the messy, everyday interactions among individuals.

Enslavers embraced the driving system because it helped them manage their fundamental problem: how to extract labor from people who had every reason to resist. The system worked because enslavers coerced and incentivized drivers to perform the dangerous, difficult job of frontline labor management and discipline. Drivers proved to be brutally effective in crushing resistance from below. They accepted the fraught requirements of the job in part because they saw that in a world where enslaved people were treated as disposable, escape was all but impossible, and rebellion seemed suicidal, being a driver was one of the only ways to survive.[5] The work of drivers was less physically debilitating. They had better access to food and other scarce material resources. They also gained social influence within their communities, which they used to build families and accrue wealth-in-people. In short, they used the perquisites of their position to forge longer lives and build social ties.

At the same time, drivers refused to be turned into mere agents of planter power, and they remained deeply embedded in their communities. Drivers saw themselves—and were seen by others—as leaders and sometimes protectors. As Big Men, they stood up for their people, helping enslaved workers protest egregious abuses, negotiate labor demands, and secure customary rights to essentials like food and rest. They used their discretion to turn a blind eye to minor acts of resistance and mitigated the violence their enslavers expected them to inflict. Sometimes they tolerated—even encouraged—strikes, slowdowns, and desertions. As fathers and husbands, drivers helped themselves and others resist the persistent threats of "social death" and natal alienation by finding connection and kinship.[6] They were among the only enslaved men able to establish the polygynous marriages to which African men aspired. Drivers served as "kings" and other crucial leaders of diasporic African "nations" that helped enslaved people create a sense of belonging and provided mutual aid across plantations. Sometimes drivers even organized and led large-scale rebellions. Taken together, the personal relationships drivers cultivated within the slave community make clear that, for them, being a driver meant much more than being an enforcer of labor discipline.

In relying on a subset of enslaved people for labor extraction and social control, enslavers created a volatile system. They knew that drivers' interests were not the same as their own and that there was always a risk drivers would collaborate with other enslaved people to sabotage or destroy the very system they had been appointed to support. To coerce drivers into doing their job, enslavers subjected them to constant surveillance and brutal discipline. Even then drivers tested the limits of their enslavers' power, with quiet acts of insubordination and open defiance.

And yet, the driving system proved effective and resilient. It survived the many attacks against it, enriching enslavers and exacting a terrible toll on drivers and other enslaved people alike. Among its most insidious effects was the way it created or reified hierarchies and divisions among the enslaved, pushing drivers and the people they supervised to see one another more as adversaries than allies.[7] Then, as now, the ruling class maintained power in part by getting oppressed people to focus on internal conflicts rather than unite against their common enemy.

It is tempting to see the driving system as the epitome of slavery's backwardness. That is how many of its contemporary critics saw it. When British antislavery activists denounced the horrors of the driving system, for instance, they did so to expose the barbarity of a world where production relied on brute force and terror. For the abolitionist James Stephen, "the odious practice of driving" was both "unspeakably cruel and destructive to the slaves" and "the most peculiar characteristic of West Indian slavery."[8]

At the time, many people liked to imagine that the driving system was a perverse feature of primitive plantation societies that would disappear after slavery was abolished, whips were replaced by wages, and new models of labor management took hold.[9] In reality, the driving system—a system designed precisely to push workers to their utter limits—was a harbinger of modern labor exploitation. Indeed, many of the quintessential features of capitalism as we know it today—the never-ending drive to maximize production and increase profits, the insatiable demands made of laborers' bodies and time, the relentless surveillance and supervision of work, and the crucial role of coercion—took shape on plantations across the Americas generations before the industrial revolution.[10]

In the end, the driving system was, as the Guyanese historian and activist Walter Rodney described the slave trade, simply capitalism without a loincloth.[11]

NOTES

INTRODUCTION

1. The most common term for this role in English-speaking plantation societies was "driver," but other terms also existed, including "head man," "superintendent," and (mainly in Barbados), "ranger."

2. For racial capitalism, see Cedric J. Robinson, *Black Marxism: The Making of the Black Radical Tradition*, 3rd ed. (Chapel Hill: University of North Carolina Press, 2020 [1983]); Justin Leroy and Destin Jenkins, "Introduction," in *Histories of Racial Capitalism*, ed. Leroy and Jenkins (New York: Columbia University Press, 2021). See also "Forum: To Remake the World: Slavery, Racial Capitalism, and Justice," *Boston Review* (2017). For the sheer physical toll of plantation labor, see Justin Roberts, "The Whip and the Hoe: Violence, Work and Productivity on Anglo-American Plantations," *Journal of Global Slavery* 6, no. 1 (2021): 108–12. For enslavers' attempts to transform enslaved laborers into commodities, see Stephanie E. Smallwood, *Saltwater Slavery: A Middle Passage from Africa to American Diaspora* (Cambridge, Mass.: Harvard University Press, 2007); Daina Ramey Berry, *The Price for Their*

Pound of Flesh: The Value of the Enslaved, from Womb to Grave, in the Building of a Nation (Boston: Beacon Press, 2017); Jennifer L. Morgan, *Reckoning with Slavery: Gender, Kinship, and Capitalism in the Early Black Atlantic* (Durham: Duke University Press, 2021). As Sidney Mintz argued, "The work regimen made the slaves into anonymous units of labour—alienated, expendable, interchangeable—as if they lacked individuality or any personal past." Mintz, *Three Ancient Colonies: Caribbean Themes and Variations* (Cambridge, Mass.: Harvard University Press, 2010), 11.

3. For slavery as a state of perpetual war, see Vincent Brown, *Tacky's Revolt: The Story of an Atlantic Slave War* (Cambridge, Mass.: Harvard University Press, 2020).

4. For the global history of what Philip D. Curtin called the "plantation complex," see Curtin, *The Rise and Fall of the Plantation Complex: Essays in Atlantic History* (New York: Cambridge University Press, 1998 [1990]). See also Michael Craton, "The Historical Roots of the Plantation Model," S&A, 5, no. 3 (1984): 189–221; Stuart B. Schwartz, ed., *Tropical Babylons: Sugar and the Making of the Atlantic World, 1450–1680* (Chapel Hill: University of North Carolina Press, 2004); Trevor Burnard, *Planters, Merchants, and Slaves: Plantation Societies in British America, 1650–1820* (Chicago: University of Chicago Press, 2015).

5. Drivers are most closely associated with sugar production in the Caribbean, where they were ubiquitous, but they were common throughout the Americas and used on plantations that produced different crops, including rice, coffee, and cotton, and on woodcutting establishments.

6. For the rise of the "integrated" sugar plantation in Barbados and the origins of the gang system, see Russell R. Menard, *Sweet Negotiations: Sugar, Slavery, and Plantation Agriculture in Early Barbados* (Charlottesville: University of Virginia Press, 2006); Simon Newman, *A New World of Labor: The Development of Plantation Slavery in the British Atlantic* (Philadelphia: University of Pennsylvania Press, 2013); Richard S. Dunn, *Sugar and Slaves: The Rise of the Planter Class in the English West Indies, 1624–1713* (Chapel Hill: University of North Carolina Press, 1972); Hilary McD. Beckles, *White Servitude and Black Slavery in Barbados, 1627–1715* (Knoxville: University of Tennessee Press, 1989); Jenny Shaw, *Everyday Life in the Early English Caribbean: Irish, Africans, and the Construction of Difference* (Athens: University of Georgia Press, 2013).

7. Antiguan planter Samuel Martin described the plantation as a "well constructed machine" with "various wheels, turning different ways, and yet all contributing to the great end proposed." Martin, *Essay upon Plantership*, 2nd ed. (London: T. Smith, 1750), 30. See also Trevor Burnard and John Garrigus, *The Plantation Machine: Atlantic Capitalism in French Saint-Domingue and British Jamaica* (Philadelphia: University of Pennsylvania Press, 2016), esp. 3–8, 40–41.

8. For "slave labor camp" rather than "plantation," see Peter H. Wood, "Slave Labor Camps in Early America: Overcoming Denial and Discovering the Gulag," in *Inequality in Early America*, ed. Carla Gardina Pestana and Sharon V. Salinger (Hanover, N.H.: University Press of New England, 1999), 222–38.

9. Richard Alsopp, *Dictionary of Caribbean English Usage* (Kingston: University of the West Indies Press, 2003), 533.

10. "Complaint of the negro Hero belonging to Pln. Kilcoy," Aug. 25, 1825, CO 116/140, TNA.

11. For amelioration, see J. R. Ward, *British West Indian Slavery, 1750–1834: The Process of Amelioration* (New York: Oxford University Press, 1988); Claudius K. Fergus, *Revolutionary Emancipation: Slavery and Abolitionism in the British West Indies* (Baton Rouge: Louisiana State University Press, 2013); Christa Dierksheide, *Amelioration and Empire: Progress and Slavery in the Plantation Americas* (Charlottesville: University of Virginia Press, 2014); Caroline Quarrier Spence, "Ameliorating Empire: Slavery and Protection in the British Colonies, 1783–1865," Ph.D. diss., Harvard University (2014); Randy M. Browne, *Surviving Slavery in the British Caribbean* (Philadelphia: University of Pennsylvania Press, 2017).

12. For the records of the fiscals and protectors of slaves, see John Lean and Trevor Burnard, "Hearing Slave Voices: The Fiscal's Reports of Berbice and Demerara-Essequebo," *Archives* 27 (2002): 120–33; Browne, *Surviving Slavery*, 2, 5–7, 34–42. Demerara and Essequibo were independent colonies for the majority of Dutch rule (though they shared the same governor and Court of Policy from 1783) but were officially united in 1812 as Demerara-Essequibo.

13. Browne, *Surviving Slavery*, 2, 5–7, 34–36; Lean and Burnard, "Hearing Slave Voices."

14. For the difficulty of recovering enslaved people's voices, perspectives, and experiences from legal records, see, among others, Emilia Viotti da Costa, *Crowns of Glory, Tears of Blood: The Demerara Slave Rebellion of 1823* (New York: Oxford University Press, 1997), 170–71, 234–42; Natalie Zacek, "Voices and Silences: The Problem of Slave Testimony in the English West Indian Law Court," S&A 24, no. 3 (2003): 24–39; Diana Paton, "Punishment, Crime, and the Bodies of Slaves in Eighteenth-Century Jamaica," *Journal of Social History* 34, no. 4 (2001): 923–54; Miles Ogborn, *The Freedom of Speech: Talk and Slavery in the Anglo-Caribbean World* (Chicago: University of Chicago Press, 2019), 35–68. For the broader methodological challenges involved in using the archives of Atlantic slavery, see Marisa J. Fuentes, *Dispossessed Lives: Enslaved Women, Violence, and the Archive* (Philadelphia: University of Pennsylvania Press, 2016); Michel-Rolph Trouillot, *Silencing the Past: Power and the Production of History* (Boston: Beacon Press, 1995); Saidiya Hartman, "Venus in Two Acts," *Small Axe* 12, no. 2 (2008): 1–14; Brian Connolly and Marisa Fuentes, "Introduction: From Archives of Slavery to Liberated Futures?" *History of the Present* 6, no. 2 (2016): 105–16.

15. J. H. Lean's quantitative analysis of these records in Berbice revealed that more than a quarter of all complaints from enslaved people were about work. Lean, "The Secret Lives of Slaves: Berbice, 1819 to 1827," Ph.D. diss., University of Canterbury (2002), 65. See also Mary Turner, "The 11 O'clock Flog: Women, Work and Labour Law in the British Caribbean," S&A 20, no. 1 (1999): 38–58.

16. For female drivers, see Diana Paton, "The Driveress and the Nurse: Childcare, Working Children and Other Work under Caribbean Slavery," *Past and Present* 246, suppl. 15 (2020): 27–28, 31–32, 42–45. See also my chapter 1.

17. For drivers in literature and historical scholarship, see Robert L. Paquette, "The Drivers Shall Lead Them: Image and Reality in Slave Resistance," in *Slavery, Secession and Southern History*, ed. Robert Louis Paquette and Louis A. Ferleger (Charlottesville: University of Virginia Press, 2000), 31–58 (esp. 33–43). For drivers in Jamaican reggae, see Jorge L. Giovannetti,

Sonidos de Condena: Sociabilidad, Historia, y Política en la Música Reggae de Jamaica (Buenos Aires: Siglo Ventiuno, 2001), 103–6.

18. Marlon James, *The Book of Night Women* (New York: Riverhead Books, 2009). James refers to enslaved Black drivers as "Johnny-jumpers" and uses "driver" for white plantation employees normally known by historians as overseers or bookkeepers. Contemporary observers rarely used "Johnny jumper," but when they did, they used it synonymously with "driver." See, for example, William Dickson, *Letters on Slavery* (London: J. Phillips, 1789), 18.

19. Eugene D. Genovese, *Roll, Jordan, Roll: The World the Slaves Made* (New York: Vintage, 1972), 365. Laurent Dubois similarly observed that drivers were both "collaborators with the master, playing a central role in the management of the plantations" and "community leaders among the slaves." Dubois, *Avengers of the New World: The Story of the Haitian Revolution* (Cambridge: Harvard University Press, 2004), 38. See also William Van Deburg, *The Slave Drivers: Black Agricultural Labor Supervisors in the Antebellum South* (Westport, Conn.: Greenwood Press, 1979); Randall L. Miller, "The Man in the Middle: The Black Slave Driver," *American Heritage* 30 (1979): 40–49; Paquette, "Drivers Shall Lead," 40–43. More recent work on drivers is cited in note 27 to this introduction.

20. John Blassingame, *The Slave Community: Plantation Life in the Antebellum South*, rev. ed. (New York: Oxford University Press, 1979), 258. For Blassingame's evolving interpretation of drivers, see Paquette, "Drivers Shall Lead," 42.

21. For the Caribbean sugar plantation as a synthesis of field and factory, see Sidney Mintz, *Caribbean Transformations* (Chicago: Aldine, 1974); Mintz, *Sweetness and Power: The Place of Sugar in Modern History* (New York: Viking, 1985). For the industrial nature of sugar production, see also Stuart B. Schwartz, "Introduction," in *Tropical Babylons*, 3; Justin Roberts, *Slavery and the Enlightenment in the British Atlantic, 1750–1807* (New York: Cambridge University Press, 2013), 287–90.

22. For ongoing debates about the relationship between slavery and capitalism—a field of study first developed by Black Marxist and radical historians, including Eric Williams, author of the pathbreaking *Capitalism and Slavery* (1944)—see, among others, Mark Harvey and Norman Geras, *Inequality and Democratic Egalitarianism: Marx's Economy and Beyond and Other Essays* (Manchester: Manchester University Press, 2018), ch. 5; Leroy and Jenkins, "Introduction"; Caitlin Rosenthal, "Capitalism When Labor Was Capital: Slavery, Power, and Price in Antebellum America," *Capitalism* 1, no. 2 (2020): 296–337. Scholarship on slavery and capitalism was reinvigorated after the publication of Cedric Robinson's influential *Black Marxism* (1983), which argued that capitalism has always been racialized. Many of the so-called new histories of capitalism focus on slavery (especially in cotton production) in the United States. See, among others, Walter Johnson, *River of Dark Dreams: Slavery and Empire in the Cotton Kingdom* (Cambridge, Mass.: Harvard University Press, 2013); Sven Beckert, *Empire of Cotton: A Global History* (New York: Vintage, 2014); Edward E. Baptist, *The Half Has Never Been Told: Slavery and the Making of American Capitalism* (New York: Basic Books, 2014); Calvin Schermerhorn, *The Business of Slavery and the Rise of American Capitalism, 1815–1860* (New Haven: Yale University Press, 2015); Sven Beckert and Seth Rockman, eds., *Slavery's Capitalism: A New History of American Economic Development* (Philadelphia:

University of Pennsylvania Press, 2016); Caitlin Rosenthal, *Accounting for Slavery: Masters and Management* (Cambridge, Mass.: Harvard University Press, 2018). For a critique of such interpretations, see Alan L. Olmstead and Paul W. Rhode, "Cotton, Slavery, and the New History of Capitalism," *Explorations in Economic History* 67 (2018): 1–17. Other important studies on slavery and capitalism in the Atlantic world include Morgan, *Reckoning with Slavery*; Diana Paton, "Gender History, Global History, and Atlantic Slavery: On Racial Capitalism and Social Reproduction," AHR 127, no. 2 (2022): 726–54; Walter Rodney, *How Europe Underdeveloped Africa* (New York: Verso, 2018 [1972]); Robin Blackburn, *The Overthrow of Colonial Slavery, 1776–1848* (New York: Verso, 1988); Robin Blackburn, *The Making of New World Slavery: From the Baroque to the Modern, 1492–1800* (New York: Verso, 1997); Dale W. Tomich, *Slavery in the Circuit of Sugar: Martinique and the World-Economy, 1830–1848*, repr. (Albany: State University of New York Press, 2016 [1990]); Joseph E. Inikori, *Africans and the Industrial Revolution in England: A Study in International Trade and Development* (New York: Cambridge University Press, 2002); Dale W. Tomich, *Through the Prism of Slavery: Labor, Capital, and World Economy* (New York: Rowman and Littlefield, 2004); Berry, *Pound of Flesh*; Burnard and Garrigus, *Plantation Machine*; Stephanie E. Jones-Rogers, *They Were Her Property: White Women as Slave Owners in the American South* (New Haven: Yale University Press, 2019); Toby Green, *A Fistful of Shells: West Africa from the Rise of the Slave Trade to the Age of Revolution* (New York: Penguin, 2020 [2019]).

23. Rosenthal, *Accounting for Slavery; Journal of Global Slavery* 6 (2021): 1–186 (special issue entitled The Management of Enslaved People on Anglo-American Plantations, 1700–1860); Roberts, *Slavery and the Enlightenment*; Bill Cooke, "The Denial of Slavery in Management Studies," *Journal of Management Studies* 40, no. 8 (2003): 1895–1918; Richard K. Fleischman et al., "Plantation Accounting and Management Practices in the US and the British West Indies at the End of Their Slavery Eras," *Economic History Review* 64, no. 3 (2011): 765–97.

24. Ira Berlin and Philip D. Morgan, eds., *Cultivation and Culture: Labor and the Shaping of Slave Life in the Americas* (Charlottesville: University of Virginia Press, 1993); Roberts, *Slavery and the Enlightenment*; Newman, *New World of Labor*.

25. For labor struggles, see, among others, Mary Turner, ed., *From Chattel Slaves to Wage Slaves: The Dynamics of Labour Bargaining in the Americas* (Bloomington: Indiana University Press, 1995).

26. Paton, "Punishment, Crime, and the Bodies of Slaves"; Diana Paton, *No Bond But the Law: Punishment, Race, and Gender in Jamaican State Formation, 1780–1870* (Durham: Duke University Press, 2004); Vincent Brown, *The Reaper's Garden: Death and Power in the World of Atlantic Slavery* (Cambridge, Mass.: Harvard University Press, 2008); Trevor Burnard, *Mastery, Tyranny, and Desire: Thomas Thistlewood and His Slaves in the Anglo-Jamaican World* (Chapel Hill: University of North Carolina Press, 2004); Fuentes, *Dispossessed Lives*; Jason T. Sharples, *The World that Fear Made: Slave Revolts and Conspiracy Scares in Early America* (Philadelphia: University of Pennsylvania Press, 2020).

27. As Robert Paquette observed, until the late twentieth century "leading historians of slavery . . . either touched on the driver perfunctorily or ignored him entirely." Paquette,

"Drivers Shall Lead," 38. Beginning in the 1970s, there was a burst of scholarship on drivers in the antebellum United States, including what remains the only monograph on drivers to date: Van Deburg's *Slave Drivers* (1979). For the Caribbean, one of the first scholars to pay close attention to drivers was the French historian Gabriel Debien. See Debien, *Les esclaves aux Antilles françaises: XVIIe–XVIIIe siècles* (Gourrbeyre, Guadeloupe, 1974), 105–17; Debien, "Sur les plantations Mauger à l'Artibonite (Saint-Domingue 1763–1803)," in *Enquêtes et documents: Nante, Afrique, Amérique* (Nantes: Centre de recherches sur l'histoire de la France atlantique, 1981), 219–314. More recent scholarship on drivers includes: Paquette, "Drivers Shall Lead"; Manuel Barcia, "Los contramayorales negros y mulatos en la Cuba decimonónica," *Boletín del Gabinete de Arqueología* 2, no. 2 (2002): 88–93; Browne, *Surviving Slavery*, ch. 3; Robert L. Paquette, "'A Horde of Brigands?' The Great Louisiana Slave Revolt of 1811 Reconsidered," *Historical Reflections* 35, no. 1 (2009): 72–96; Keith Mason, "The Absentee Planter and the Key Slave: Privilege, Patriarchalism, and Exploitation in the Early Eighteenth-Century Caribbean," WMQ 70, no. 1 (2013): 79–102; David Stefan Doddington, *Contesting Slave Masculinity in the American South* (New York: Cambridge University Press, 2018), ch. 2; Laura R. Sandy, *The Overseers of Early American Slavery: Supervisors, Enslaved Labourers, and the Plantation Enterprise* (New York: Routledge, 2020), ch. 6; Paton, "Driveress," 27–28, 31–32, 42–45.

28. For a thoughtful discussion of "what slavery can teach us about the history of business" and "the ways business history can help us to understand slavery," see Rosenthal, *Accounting for Slavery*, 187–98 (quotation, 189).

29. For "social death" and natal alienation, see Orlando Patterson, *Slavery and Social Death: A Comparative Study* (Cambridge, Mass.: Harvard University Press, 1982). My approach builds on Vincent Brown's argument that social death was "a compelling metaphysical threat" rather than a permanent condition of enslavement or accurate description of social life under slavery. Brown, "Social Death and Political Life in the Study of Slavery," AHR 114, no. 5 (2009): 1231–49 (quotation, 1244). See also Smallwood, *Saltwater Slavery*; Michael L. Dickinson, *Almost Dead: Slavery and Social Rebirth in the Black Urban Atlantic, 1680–1807* (Athens: University of Georgia Press, 2020).

30. Diasporic national groups represented an ongoing process of ethnogenesis or group identity construction, rather than the direct continuation of African polities or ethnicities. In most cases the diaspoic "nations" that emerged in the Americas did not exist as polities in Africa, where people had more localized identities. For different perspectives on "nation" and ethnicity in the African diaspora, see Douglas B. Chambers, "Ethnicity in the Diaspora: The Slave-Trade and the Creation of African 'Nations' in the Americas," S&A 22, no. 3 (2001): 25–39; Paul E. Lovejoy, "Ethnic Designations of the Slave Trade and the Reconstruction of the History of Trans-Atlantic Slavery," in *Trans-Atlantic Dimensions of Ethnicity in the African Diaspora*, ed. Lovejoy and David Trotman (New York: Continuum, 2003), 9–42; Gwendolyn Midlo Hall, *Slavery and African Ethnicities in the Americas: Restoring the Links* (Chapel Hill: University of North Carolina Press, 2005); Alexander X. Byrd, "Eboe, Country, Nation, and Gustavus Vassa's 'Interesting Narrative,'" WMQ 63, no. 1 (2006): 123–48; James H. Sweet, "Defying Social Death: The Multiple Configurations of African Slave Family in the Atlantic

World," WMQ 70, no. 2 (2013): 251–72; Walter C. Rucker, *Gold Coast Diasporas: Identity, Culture, and Power* (Bloomington: Indiana University Press, 2015). For ethnogenesis, see "Forum: Ethnogenesis," WMQ 68, no. 2 (2011), esp. the introductory essay by James Sidbury and Jorge Cañizares-Esguerra, "Mapping Ethnogensis in the Early Modern Atlantic," 181–208; John Thornton, *Africa and Africans in the Making of the Atlantic World, 1400–1800*, 2nd. ed (New York: Cambridge University Press, 1998), 195–205; Gomez, *Exchanging Our Country Marks*; Chambers, "Ethnicity in the Diaspora"; Lovejoy and Trotman, eds., *Ethnicity in the African Diaspora;* James Sidbury, *Becoming African in America: Race and Nation in the Early Black Atlantic* (New York: Oxford University Press, 2007); Sharples, *World That Fear Made*, ch. 4.

31. For conflict within the "slave community," a concept first developed in John Blassingame, *The Slave Community*, see, among others, Dylan C. Penningroth, *The Claims of Kinfolk: African American Property and Community in the Nineteenth-Century South* (Chapel Hill: University of North Carolina Press, 2004); Aviva Ben-Ur, "Bound Together? Reassessing the 'Slave Community' and 'Resistance' Paradigms," *Journal of Global Slavery* 3, no. 3 (2018): 195–210; Jeff Forret, *Slave Against Slave: Plantation Violence in the Old South* (Baton Rouge: Louisiana State University Press, 2015); Justin Roberts, "The 'Better Sort' and the 'Poorer Sort': Wealth Inequalities, Family Formation and the Economy of Energy on British Caribbean Sugar Plantations, 1750–1800," S&A 35, no. 3 (2014): 458–73.

32. For Big Man politics and wealth-in-people in Africa and the diaspora, including references to important scholarship, see my chapter 3.

33. Browne, *Surviving Slavery.*

SOURCES AND METHOD

1. Michel-Rolph Trouillot, *Silencing the Past: Power and the Production of History* (Boston: Beacon Press, 1995); Marisa Fuentes, *Dispossessed Lives: Enslaved Women, Violence, and the Archive* (Philadelphia: University of Pennsylvania Press, 2016); Saidiya Hartman, "Venus in Two Acts," *Small Axe* 12, no. 2 (2008): 1–14; Brian Connolly and Marisa Fuentes, "Introduction: From Archives of Slavery to Liberated Futures?" *History of the Present* 6, no. 2 (2016): 105–16.

2. For amelioration, see J. R. Ward, *British West Indian Slavery, 1750–1834: The Process of Amelioration* (New York: Oxford University Press, 1988); Claudius K. Fergus, *Revolutionary Emancipation: Slavery and Abolitionism in the British West Indies* (Baton Rouge: Louisiana State University Press, 2013); Christa Dierksheide, *Amelioration and Empire: Progress and Slavery in the Plantation Americas* (Charlottesville: University of Virginia Press, 2014); Randy M. Browne, *Surviving Slavery in the British Caribbean* (Philadelphia: University of Pennsylvania Press, 2017).

3. For the offices of the fiscal and protector of slaves and these records, see John Lean and Trevor Burnard, "Hearing Slave Voices: The Fiscal's Reports of Berbice and Demerara-Essequebo," *Archives* 27 (2002): 120–33; Browne, *Surviving Slavery*, 2, 5–7, 34–42.

4. Emilia Viotti da Costa, *Crowns of Glory, Tears of Blood: The Demerara Slave Rebellion of 1823* (New York: Oxford University Press, 1997), 170–71, 234–42; Browne, *Surviving Slavery*, 56–68. See also Natalie Zacek, "Voices and Silences: The Problem of Slave Testimony in the English West Indian Law Court," S&A 24, no. 3 (2003): 24–39; Miles Ogborn, *The Freedom of Speech: Talk and Slavery in the Anglo-Caribbean World* (Chicago: University of Chicago Press, 2019), 35–68; Marjoleine Kars, *Blood on the River: A Chronicle of Mutiny and Freedom on the Wild Coast* (New York: New Press, 2000), 246–52.

5. Unless noted otherwise, all translations are my own.

6. Peter Thompson, "Henry Drax's Instructions on the Management of a Seventeenth-Century Barbadian Sugar Plantation," WMQ 66, no. 3 (2009): 565–604. William Belgrove expanded and amended Drax's instructions, likely written in 1679, as *A Treatise upon Husbandry or Planting . . .* (Boston: D. Fowle, 1755).

7. For the origins of slave registration and the nature of this evidence, see B. W. Higman, *Slave Populations in the British Caribbean, 1807–1834* (Baltimore: Johns Hopkins University Press, 1984), 6–36.

8. Some of these records are available in digitized form at Ancestry.co.uk.

9. Higman, *Slave Populations*, 333, 667; Richard S. Dunn, *A Tale of Two Plantations: Slave Life and Labor in Jamaica and Virginia* (Cambridge, Mass.: Harvard University Press, 2014), 142–43, 432; Browne, *Surviving Slavery*, 226–27n10.

10. For this approach, see Tessa Murphy, "Centering Slavery in the Age of Abolition: The St. Lucia Registry of Plantation Slaves as Archival Source" (forthcoming).

11. For (British) Caribbean slave narratives, which are less numerous than those from the United States, see Nicole N. Aljoe, *Creole Testimonies: Slave Narratives from the British West Indies, 1709–1838* (New York: Palgrave Macmillan, 2012).

CHAPTER 1. THE DRIVING SYSTEM

1. For the centrality of whipping in discussions about slavery, see Justin Roberts, "The Whip and the Hoe: Violence, Work and Productivity on Anglo-American Plantations," *Journal of Global Slavery* 6, no. 1 (2021): 108–12; Diana Paton, *No Bond but the Law: Punishment, Race, and Gender in Jamaican State Formation, 1780–1870* (Durham: Duke University Press, 2004), 20.

2. For tally sticks as a key part of "the larger accounting systems of the plantation," see Caitlin Rosenthal, *Accounting for Slavery: Masters and Management* (Cambridge, Mass.: Harvard University Press, 2018), 35. Sometimes, white plantation authorities tracked production themselves with tallies. For example, James Alexander described a group of enslaved laborers on a sugar plantation in Essequibo who worked under the supervision of a driver armed with "a small cane" as well as "a white book-keeper," or junior overseer, who "held in his hand a board containing a register of names, and certain little pegs to mark off the tasks performed." Alexander, *Transatlantic Sketches, Comprising Visits to the Most Interesting Scenes in North and South America, and the West Indies*, vol. 1 (London: Richard Bentley, 1833), 98.

Drivers also sometimes used tallies to count the number of lashes they gave other enslaved people. For example, when one driver in Demerara was called by the protector of slaves to respond to a complaint from an enslaved man, he produced a tally and said he gave the man "the number of marks upon this Tally." June 12, 1833, "Appendix to Protector's Report," CO 116/161, 7.

3. Henry Whiteley, *Three Months in Jamaica, in 1832: Comprising a Residence of Seven Weeks on a Sugar Plantation* (London: J. Hatchard, 1833), 9–10.

4. For the growth of numeracy and the greater emphasis on new kinds of accounting, such as work logs, to track production in the late eighteenth century, see Justin Roberts, *Slavery and the Enlightenment in the British Atlantic, 1750–1807* (New York: Cambridge University Press, 2013), esp. 56–68. See also Rosenthal, *Accounting for Slavery*.

5. Samuel Martin, *Essay upon Plantership*, 2nd ed. (London: T. Smith, 1750), 30. See also Richard B. Sheridan, "Samuel Martin, Innovating Sugar Planter of Antigua 1750–1776," *Agricultural History* 34, no. 3 (1960): 126–39.

6. As John W. Blassingame observed, drivers were "almost literally shot at from all sides." Blassingame, *The Slave Community: Plantation Life in the Antebellum South*, rev. ed. (New York: Oxford University Press, 1979), 258.

7. Quoted in Gabriel Debien, *Les esclaves aux Antilles françaises, XVIIe–XVIIIe siècles* (Basse-Terre, Guadeloupe: Société d'histoire de la Guadeloupe, 1974), 128.

8. M. Poyen de Sainte-Marie, *De l'exploitation des sucreries, ou Conseils d'un vieux planteur aux jeunes agriculteurs des colonies* (Pointe-à-Pitre, Guadeloupe: Imprimerie de la République, 1802 [1792]), 3–4.

9. James H. Hammond, quoted in Leslie Howard Owens, *This Species of Property: Slave Life and Culture in the Old South* (New York: Oxford University Press, 1976), 121 ("most important negro"); Thomas Roughley, *The Jamaica Planter's Guide* ... (London: Longman, Hurst, Rees, Orme, and Brown, 1823), 79 ("most important personage"), 80–81. See also Robert L. Paquette, "The Drivers Shall Lead Them: Image and Reality in Slave Resistance," in *Slavery, Secession, and Southern History,* ed. Robert L. Paquette and Lou Ferleger (Charlottesville: University of Virginia Press, 2000), 32; Philip D. Morgan, *Slave Counterpoint: Black Culture in the Eighteenth-Century Chesapeake and Lowcountry* (Chapel Hill: University of North Carolina Press, 1998), 343–44; Ruud Beeldsnijder, *"Om werk van jullie te hebben": Plantageslaven in Suriname, 1730–1750* (Utrecht, Netherlands: Vakgroep Culturele Antropologie, 1994), ch. 7.

10. Alexander Barclay, *A Practical View of the Present State of Slavery in the West Indies* ... (London: Smith, Elder, 1826), 40.

11. Bernard Martin Senior, *Jamaica, as It Was, as It Is, and as It May Be* ... (London: T. Hurst, 1835), 60.

12. For sugar production in this period, see Stuart B. Schwartz, *Sugar Plantations in the Formation of Brazilian Society: Bahia, 1550–1835* (New York: Cambridge University Press, 1985), ch. 1; Stuart B. Schwartz, ed., *Tropical Babylons: Sugar and the Making of the Atlantic World, 1450–1680* (Chapel Hill: University of North Carolina Press, 2004); Arlindo Manuel Caldeira, "Learning the Ropes in the Tropics: Slavery and the Plantation System on the Island

of São Tomé," *African Economic History* 39, no. 1 (2011): 35–71. The largest sugar producer in the Americas until the late seventeenth century was Brazil, where a typical operation in the late sixteenth and early seventeenth centuries had 100–120 enslaved laborers, divided between about 60 people tied to the mill (*engenho*) and another 40–60 people owned by dependent cane farmers (*lavradores de cana*). Schwartz, "Inntroduction," in Schwartz, ed., *Tropical Babylons*, 18. See also Schwartz, *Sugar Plantations*.

13. Stephanie E. Smallwood, "African Guardians, European Slave Ships, and the Changing Dynamics of Power in the Early Modern Atlantic," WMQ 64, no. 4 (2007): 679–716. Simon Newman hypothesized that when RAC captives were sold in Barbados, guardians "may have been promoted more quickly into positions of authority on plantations, as drivers or even as skilled artisans in sugar production." Newman, *A New World of Labor: The Development of Plantation Slavery in the British Atlantic* (Philadelphia: University of Pennsylvania Press, 2013), 201.

14. For mestre de açúcar and similar specialists, see Schwartz, *Sugar Plantations*, 24–25, 66–69, 156; Alberto Vieira, "Sugar Islands: The Sugar Economy of Madeira and the Canaries, 1450–1650," in *Tropical Babylons*, 60; Genaro Rodríguez Morel, "The Sugar Economy of Española in the Sixteenth Century," in *Tropical Babylons*, 100; Stuart B. Schwartz, "A Commonwealth Within Itself: The Early Brazilian Sugar Industry, 1550–1670," in *Tropical Babylons*, 177, 189–90. For the role of similar skilled enslaved workers in the early Barbadian sugar industry, see Eric Otremba, "Inventing Ingenios: Experimental Philosophy and the Secret Sugar-Makers of the Seventeenth-Century Atlantic," *History and Technology* 28, no. 2 (2012): 119–47 (esp. 131–36).

15. The earliest clear reference I have found to an enslaved driver is from Colonel Henry Drax's instructions for the management of his plantations in Barbados (Drax Hall and Hope), which were "probably written in 1679," according to Peter Thompson. Drax referred to a man named Moncky Nocco, whom he described as "an Excellent Slave" and "head overseer." Thompson, "Henry Drax's Instructions on the Management of a Seventeenth-Century Barbadian Sugar Plantation," WMQ 66, no. 3 (2009): 565 ("probably written"), 577, 600 ("Moncky Nocco"). To the best of my knowledge, the first written use of "driver" came two generations later, when William Belgrove expanded and amended Drax's instructions as *A Treatise upon Husbandry or Planting* . . . (Boston: D. Fowle, 1755). Among several enslaved men with specialized positions, Belgrove mentioned "two Drivers . . . to overlook the others." Later, he referred to them as the "chief Driver" and "under Driver" and indicated that they both received salaries. In a different section, he referred to enslaved "Field Overseers," or "black Overseers," who were almost certainly also drivers. Belgrove, *Treatise*, 41 ("two drivers"), 44 ("chief Driver"), 64 ("Field Overseers"). See also Thompson, "Drax's Instructions," 578. Richard Ligon, who lived and worked in Barbados from 1647 to 1651, when the sugar boom was just beginning, described "subordinate Overseers" in charge of "severall Gangs," but these overseers appear to have been white servants. Ligon, *A True and Exact History of the Island of Barbados* . . . (London: Humphrey Moseley, 1657), 113–15. Both free and enslaved men were employed as drivers in the early Brazilian sugar industry, though the timing and evolution of the position there is obscure. See Schwartz, *Sugar Plantations*, 146, 148, 318–20.

16. For different perspectives on these transformations in Barbados—often called the "sugar revolution"—and their role in the broader evolution of sugar production and plantation production, see Russell R. Menard, *Sweet Negotiations: Sugar, Slavery, and Plantation Agriculture in Early Barbados* (Charlottesville: University of Virginia Press, 2006); B. W. Higman, "The Sugar Revolution," *Economic History Review* 53, no. 2 (2000): 213–36; John J. McCusker and Russell R. Menard, "The Sugar Industry in the Seventeenth Century: A New Perspective on the Barbadian 'Sugar Revolution,'" in *Tropical Babylons*, 289–330; Newman, *New World of Labor*; Trevor Burnard, *Planters, Merchants, and Slaves: Plantation Societies in British America, 1650–1820* (Chicago: University of Chicago Press, 2019), ch. 1; Richard S. Dunn, *Sugar and Slaves: The Rise of the Planter Class in the English West Indies, 1624–1713* (Chapel Hill: University of North Carolina Press, 1972); Richard B. Sheridan, *Sugar and Slavery: An Economic History of the British West Indies, 1623–1775* (Kingston: University of West Indies Press, 1974); Hilary McD. Beckles, *White Servitude and Black Slavery in Barbados, 1627–1715* (Knoxville: University of Tennessee Press, 1989); Philip D. Curtin, *The Rise and Fall of the Plantation Complex: Essays in Atlantic History* (New York: Cambridge University Press, 1998), ch. 6; David Eltis, *The Rise of African Slavery in the Americas* (New York: Cambridge University Press, 2000), ch. 8.

17. Menard, *Sweet Negotiations*, 94–95.

18. Historians generally agree, as John McCusker and Russell Menard argue, that gang labor was "the integrated plantation's hallmark and the major source of its productivity advantage over the dispersed system" of sugar production that predated it, but there is no consensus as to exactly when the gang system emerged. McCusker and Menard assert that "there is little evidence" that gang labor existed in the seventeenth century (the earliest evidence for the use of gangs on sugar plantations that Menard found dates from the 1740s), but other historians note that gang labor was mentioned as early as the 1650s in relation to Barbados. McCusker and Menard, "Barbadian 'Sugar Revolution,'" 301 (quotations), 321n38; Menard, *Sweet Negotiations*, 96; Burnard and Garrigus, *Plantation Machine*, 4. For the productivity of gang labor, see Eltis, *Rise of African Slavery*, 220–21.

19. For gang labor, see Roberts, *Slavery and the Enlightenment*, ch. 3; Philip D. Morgan, "Task and Gang Systems: The Organization of Labor on New World Plantations," in Stephen Innes, ed., *Work and Labour in Early America* (Chapel Hill: University of North Carolina Press, 1988), 189–220.

20. As James Craskell wrote in a 1763 letter, skilled positions for white employees were "dispensed with" to save money when there were "capable negroes to execute their offices." Quoted in David Beck Ryden, *West Indian Slavery and British Abolition, 1783–1807* (Cambridge: Cambridge University Press, 2009), 142n23. See also Debien, *Les esclaves*, 120; Roberts, *Slavery and the Enlightenment*, 209.

21. Morgan, "Gang and Task"; B. W. Higman, *Slave Populations in the British Caribbean, 1807–1834* (Baltimore: Johns Hopkins University Press, 1984), 179–80; Paquette, "Drivers Shall Lead," 31–32; Morgan, *Slave Counterpoint*, 220–22.

22. "Return of Slaves attached to Plantation Woordsburg . . . ," Dec. 8, 1817, T 71/437, 40–41, TNA.

23. "List of Male Slaves, belonging to plantations Best & Phoenix . . . ," and "List of Female Slaves, belonging to plantations Best & Phoenix . . . ," May 31, 1817, T 71/392, 929–45, TNA.

24. Roberts, *Slavery and the Enlightenment*, 133–46; Higman, *Slave Populations*, 161–68; Newman, *New World of Labor*, 204–10. For contemporary descriptions of the composition of gangs, see John Stewart, *A View of the Present State of the Island of Jamaica* (Edinburgh: Oliver and Boyd, 1823), 231; Roughley, *Planter's Guide*, 99–110.

25. Higman, *Slave Populations*, 169–70 (quotation, 169); Roberts, *Slavery and the Enlightenment*, 209, 231, 243.

26. Janet Henshall Momsen, "Gender Roles in Caribbean Agricultural Labour," in *Labour in the Caribbean: From Emancipation to Independence*, ed. Malcolm Cross and Gad Heuman (London: Macmillan Caribbean, 1992), 142–43; Barbara Bush, *Slave Women in Caribbean Society, 1650–1838* (Bloomington: Indiana University Press, 1990), 33–45; Marietta Morrissey, *Slave Women in the New World: Gender Stratification in the Caribbean* (Lawrence: University Press of Kansas, 1989), 67, 74–75; Higman, *Slave Populations*, 189–92; Claire Robertson, "Africa into the Americas? Slavery and Women, the Family, and the Gender Division of Labor," in *More Than Chattel: Black Women and Slavery in the Americas*, ed. David Barry Gaspar and Darlene Clark Hine (Bloomington: Indiana University Press, 1996), 21–22; Jennifer L. Morgan, *Laboring Women: Reproduction and Gender in New World Slavery* (Philadelphia: University of Pennsylvania Press, 2004), ch. 5; Bernard Moitt, *Women and Slavery in the French Antilles, 1635–1848* (Bloomington: Indiana University Press, 2001), 36–38, 43; Lucille Mathurin Mair, *A Historical Study of Women in Jamaica, 1655–1844*, ed. Hilary McD. Beckles and Verene A. Shepherd (Kingston: University of the West Indies Press, 2006), 198–206; Roberts, *Slavery and the Enlightenment*, 236; Jennifer L. Morgan, *Reckoning with Slavery: Gender, Kinship, and Capitalism in the Early Black Atlantic* (1 Durham: Duke University Press, 2021), 38.

27. For female drivers and children's gangs, see Diana Paton, "The Driveress and the Nurse: Childcare, Working Children and Other Work Under Caribbean Slavery," *Past and Present* 246, suppl. 15 (2020): 27–28, 31–32, 42–45; Roberts, *Slavery and the Enlightenment*, 141–42, 155–56; Dale W. Tomich, *Slavery in the Circuit of Sugar: Martinique and the World Economy*, 2nd ed. (Albany: State University of New York Press, 2016), 317–19; Jerome Teelucksingh, "The 'Invisible Child' in British West Indian Slavery," S&A 27, no. 2 (2006): 242–44.

28. Paton, "Driveress," 43.

29. Paton, "Driveress," 28, 44–45; William Dickson, *Letters on Slavery . . .* (London: J. Phillips, 1789), 12; Tomich, *Slavery in the Circuit of Sugar*, 318–19; Teelucksingh, "'Invisible Child,'" 242–44; Coleen A. Vasconcellos, *Slavery, Childhood, and Abolition in Jamaica, 1788–1838* (Athens: University of Georgia Press, 2015), 30.

30. Robert Renny, *An History of Jamaica . . .* (London: J. Cawthorn, 1807), 176.

31. [David Collins], *Practical Rules for the Management and Medical Treatment of Negro Slaves . . .* (London: J. Barfield, 1803), 181. See also Roughley, *Planter's Guide*, 105.

32. Poyen de Sainte-Marie, quoted in Moitt, *Women and Slavery*, 43.

33. Madeleine Spencer: "[Return of Slaves attached to] Union [plantation] . . . ," Nov. 22, 1815, T 71/379, 697, TNA; Sylvia: "List of Female Slaves belonging to Pl. Batseba's Lust . . . ," Aug. 26, 1827, T 71/394, 1823, TNA.

34. Roughley, *Planter's Guide*, 105–7; Charles Johnston, "A Few Disjointed Facts Connected with Slavery in Jamaica," in *The Tourist; or Sketch Book of the Times* 1, no. 1 (1833): 142; Tomich, *Slavery in the Circuit of Sugar*, 343; Moitt, *Women and Slavery*, 42–43; Paton, "Driveress," 45.

35. Roughley, *Planter's Guide*, 106, 109.

36. Roberts, *Slavery and the Enlightenment*, 155–57.

37. George Pinckard, *Notes on the West Indies* (London: Longman, Hurst, Rees, and Orme, 1806), 3:179.

38. Sept. 10, 1829, *Protectors of Slaves Reports . . .* , PP 1830–31 (262), 84.

39. For slave registration, see Higman, *Slave Populations*, 6–36; Tessa Murphy, "Centering Slavery in the Age of Abolition: The St. Lucia Registry of Plantation Slaves as Archival Source" (forthcoming)

40. Higman, *Slave Populations*, 192–93. Higman hypothesized that "the unusual importance of female drivers in Barbados must be traced to the early age at which Barbadian children were introduced to field labor and the resulting large squads of children under 15 years of age to be supervised." Ibid., 193.

41. "List of Female Slaves belonging to plant Le Resouvenir . . . ," Aug. 20, 1817, T 71/392, 1090, TNA; John Smith diary, entries for Oct. 13 and Oct. 16, 1821, in Rodney Van Cooten, "Van Cooten Voices," at https://www.vc.id.au/fh/smithdiary1821.html#r1821 (last accessed Mar. 18, 2023).

42. Feb. 22, 1832, CO 330/28, 166, TNA; Higman, *Slave Populations*, 192.

43. Roberts, *Slavery and the Enlightenment*, 156–57.

44. For enslaved women's archival erasure, the pervasive silences of the archive, and the methodological challenges of using problematic and fragmentary sources to understand Black women's lives, see Marisa J. Fuentes, *Dispossessed Lives: Enslaved Women, Violence, and the Archive* (Philadelphia: University of Pennsylvania Press, 2016). See also Morgan, *Reckoning with Slavery*.

45. Roughley, *Planter's Guide*, 80–81.

46. Barclay, *Practical View*, 39–40.

47. A. C. Carmichael, *Domestic Manners and Social Condition of the White, Coloured, and Negro Population of the West Indies* (London: Whittaker, Treacher, 1833), 2:123 ("selected"); P. J. Laborie, *The Coffee Planter of Saint Domingo* (London: T. Cadell and W. Davies, 1798), 164 ("perfectly"). See also Debien, *Les esclaves*, 123.

48. Higman, *Slave Populations*, 189, 192, 590, 596, 598, 600, 602; Michael Craton, *Searching for the Invisible Man: Slaves and Plantation Life in Jamaica* (Cambridge, Mass.: Harvard University Press, 1978), 149, 187, 201–2; Randy M. Browne, *Surviving Slavery in the British Caribbean* (Philadelphia: University of Pennsylvania Press), 73; Roberts, *Slavery and the Enlightenment,* 213; Paton, "Driveress and the Nurse," 43–44; James Clifton, "The Rice Driver: His Role in Slave Management," *South Carolina Historical Magazine* 82, no. (4): 332–33.

49. Roughley, *Planter's Guide*, 25 ("the head driver"), 80–81 ("so many points").

50. Richard S. Dunn, *A Tale of Two Plantations: Slave Life and Labor in Jamaica and Virginia* (Cambridge, Mass.: Harvard University Press, 2014), 143, 432 (appendix 16, "The Occupation, Health, and Longevity of Mesopotamia Adult Slaves, 1762–1833").

51. For an extreme case, see the eighty-two-year-old driver, André Pombeau, on the Mon Repos sugar plantation in St. Lucia. Dec. 16, 1815, T 71/379, image 459 on Ancestry.co .uk, https://www.ancestry.co.uk/imageviewer/collections/1129/images/CSUK1812_133722 -00458?ssrc=&backlabel=Return (last accessed Mar. 19, 2023).

52. Browne, *Surviving Slavery*, 73–74.

53. For seasoning, see Nicholas Radburn, "'[M]anaged at First as if They Were Beasts': The Seasoning of Enslaved Africans in Eighteenth-Century Jamaica," *Journal of Global Slavery* 6, no. 1 (2021): 11–30; Stephanie Smallwood, *Saltwater Slavery: A Middle Passage from Africa to American Diaspora* (Cambridge, Mass.: Harvard University Press, 2007), 193–200; Vincent Brown, *The Reaper's Garden: Death and Power in the World of Atlantic Slavery* (Cambridge, Mass.: Harvard University Press, 2008), 48–51; Alexander X. Byrd, *Captives and Voyagers: Black Migrants Across the Eighteenth-Century British Atlantic World* (Baton Rouge: Louisiana State University Press, 2008), ch. 3; Dunn, *Two Plantations*, 157–59.

54. Robin Blackburn, *The Making of New World Slavery: From the Baroque to the Modern, 1492–1800* (New York: Verso, 1997), 339; Brown, *Reaper's Garden*, 50.

55. Michael Tadman, "The Demographic Cost of Sugar: Debates on Slave Societies and Natural Increase in the Americas," AHR 105, no. 5 (2000): 1540. See also Ward, *British West Indian Slavery*, 82, 125.

56. Brown, *Reaper's Garden*, 54-55; Vasconcellos, *Slavery, Childhood, and Abolition*, 17–18; Sasha Turner, *Contested Bodies: Pregnancy, Childrearing, and Slavery in Jamaica* (Philadelphia: University of Pennsylvania Press, 2017), 173; Higman, *Slave Populations*, 26–30, 319, 344–45.

57. Eltis, *Rise of African Slavery*, 89.

58. Roberts, "Whip and the Hoe."

59. Dunn, *Two Plantations*, 142–43, 432 (appendix 16: "The Occupation, Health, and Longevity of Mesopotamia Adult Slaves, 1762–1833"); Brown, *Reaper's Garden*, 52; Roberts, *Slavery and the Enlightenment*, 167–70.

60. Kristrina A. Shuler, "Life and Death on a Barbadian Sugar Plantation: Historic and Bioarchaeological Views of Infection and Mortality at Newton Plantation," *International Journal of Osteoarchaeology* 21, no. 1 (2011): 66–81.

61. John E. Crowley, "Sugar Machines: Picturing Industrialized Slavery," AHR 121, no. 1 (2016): 403–36 ("killing labor," 426). As B. W. Higman concluded, the most important factors that contributed to the notoriously high mortality rates on sugar plantations "were the extreme hours of heavy labor and the brutality of the gang-driving system." Higman, *Slave Populations*, 374. See also Tadman, "Demographic Cost of Sugar"; Brown, *Reaper's Garden*; Roberts, "Whip and the Hoe."

62. For important shifts, including the rise of pro-natalism, after the abolition of the transatlantic slave trade, see Turner, *Contested Bodies*; Katherine Paugh, *The Politics of Reproduction: Race, Medicine, and Fertility in the Age of Abolition* (New York: Oxford University Press, 2017); Vasconcellos, *Slavery, Childhood, and Abolition*.

63. "The most important occupational mortality differential," B. W. Higman found, "was that between field laborers and 'privileged' drivers, skilled tradespeople, and

domestics." Higman, *Slave Populations*, 333 (quotation), 667 (also table S9.28, "Slave Age-Specific Death Rates by Sex, Birthplace, Occupation, and Crop-type: St. Lucia, 1815–19").

64. Dunn, *Two Plantations*, 432 (appendix 16, "The Occupation, Health, and Longevity of Mesopotamia Adults Slaves, 1763–1833"). See also Martin Forster and Simon D. Smith, "Surviving Slavery: Mortality at Mesopotamia, a Jamaican Sugar Estate, 1762–1832," *Journal of the Royal Statistical Society* 174, no. 4 (2011): 923.

65. Higman, *Slave Populations*, 334.

66. Higman, *Slave Populations*, 224 ("mere rag"); Robert S. Duplessis, "What Did Slaves Wear? Textile Regimes in the French Caribbean," *Monde(s)* 1 (2012): 181.

67. Henry Thomas De La Beche, *Notes on the Present Condition of the Negroes in Jamaica* (T. Cadell, 1825), 11–12; Craton, *Invisible Man*, 176, 211; Robert S. Starobin, "Privileged Bondsmen and the Process of Accommodation: The Role of Houseservants and Drivers as Seen in Their Own Letters," *Journal of Social History* 5, no. 1 (1971): 61. For the shift from ready-made clothing to providing enslaved people with materials to make their own clothes, see Higman, *Slave Populations*, 224–25.

68. Debien, *Les esclaves*, 130–31; Laborie, *Coffee Planter of Saint Domingo*, 166; Paquette, "Drivers Shall Lead," 32; Gert Oostindie, *Roosenburg en Mon Bijou: Twee Surinaamse Plantages, 1720–1870* (Dordrecht, Netherlands: Foris, 1989), 165; Beeldsnijder, *Plantageslaven in Suriname,*157; Mark Smith, *Mastered by the Clock: Time, Slavery, and Freedom in the American South* (Chapel Hill: University of North Carolina Press, 1997), 2, 144; Moitt, *Women and Slavery*, 39; Alvin O. Thompson, *Unprofitable Servants: Crown Slaves in Berbice, Guyana, 1803–1831* (Kingston: University of the West Indies Press, 2002), 11.

69. Laborie, *Coffee Planter*, 165.

70. [Collins], *Practical Rules*, 129–30. Enslavers often commented on their efforts to distinguish drivers from other enslaved people and enhance their "authority." Grenada sugar planter Gordon Turnbull, for instance, said that drivers "ought to be particularly encouraged, and invested with some authority over the rest of the negroes." Quoted in Roberts, *Slavery and the Enlightenment*, 202. See also Debien, *Les esclaves*, 127.

71. Higman, *Slave Populations*, 203; Newman, *New World of Labor*, 238; William Van Deburg, *The Slave Drivers: Black Agricultural Labor Supervisors in the Antebellum South* (Westport, Conn.: Greenwood Press, 1979), 51; Jean Baptise Labat, *Nouveau voyage aux isles de l'Amerique . . .*, vol. 3 (Paris, 1722), 436; J. Harry Bennett Jr., *Bondsmen and Bishops: Slavery and Apprenticeship on the Codrington Plantations of Barbados, 1710–1838* (Berkeley: University of California Press, 1958), 18; Randall Miller, "The Man in the Middle: The Black Slave Driver," *American Heritage* 30, no. 6 (1979): 276.

72. "Examination of the Negro Woman Rosetta," June 4, 1819, CO 116/138, 54, TNA ("washerwoman"); B. W. Higman, *Montpelier, Jamaica: A Plantation Community in Slavery and Freedom, 1739–1912* (Kingston: University of the West Indies Press, 1998), 275 ("servant boy"). See also Clifton, "Rice Driver," 345; Miller, "Man in the Middle," 276; Craton, *Invisible Man*, 211.

73. Alex van Stipriaan, *Surinaams Contrast* (Leiden: Brill, 1993), 282.

74. John Williamson, *Medical and Miscellaneous Observations, Relative to the West India Islands*, vol. 1 (Edinburgh: Alex Smellie, 1817), 1:363; Clifton, "Rice Driver," 347; Higman, *Montpelier*, 275.

75. Debien, *Les esclaves*, 127 ("better housed"); Labat, *Nouveau voyage*, 3:436; Miller, "Man in the Middle," 276; Van Deburg, *Slave Drivers*, 51.

76. Higman, *Slave Populations*, 221–22.

77. Henry Nelson Coleridge, *Six Months in the West Indies, in 1825* (London: John Murray, 1826), 126; Clifton, "Rice Driver," 345–46; Higman, *Slave Populations*, 221–22; Michael Mullin, *Africa in America: Slave Acculturation and Resistance in the American South and the British Caribbean, 1736–1831* (Urbana: University of Illinois Press, 1994), 147–48; Paquette, "Drivers Shall Lead," 32.

78. Williamson, *Medical and Miscellaneous Observations*, 363.

79. Quoted in Clifton, "Rice Driver," 344.

80. Higman, *Slave Populations*, 204–18; Nicholas Crawford, *Sustaining Slavery: Food Provisioning, Power, and Protest in the British Caribbean, c. 1784–1834* (in progress); Brown, *Reaper's Garden*, 54, 56–57.

81. Belgrove, *Treatise upon Husbandry*, 66. See also Labat, *Nouveau voyage*, 436; Clifton, "Rice Planter," 344–45; Van Deburg, *Slave Drivers*, 51; Higman, *Slave Populations*, 207, 209; Newman, *New World of Labor*, 204, 231; Roberts, *Slavery and the Enlightenment*, 244–45; Eugene Genovese, *Roll, Jordan, Roll: The World the Slaves Made* (New York: Vintage, 1972), 370.

82. Quoted in Debien, *Les esclaves*, 127.

83. Clifton, "Rice Driver," 346.

84. Mary Turner, *Slaves and Missionaries: The Disintegration of Jamaican Slave Society, 1787–1834* (Kingston: University of West Indies Press, 1998), 42; Craton, *Testing the Chains*, 54; Roderick McDonald, *The Economy and Material Culture of Slaves: Goods and Chattels on the Sugar Plantations of Jamaica and Louisiana* (Baton Rouge: Louisiana State University Press, 1993), 23.

85. For "social death" as the basic condition of slavery, see Orlando Patterson, *Slavery and Social Death: A Comparative Study* (Cambridge, Mass.: Harvard University Press, 1982). For social death as "a compelling metaphysical threat," rather than an actual condition, see Vincent Brown, "Social Death and Political Life in the Study of Slavery," AHR 114, no. 5 (2009): 1231–49 (quotation, 1244).

86. According to *Voyages*, 64.5 percent of all captives in the slave trade were male (www .slavevoyages.org, accessed March 9, 2023). For an overview of sex ratios in the transatlantic slave trade (and American slave societies), and references to more specialized scholarship, see Richard Follett, "The Demography of Slavery," in *The Routledge History of Slavery*, ed. Gad Heuman and Trevor Burnard (New York: Routledge, 2011), 124–29. Sex ratios varied over the course of the slave trade, but in sugar-producing Caribbean slave societies, men were almost always purchased at much higher rates than women (Follet's examples range from 165:100 to 220:100). Jennifer Morgan recently called attention to the problematic nature of surviving evidence for sex ratios in the transatlantic slave trade, noting that out of the 36,110 voyages

documented in *Voyages* as of November 2020, only 3,426 record sex ratios, thus "erasing women from the records of more than 95 percent of all slave-trading voyages to North America or 85 percent of all slave-trading voyages to the Caribbean." Morgan has also emphasized "the significant presence of women in the slave trade before 1700," when the "numbers of women and men were relatively balanced, with women sometimes constituting majorities." Morgan, *Reckoning with Slavery*, ch. 1 (quotations, 52, 32). See also David Eltis and Stanley L. Engerman, "Was the Slave Trade Dominated by Men?" *Journal of Interdisciplinary History* 23, no. 2 (1992): 237–57; Herbert S. Klein, "African Women in the Atlantic Slave Trade," in *Women and Slavery in Africa*, ed. Claire C. Robertson and Martin A. Klein (Madison: University of Wisconsin Press, 1983), 29–38; G. Ugo Nwokeji, "African Conceptions of Gender and the Slave Trade," WMQ 58, no. 1 (2001): 47–68.

87. As Diana Paton observed, "In almost all plantation societies until late in the era of slavery, the majority of enslaved people were men." Paton, "Gender History, Global History, and Atlantic Slavery: On Racial Capitalism and Social Reproduction," AHR 127, no. 2 (2022): 742. For sex ratios and male majorities in American slave societies, see also Follett, "Demography of Slavery"; Higman, *Slave Populations*, 115–20; Laird W. Bergad, *The Comparative Histories of Slavery in Brazil, Cuba, and the United States* (New York: Cambridge University Press, 2007), 96–113 (esp. 111); Schwartz, *Sugar Plantations*, 346–48; David Geggus, "Slave Society in the Sugar Plantation Zones of Saint Domingue and the Revolution of 1791–93," S&A 20, no. 2 (1999): 35; Richard Follet, *The Sugar Masters: Planters and Slaves in Louisiana's Cane World, 1820–1860* (Baton Rouge: Louisiana State University Press, 2005), 50–51.

88. Randy M. Browne and Trevor Burnard, "Husbands and Fathers: The Family Experience of Enslaved Men in Berbice, 1819–1834," *New West Indian Guide* 91, nos. 3–4 (2017): 193–222. For similar dynamics in Virginia, see Sarah S. M. Pearsall, *Polygamy: An Early American History* (New Haven: Yale University Press, 2019), 137.

89. Higman, *Slave Populations*, 370–71; B. W. Higman, "The Slave Family and Household in the British West Indies, 1800–1834," *Journal of Interdisciplinary History* 6, no. 2 (1975): 275, 284–85; Justin Roberts, "The 'Better Sort' and the 'Poorer Sort': Wealth Inequalities, Family Formation and the Economy of Energy on British Caribbean Sugar Plantations, 1750–1800," S&A 35, no. 3 (2014): 468–69. Pearsall, *Polygamy*, 139.

90. Roberts, *Slavery and the Enlightenment*, 252.

91. For Big Men politics and drivers' pursuit of wealth-in-people, including references to important scholarship, see my chapter 3.

92. Thompson, "Henry Drax's Instructions," 565–604 (quotation, 600). See also Morgan, *Laboring Women*, 120. For drivers' "masculine provider role" in the U.S. South, see David Doddington, *Contesting Slave Masculinity in the American South* (New York: Cambridge University Press, 2018), 70–75.

93. For the connection between material inequalities and social hierarchies, see Roberts, "The 'Better Sort' and the 'Poorer Sort.'"

94. Robert Scott, quoted in Higman, *Slave Populations*, 169.

95. Sainte-Marie, *De l'exploitation des sucreries*, 3, 13.

96. Sainte-Marie, *De l'exploitation des sucreries*, 3.

97. Sainte-Marie, *De l'exploitation des sucreries*, 13; Labat, *Nouveau voyage*, 416; Debien, *Les esclaves aux Antilles françaises*, 129; Paquette, "Drivers Shall Lead," 32.

98. Roberts, *Slavery and the Enlightenment*, esp. 30–31, 56–58; Rosenthal, *Accounting*.

99. "Complaint of the Negro William . . . ," Jan. 17, 1826, CO 116/140, TNA.

100. "Complaint of the Negro William. . . ."

101. "Complaint of the Negro William. . . ." According to the manager, William had "in sundry instances deceived & told me lies & I threatened to punish him if he repeated this conduct."

102. Dec. 1, 1830, CO 116/147, 144–47, TNA. The manager claimed that he was only able to make "2 and 1/5" hogsheads of sugar, which was half of what he could produce if Smart's gang cut as much cane as they were ordered to cut.

103. The earliest record of Sondag (or Zondag) is an 1817 slave registration return, which lists him as a thirty-six-year-old driver born in Berbice. "Return of Slaves attached to Plantation L'Esperance . . . ," Dec. 4, 1817, T 71/437, 166, TNA.

104. "Complaint of the Negro January . . . ," August 15, 1825, CO 116/140, TNA.

105. "Complaint of the Negro January. . . ."

106. "Complaint of the Negro January. . . ." An 1810 law set a limit of thirty-nine lashes, which did not apply to members of the colonial government. "Proclamation of Acting-Governor Dalrymple," Nov. 14, 1810, in Alvin O. Thompson, *A Documentary History of Slavery in Berbice, 1796–1834* (Georgetown, Guyana: Free Press, 2002), 197–98.

107. "Complaint of the Negro January. . . ."

108. Thomas Cooper, *Facts Illustrative of the Condition of the Negro Slaves in Jamaica* (London: J. Hatchard and Son, 1824), 49–50.

109. An 1817 slave registration return listed Marquis as a forty-five-year-old African driver. "Return of Slaves, attached to Plantation Blyendaal . . . ," Dec. 30, 1817, T 71/437, 313, TNA.

110. "Complaint of the Negroes February, David, Mars, Lubin, Water, Isaac, Hendrick, Lauw, & Daphne . . . ," July 21, 1826, CO 116/141, TNA. For another case in which a manager was accused of regularly going into the fields and flogging the driver with the driver's own whip, see "Enquiry Instituted by authority of His Honor N. Musgrave President of the courts of Justice, into the circumstance of thirty five negroes (14 men & 25 women) belonging to the Sugar Plantation Herstelling . . . having absconded from said property, and taken refuge, in the woods aback of said estate . . . ," Apr. 14, 1825, CO 116/140, TNA.

111. Gloria Garcia Rodriguez, *Voices of the Enslaved in Nineteenth-Century Cuba: A Documentary History* (Chapel Hill: University of North Carolina Press, 2011), 152–55 (quotation, 155). In a similar case from a Jamaican plantation, whenever the overseer thought that the driver did not whip other slaves "hard enough," the overseer would sometimes "knock the driver down with his own hand" and at other times subject the driver to a severe whipping. "Minutes of the Evidence taken before a committee of the House of Commons, being a select committee, appointed to take the examination of witnesses respecting the African Slave Trade," 1791, in *House of Commons Sessional Papers of the Eighteenth Century*, vol. 82, ed. Sheila Lambert (Wilmington, Del.: Scholarly Resources, 1975), 71.

112. Whiteley, *Three Months in Jamaica*, 10.

113. "Examination of *Francis Newtown*," enclosure in Governor Probyn to Earl Bathurst, July 8, 1817, *Papers Relating to the Treatment of Slaves in the Colonies . . .* , PP 1818 (247), 3–4.

114. For demotion, see my chapter 4.

115. "At a meeting of the Magistrates, held in Charlestown . . . ," Jan. 23, 1830, enclosure in "Copy of a Dispatch from Governor Maxwell to Secretary Sir George Murrary," July 7, 1830, *Slaves*, vol. 2, PP 1830–31 (16), 26.

116. Diary of Pierre Dessalles, Feb. 1, 1840, in *Sugar and Slavery, Family and Race: The Letters and Diary of Pierre Dessalles, Planter in Martinique, 1808–1856*, ed. and trans. Elborg Forster and Robert Forster (Baltimore: Johns Hopkins University Press, 1996), 136–37.

117. Samuel George Morton, "Diary of Trip to the West Indies," 13, Samuel George Morton Papers, Mss.B.M843, American Philosophical Society, Philadelphia.

118. James Williams, *Narrative of James Williams, An American Slave . . .* (New York: American Anti-Slavery Society, 1838), 43.

119. Complaint No. 14, April 24, 1830, CO 116/145, 264.

120. Solomon Northup, *Twelve Years a Slave . . .* (Auburn: Derby and Miller, 1853), 194.

121. Johnston, "Slavery in Jamaica," 146.

122. For McMahon, see Karst de Jong, "The Irish in Jamaica During the Long Eighteenth Century (1698–1836)," Ph.D. diss, Queens University Belfast (2017), 176–84.

123. Benjamin McMahon, *Jamaica Plantership* (London: Effingham Wilson, 1839), 47–48.

124. William Wilberforce, *An Appeal to the Religion, Justice, and Humanity of the Inhabitants of the British Empire, in Behalf of the Negro Slaves in the West Indies* (London: J. Hatchard and Son, 1823), 12.

125. Cooper, *Facts Illustrative*, 50, 55.

126. James Stephen, *The Slavery of the British West India Colonies Delineated*, vol. 2 (London: Saunders and Benning, 1830), 202–12 (quotations, 205).

127. "Examination of a complaint preferred by the negroes *Opdam* and *Edam* . . . ," Feb. 6, 1821, CO 116/138, 76, TNA.

128. "Complaint of the Negroes February, David, Mars, Lubin, Water, Isaac, Hendrick, Lauw, & Daphne. . . ."

129. R. Kennedy to W. Kewley, July 15, 1826, CO 116/141, TNA.

130. "Enquiry Instituted by authority of His Honor N. Musgrave."

131. R. Kennedy to W. Kewley.

132. R. Kennedy to W. Kewley. Hussar left Herstelling and traveled to New Amsterdam, where he planned to appeal to the plantation's attorney. But before he could reach the attorney, he ran into the fiscal, "just as he was stepping in the yacht" to travel to Herstelling. As it turned out, the attorney had received a letter from Hussar's manager, who claimed that Hussar's gang was working so poorly that he would be unable to continue producing sugar unless there was "some judicial inquiry into the cause of their delinquency." After conducting a detailed investigation and taking testimony from the manager, Hussar, another driver, and other enslaved laborers, the fiscal concluded that the people on Herstelling had no excuse for not cutting as much

sugarcane as the manager demanded. It was, he explained, his duty "to take measures to force them to labour in equal measure with other well disposed negroes." And because he ultimately blamed their "spirit of opposition" on Hussar's "incorrigible" conduct, the fiscal sentenced Hussar to fifty lashes "for the double fault of labor & absenting himself from the Estate."

CHAPTER 2. DRIVING

1. Sept. 24, 1826, CO 116/141, TNA. There were 214 enslaved people on plantation Essendam (combined with the neighboring plantation Sans Souci) in 1825. "Return of Slaves . . . attached to Plant. Essendam & Sans Souci . . . ," Mar. 22, 1825, T 71/442, 73–76, TNA.

2. Sept. 24, 1826. An 1819 slave registration return lists Tobias as a thirty-three- to thirty-four-year-old carpenter, born in Berbice, and Max as a forty-two- to forty-three-year-old field laborer, born in Africa. "Return of Slaves attached to Plantation Essendam & Sans Souci . . . ," May 8, 1819, T 71/438, 695, TNA.

3. Sept. 24, 1826.

4. For "slave labor camp" rather than "plantation," see Peter H. Wood, "Slave Labor Camps in Early America: Overcoming Denial and Discovering the Gulag," in *Inequality in Early America*, ed. Carla Gardina Pestana and Sharon V. Salinger (Hanover, N.H.: University Press of New England, 1999), 222–38.

5. On amelioration, see J. R. Ward, *British West Indian Slavery, 1750–1834: The Process of Amelioration* (New York: Oxford University Press, 1988).

6. See, for example, "List of Offences committed by male and Female Plantation Slaves in the Island of Trinidad . . . from the 24th June 1824 to the 24th June 1826 . . . ," in PP 1826–27 (008), 261–62; "List of Offences committed by Male and Female Plantation Slaves . . . ," St. Lucia, 1828, in PP 1829 (335), 64; "Abstract of Offences Committed by Male and Female Plantation Slaves, January 1–May 14, 1830," CO 116/145, 266–67, TNA.

7. "List of Offences committed by male and Female Plantation Slaves in the Island of Trinidad"; "List of Offences committed by Male and Female Plantation Slaves . . . ," St. Lucia, 1828; "Abstract of Offences Committed by Male and Female Plantation Slaves." See also Randy M. Browne, *Surviving Slavery in the British Caribbean* (Philadelphia: University of Pennsylvania Press, 2017), 90.

8. Henry Whiteley, *Three Months in Jamaica, in 1832: Comprising a Residence of Seven Weeks on a Sugar Plantation* (J. Hatchard, 1833), 2 ("no clear"), 3 (all other quotations). Next to cane holing, manuring was the most physically demanding job on Caribbean plantations. See Justin Roberts, *Slavery and the Enlightenment in the British Atlantic, 1750–1807* (New York: Cambridge University Press, 2013), 113–17.

9. As Anthony Kaye observed, "The driver's problem was how to exercise power over field laborers when he had no more than a slave's authority." Kaye, *Joining Places: Slave Neighborhoods in the Old South* (Chapel Hill: University of North Carolina Press, 2007), 141.

10. May 22, 1790, "Minutes of the Evidence taken before a committee of the House of Commons," in *House of Commons Sessional Papers of the Eighteenth Century*, vol. 82, ed. Sheila Lambert (Wilmington, Del.: Scholarly Resources, 1975, 262.

11. Hunton Love, quoted in Richard J. Follett, *The Sugar Masters: Planters and Slaves in Louisiana's Cane World, 1820–1860* (Baton Rouge: Louisiana State University Press, 2005), 135.

12. The 1824 Order in Council, which was the "imperial government's blueprint" for amelioration and, specifically, for new slave codes in several British colonies, prohibited drivers and other labor supervisors from carrying "a whip, cat, or other instrument of a like nature for the purpose of impelling, or coercing any slave, or slaves to perform any labour of any kind." Quoted in Mary Turner, "Modernizing Slavery: Investigating the Legal Dimension," *New West Indian Guide* 73, nos. 3–4 (1999): 8–9. See also Browne, *Surviving Slavery*, 48.

13. For abolitionist portrayals of drivers, see Robert L. Paquette, "The Drivers Shall Lead Them: Image and Reality in Slave Resistance," in *Slavery, Secession and Southern History*, ed. Robert Louis Paquette and Louis A. Ferleger (Charlottesville: University of Virginia Press, 2000), 38–43.

14. Mary Prince, *The History of Mary Prince, a West Indian Slave* . . . (London: F. Westley and A. H. Davis, 1831), 16

15. White plantation authorities began to emphasize the close measuring and tracking of work versus rest time in the late eighteenth century as part of a broader agricultural improvement movement designed to maximize productivity. See Roberts, *Slavery and the Enlightenment*, 26–32, 68–78.

16. "Special Sessions for Trial of Slaves," Nov. 22, 1823, in *Third Report of the Commissioner of Inquiry into the Administration of Civil and Criminal Justice in the West Indies*, PP 1826–27 (36), 72–73.

17. Robert Renny, *An History of Jamaica* . . . (London: J. Cawthorn, 1807), 177, 324; Whiteley, *Three Months*, 14; Ashton Warner and Samuel Strickland, *Negro Slavery Described by a Negro: Being the Narrative of Ashton Warner, a Native of St. Vincent's* (London: Samuel Maunder, 1831), 33–34; James Kelly, *Voyage to Jamaica, and Seventeen Years' Residence in That Island* (Belfast: J. Wilson, 1838), 32–33; Benjamin MacMahon, *Jamaica Plantership* (London: Wilson, 1839), 19–20, 31, 34–35.

18. Strikethrough in the original. Feb. 23, 1831, CO 258/8, 186–92, TNA. For a similar case from St. Christopher, see *Third Report*, 72–73. The use of "combine" suggests organized labor bargaining; "combination" was a contemporary term for a trade union.

19. "Examination of the Negro Woman Laura," June 4, 1819, CO 116/138, 55, TNA.

20. For a comparison of task and gang labor, see Philip D. Morgan, "Task and Gang Systems: The Organization of Labor on New World Plantations," in *Work and Labor in Early America,* ed. Stephen Innes (Chapel Hill: University of North Carolina Press, 1988), 189–220. As Morgan observed, during the period of amelioration there was a shift from gang to task labor on sugar plantations in colonies where the British government had greater leverage, including Trinidad, Demerara-Essequibo, and Berbice. Ibid., 197, 202, 207–8. See also Roberts, *Slavery and the Enlightenment*, 152–53.

21. "Examination of the negro *Louis* . . . ," 1819, CO 116/138, 59–60, TNA. Louis also told the fiscal "that the driver always point[ed] at him, although he never gave cause for such dealings," which suggests that the conflict between Louis and La Fleur had deeper, personal roots.

For their ages and birthplaces, see "Return of Slaves attached to plantation The Friends . . . ,"
Dec. 30, 1817, T 71/437, 378–89, TNA.

22. Nov. 2, 1833, CO 300/32, 448–50, TNA.

23. Nov. 2, 1833, CO 300/32, 448–50, TNA.

24. William Dickson, *Letters on Slavery . . .* (London: J. Phillips, 1789), 23.

25. Whiteley, *Three Months*, 14.

26. James Stephen, *The Slavery of the British West India Colonies Delineated*, vol. 2 (London: Saunders and Benning, 1830), 240.

27. Nov. 29, 1833, and Dec. 7, 1833, CO 116/162, 101–6, TNA.

28. Nov. 29, 1833, and Dec. 7, 1833.

29. May 13, 1833, CO 300/31, 361–62 (Anne's complaint), 363–63 (Juan Joseph's complaint), TNA.

30. Feb. 25, 1833, CO 116/152, 102–5, TNA.

31. Aug. 22, 1832, CO 116/151, 109–12, TNA.

32. John E. Crowley, "Sugar Machines: Picturing Industrialized Slavery," AHR 121, no. 1 (2016): 426.

33. Aug. 22, 1832.

34. Feb. 5, 1834, CO 300/33, 305, TNA. Félicité appealed to the protector alongside four other people from the same plantation, though the other complaints focused on the manager rather than the driver.

35. Nov. 13, 1832, CO 116/151, 166–68, TNA. The manager was ill the day Daniel reported the man, Murphy, but promised to have him punished as soon as he was better (supposedly he was "always present when corporal punishment [was] inflicted"). About a week later, Murphy was again "troublesome," refusing Daniel's order to work the *koker* (sluice) because he said it was not his turn and "the strong hands should be selected instead." At that point, the manager followed through on his threat to have Murphy punished and gave him fourteen lashes.

36. Oct. 17, 1833, CO 116/153, 81–84, TNA.

37. "Examination of a Complaint Preferred by the Negro Welcome," June 28, 1822, CO 116/138, 123–24, TNA; "Return of Slaves attached to Plantation Vryberg . . . ," Feb. 22, 1819, T 71/438, 694, TNA; "Return of Slaves attached to Plantation Vryberg . . . ," Mar. 22, 1822, T 71/440, 743–44, TNA.

38. "Complaint Preferred by the Negro Welcome."

39. Journal of Pierre Dessalles, April 15, 1842, excerpted in *Sugar and Slavery, Family and Race: The Letters and Diary of Pierre Dessalles, Planter in Martinique, 1808–1856*, ed. and trans. Elborg Forster and Robert Forster (Baltimore: Johns Hopkins University Press, 1996), 164.

40. For insolence and insulting speech, see Diana Paton, "Gender, Language, Violence and Slavery: Insult in Jamaica, 1800–1838," *Gender and History* 18, no. 2 (2006): 246–65. See also Miles Ogborn, *The Freedom of Speech: Talk and Slavery in the Anglo-Caribbean World* (Chicago: University of Chicago Press, 2019).

41. Aug. 9, 1832, CO 300/30, 167–69, TNA.

42. Nov. 21, 1833, CO 116/153, 158–61, TNA.

43. "Complaint, No. 17," Oct. 23, 1829, CO 116/145, 236, TNA.

44. "We" may have meant either the driver and white plantation authorities or the driver and other enslaved people. Woensdag readily admitted that other enslaved people on the estate did not like him. When the day's work was done on Christmas Eve—the day of the argument with the driver—he refused to join them when they gathered to receive rum from the manager-attorney because, he reported, "the negroes said they did not care about me." Later that night, "when they began to dance," Woensdag attempted to join them, only to be, he said, "pushed out of the dance finding I was a poor fellow without a mother or family."

45. "Complaint of the Negro Woensdag . . . ," Jan. 7, 1825, CO 116/140, TNA.

46. "Complaint of the Negro Woensdag."

47. Journal of Pierre Desalles, April 15, 1842.

48. Feb. 7, 1834, CO 300/33, 308–10, TNA.

49. "Complaint of the Slave Albinus . . . ," June 18, 1830, CO 116/156, 146–48, TNA. In response, the manager had him locked in the hospital until the next morning, when he was given thirty-five lashes.

50. June 22, 1830, CO 116/156, 118–23, TNA.

51. The protector noted for the sake of his Colonial Office superiors that "no greater insult can be offered by one negro to another than a curse of his family." June 22, 1830, CO 116/156, 118–23, TNA.

52. ["Extracts from] Copy of the Records of Proceedings in Complaints Against and By Slaves," August 1830, CO 116/156; "[Extracts from] Copy of the Records of Proceedings in Complaints Against and By Slaves," May 1831, CO 116/156, TNA.

53. Jean Baptiste Labat, *Nouveau voyage aux isles de l'Amerique . . .* , vol. 3 (Paris, 1722).

54. Journal of Pierre Desalles, July 4, 1840, entry, in *Letters and Diary of Pierre Dessalles*, 142–43.

55. Apr. 2, 1768, *Saint Jago Intelligencer*, American Antiquarian Society. For a similar case from Louisiana in 1838, where an enslaved man murdered a driver and then fled, see Leslie Howard Owens, *This Species of Property: Slave Life and Culture in the Old South* (New York: Oxford University Press, 1976), 122–23.

56. Randall Miller, "The Man in the Middle: The Black Slave Driver," *American Heritage* 30, no. 6 (1979): 279.

57. In another case from Mississippi, an enslaved woman named Ursula tried at least twice to enlist the help of two other women to kill their driver with hoes or axes. Jeff Forret, *Slave Against Slave: Plantation Violence in the Old South* (Baton Rouge: Louisiana State University Press, 2015), 179.

58. James Clifton, "The Rice Driver: His Role in Slave Management," *South Carolina Historical Magazine* 82, no. (4): 350; Charles Joyner, *Down by the Riverside: A South Carolina Slave Community* (Urbana: University of Illinois Press, 1984), 66–67.

59. In Cuba, enslaved Africans were often identified by their purported ethnic or "national" identification "as a form of surname to distinguish between slaves with the same first name." Gloria García Rodríguez, *Voices of the Enslaved in Nineteenth-Century Cuba: A Documentary History*, trans. Nancy L. Westgate (Chapel Hill: University of North Carolina Press, 2011), 25.

60. Nov. 11, 1829, 1246/C, Miscelánea de Expedientes, Archivo Nacional de Cuba, in García Rodríguez, *Voices of the Enslaved*, 122–23. According to other witnesses, José also neglected to feed and give water to the horses, despite a warning from another man that he would "be in big trouble" if Francisco found out. For José's sentence, see García Rodriguez, *Voices*, 200n13.

61. *Re Negro Pedro*, 10 *Louisiana Historical Quarterly*, July 1774, in *Judicial Cases Concerning American Slavery and the Negro*, ed. Helen Tunnicliff Catterall, vol. 3 (Washington: Carengie Institution, 1932), 431. See also Forret, *Slave Against Slave*, 179.

62. Quoted in Manuel Barcia, "Los contramayorales negros y mulatos en la Cuba decimonónica," *Boletin del Gabinete de Arqueología* 2, no. 2 (2002): 91.

63. For labor bargaining, see *From Chattel Slaves to Wage Slaves: The Dynamics of Labour Bargaining in the Americas*, ed. Mary Turner (Bloomington: Indiana University Press, 1995).

64. "Compliant No. 3," Jan. 2, 1827, CO 116/143, 177–79, TNA.

65. The first available slave registration return for plantation De Dankbaarheid (later combined with plantation St. Jan to become plantation Highbury), in 1817, listed Hendrick as a forty-five-year-old "First Driver" born in Berbice. "Return of slaves attached to Plantation de Dankbaarheid . . . ," Nov. 29, 1817, T 71/437, 28, TNA.

66. "Compliant No. 3."

67. "Complaint No. 3." In response to the complaint that they were not allowed to bury Samba, the protector "thought it no more but decent that the estate's negroes should bury their dead, and not the negroes belonging to other estates."

68. "Complaint No. 3."

69. The manager also ordered five men out of the trench and sent them to dig cane holes, the most physically demanding job on a plantation. For cane holing, see Roberts, *Slavery and the Enlightenment*, 105–10; Simon Newman, *A New World of Labor: The Development of Plantation Slavery in the British Atlantic* (Philadelphia: University of Pennsylvania Press, 2013), 206–7.

70. Oct. 11, 1830, CO 116/147, 121–25, TNA. The manager denied having beaten the men in the field and attributed their complaint to "the influence of two [former] Overseers over the negroes." He claimed, "[The overseers'] characters were so bad it was necessary to dismiss them and I presume they have instigated the negroes to complain." The protector did not believe the manager and referred the case to criminal court, where the manager was convicted of beating two enslaved men and sentenced to pay ten pounds sterling. See "R. Samuel, Acting Protector of Slaves, Versus Hugh Roarke Manager of Plantn. Enfield," Dec. 24, 1830, CO 116/148, 294, TNA. An 1817 slave registration return listed Hull as a thirty-four-year-old African field laborer. "Return of Slaves attached to Plantation Enfield . . . ," Dec. 31, 1817, T 71/437, 106, TNA.

71. As Mary Turner observed, white plantation authorities "had every incentive to arrive at informal deals with headmen and drivers about the slaves' terms of work." Turner, "Introduction," in *Chattel Slaves to Wage Slaves*, 8.

72. "Examination of the negro *Samuel* . . . ," Jan. 2, 1821, CO 116/138, 74, TNA; "Answer of Mr. Spangenburg to the complaint of Samuel," CO 116/138, 18, TNA. Samuel was registered

as a forty-one-year-old African in 1819, when he was owned by Maria Burgers, and again as forty-one in 1822. "Return of Slaves, the Property of Maria Burgers," Feb. 20, 1819, T 71/438, 51–52; "Return of Slaves the Property of F. Alidus Spangenberg . . . ," Feb. 27, 1822, T 71/440, 637, TNA.

73. "Examination of the negro *Samuel*"; "Answer of Mr. Spangenburg."

74. "Complaint No. 36," Jan. 1, 1828, CO 116/144, 84–85, TNA. Even after his complaint was dismissed, Drenna did not back down. When he was ordered to take everyone back to the plantation, "he flatly refused to quit Town, and followed up such refusal by conducting the whole party to the jail," where they may have had friends or kin in confinement.

75. Mar. 14, 1834, CO 330/33, 336, TNA.

76. Whiteley, *Three Months*, 5.

77. "Complaint No. 12," Dec. 5, 1831, CO 258/10, 214, TNA.

78. Browne, *Surviving Slavery*, 49, 51.

79. John Stewart, *A View of the Past and Present State of the Island of Jamaica* . . . (Edinburgh: Oliver and Boyd, 1823), 346–47. See also [David Collins], *Practical Rules for the Management and Medical Treatment of Negro Slaves, in the Sugar Colonies* . . . (London: J. Barfield, 1803), 201–2; Kelly, *Voyage to Jamaica*, 33.

80. June 12, 1833, "Appendix to Protector's Report," CO 116/161, 7, TNA.

81. "Complains [*sic*] of *Jack, Boast, Jem, Tancra, Trim, Harry, and Peter*," Dec. 24, 1821, CO 116/138, 93–94, TNA; "Return of Slaves attached to Plantation Nigg . . . ," Feb. 22, 1819, T 71/438, 355–56, TNA. Understandably, Watson denied having "not cut them in consequence of knowing they were in the right," and he claimed that his manager had told him that when he was to flog people, "they should be burnt, but not cut." Some drivers conspired with other enslaved people to fake whippings they were ordered to inflict. Solomon Northup, who worked as a driver on a Louisiana sugar plantation, explained: "During my eight years' experience as a driver, I learned to handle the whip with marvelous dexterity and precision, throwing the lash within a hair's breadth of the back, the ear, the nose, without, however, touching either of them. If Epps [Northup's purported owner] was observed at a distance, or we had reason to apprehend he was as sneaking somewhere in the vicinity, I would commence plying the lash vigorously, when, according to arrangement, they would squirm and screech as if in agony, although not one of them had in fact been even grazed." Northup, *Twelve Years a Slave* (Auburn: Derby and Miller, 1853), 226–27.

82. "Complaint of the Negro *Tommy*," Feb. 9–10, 1819, CO 116/138, 32–34, TNA. The fiscal did not order the drivers to be punished, perhaps because he did not believe Tommy's claim that they "favoured" him.

83. Sept. 21, 1832, CO 116/160, 340–46, TNA. The 1831 consolidated slave code prohibited floggings of more than fifteen lashes.

84. Sept. 21, 1832.

85. Sept. 24, 1826.

86. An 1825 slave registration return listed 214 enslaved people on Essendam. "Return of slaves . . . attached to Plant. Essendam & Sans Souci . . . ," Mar. 22, 1825, T 71/442, 73–76, TNA.

87. Sept. 24, 1826.

88. Sept. 24, 1826.

89. Sept. 24, 1826.

CHAPTER 3. BIG MEN

1. Richard S. Dunn, *A Tale of Two Plantations: Slave Life and Labor in Jamaica and Virginia* (Cambridge, Mass.: Harvard University Press, 2014), 231–34, 330 (quotations, 231). See also Katharine Gerbner, *Christian Slavery: Conversion and Race in the Protestant Atlantic World* (Philadelphia: University of Pennsylvania Press, 2018), 190–92.

2. Robert L. Paquette, "The Drivers Shall Lead Them: Image and Reality in Slave Resistance," in *Slavery, Secession and Southern History*, ed. Robert Louis Paquette and Louis A. Ferleger (Charlottesville: University of Virginia Press, 2000), 40, 49–50; Laurent Dubois, *Avengers of the New World: The Story of the Haitian Revolution* (Cambridge, Mass.: Harvard University Press, 2005), 38.

3. Alexander Barclay, *A Practical View of the Present State of Slavery in the West Indies* (London: Smith, Elder, 1826), 40. See also Thomas Roughley, *The Jamaica Planter's Guide* (London: Longman, Hurst, Rees, Orme, and Brown, 1823), 81.

4. As Benjamin N. Lawrence, Emily Lynn Osborn, and Richard L. Roberts observed regarding African employees of colonial states, "Africans who rendered services to Europeans often strategically used their influence and authority to enhance their personal wealth, political power, and status." Lawrence, Osborn, and Roberts, "Introduction: African Intermediaries and the 'Bargain' of Collaboration," in *African Employees in the Making of Colonial Africa*, ed. Lawrence, Osborn, and Roberts (Madison: University of Wisconsin Press, 2006), 4.

5. Among the first scholars to apply the concept of wealth-in-people to precolonial Africa were Suzanne Miers and Igor Kopytoff in their "African 'Slavery' as an Institution of Marginality," in *Slavery in Africa: Historical and Anthropological Perspectives*, ed. Miers and Kopytoff (Madison: University of Wisconsin Press, 1977), 3–81. Since then, Africanists have found the concept to be interpretively powerful and flexible enough to work in a wide variety of locations and time periods. In his study of Angola in the era of the transatlantic slave trade, for example, Joseph C. Miller explained that "a wealthy man increased productivity by organizing and controlling people," or "aggregating human dependents." Miller, *Way of Death: Merchant Capitalism and the Angolan Slave Trade, 1730–1830* (Madison: University of Wisconsin Press, 1997), 47 "(a wealthy man"), 43 ("aggregating"). Jan M. Vansina, in an influential study of Bantu-speaking societies in equatorial Africa, similarly argued for the persistence of Big Man politicking despite major historical shifts and concluded that even "after centuries of trading, goods still retained their value as items for use rather than exchange. Whenever possible, wealth in goods was still converted into followers." Vansina, *Paths in the Rainforests: Toward a History of Political Tradition in Equatorial Africa* (Madison: University of Wisconsin Press, 1990), 237, 251. See also Sean Stilwell, *Slavery and Slaving in African History* (New York: Cambridge University Press, 2014), 15–19, 44, 46, 49–50, 63–66; John K. Thornton, *Africa and Africans in the Making of the Atlantic World, 1400–1800* (New York: Cambridge University Press, 1998),

ch. 3. Even scholars who have critiqued elements of the wealth-in-people model and some of its applications have still generally found the concept compelling. Important critiques and revisions include Jane I. Guyer, "Wealth in People and Self-Realization in Equatorial Africa," *Man* 28, no. 2 (1993): 243–65; Guyer, "Wealth in People, Wealth in Things—Introduction," *Journal of African History* 36, no. 1 (1995): 83–90; Jane I. Guyer and Samuel M. Eno Belinga, "Wealth in People as Wealth in Knowledge: Accumulation and Composition in Equatorial Africa," *Journal of African History* 36, no. 1 (1995): 91–92, 106–7; Neil Kodesh, "Networks of Knowledge: Clanship and Collective Well-Being in Buganda," *Journal of African History* 49, no. 2 (2008): 197–216; Kathryn M. de Luna, "Affect and Society in Precolonial Africa," *International Journal of African Historical Studies* 46, no. 1 (2013): 123–50.

6. Guyer, "Introduction," 84.

7. For "gendered Atlanticization," or "the masculinazation of sociopolitical power during the Atlantic Age," see Ndubueze L. Mbah, *Emergent Masculinities: Gendered Power and Social Change in the Biafran Atlantic Age* (Athens: Ohio University Press, 2019), 9. Sean Stilwell has similarly argued that during this period the transatlantic "slave trade made African big men that much bigger." Stilwell, *Slavery and Slaving*, 49–50, 144, 149–50 (quotation, 49).

8. Miers and Kopytoff, "African 'Slavery'"; Vansina, *Paths*, 73–83. As Guyer argued, wealth-in-people was not simply an accumulative process whereby Big Men sought to get more wives, children, and followers but a compositional process in which leaders recognized the "qualitatively different dimensions" of individual people and valued them as "assets" differentiated by individual qualities and personal attributes. Guyer, "Wealth in People and Self-Realization," 246. See also Guyer and Belinga, "Wealth in People as Wealth in Knowledge," esp. 108–10. For wealth in material goods and currencies, see also Guyer, "Introduction"; Toby Green, *A Fistful of Shells: West Africa from the Rise of the Slave Trade to the Age of Revolution* (New York: Penguin, 2019).

9. Jean-François Bayart, *The State in Africa: Politics of the Belly*, 2nd ed. (Cambridge: Polity Press, 2009 [French, 1989]), esp. 22–23; Bayart, "Africa in the World: A History of Extraversion," *African Affairs* 99, no. 395 (2000): 217–67; Lisa A. Lindsay, "Extraversion, Creolization, and Dependency in the Atlantic Slave Trade," *Journal of African History* 55, no. 2 (2014): 135–45; Miller, *Way of Death*, ch. 3; Vansina, *Paths*, 93–94.

10. For wealth-in-people as it relates to marriage and social networks, see Caroline H. Bledsoe, *Women and Marriage in Kpelle Society* (Stanford: Stanford University Press, 1976). See also Stilwell, *Slavery and Slaving*, 24–26, 67–69, 96–97; Robin Law, *The Oyo Empire c. 1600–c. 1836: A West African Imperialism in the Era of the Atlantic Slave Trade* (Oxford: Clarendon Press, 1977), 62–64; Vansina, *Paths*, 73–83; Thornton, *Africa and Africans*, 85-86.

11. For the creolization debate—sparked in large part by Sidney W. Mintz and Richard Price, *The Birth of African American Culture: An Anthropological Perspective* (1976), see Roderick McDonald and Michelle Craig McDonald, "Creolization," *Oxford Bibliographies in Atlantic History* (New York: Oxford University Press), https://doi.org/10.1093/OBO/9780199730414-0016. My approach here is informed by that of scholars such as Vincent Brown, who emphasized the advantages of "examining the politics of practical behavior" because it "calls attention to people's strategies for using cultural practices to fulfill a variety of

pressing needs in difficult and dangerous circumstances." Like Brown, I start from the premise that "rather than ask of a cultural practice or idea, 'How African is it?'"—or where precisely in Africa a particular practice or idea originated—it is "more useful to ask, 'What was it used for? What were its consequences?'" Brown, *The Reaper's Garden: Death and Power in the World of Atlantic Slavery* (Cambridge, Mass.: Harvard University Press), 7–8.

12. For low population densities and wealth-in-people, see Thornton, *Africa and Africans*, 74–76.

13. See, among others, Lindsay, "Extraversion, Creolization, and Dependency."

14. Dunn, *Two Plantations*, 236, 330, 333–36. For Tacky's Revolt, see Vincent Brown, *Tacky's Revolt: The Story of an Atlantic Slave War* (Cambridge, Mass.: Harvard University Press, 2020).

15. Dunn, *Two Plantations*, 335–36 (quotations, 336). For provisioning, see Nicholas Crawford, *Sustaining Slavery: Food Provisioning, Power, and Protest in the British Caribbean, c. 1784–1834* (in progress).

16. "Investigation of the Complaint of Nine Negro Men . . . ," Feb. 1, 1819, CO 116/138, 5–8, TNA. "Return of Slaves attached to Plant[ation] Bien Content . . . ," Dec. 22, 1817, T 71/437, 316–17, TNA.

17. "Complaint of Nine Negro Men."

18. "Complaint of the Negro Hero . . . ," Aug. 25, 1825, CO 116/140, TNA.

19. "Complaint of Nine Negro Men." A subsequent complaint from three people against the same owner for several abuses—including meager allowances of food and clothing—suggests that any change after the February 1819 complaint was short lived. "Examination of the negroes *Sam, Louis*, and *David* . . . ," Aug. 18, 1820, CO 116/138, 67, TNA.

20. May 8, 1830, CO 116/146, 131–34, TNA.

21. May 8, 1830. When the deputy protector traveled to the plantation to investigate, "one half of the gang declared the complaint to be true whilst the rest asserted it to be false." He then "enquired of the most intelligent slaves what was the cause of the dissatisfaction amongst some of the slaves," and they told him "that there was little to complain of with respect to food, the fact was the old driver had lately died and the new one was in the habit of listening to all the little disputes of the slaves and immediately ran to tell Mr. de Quay the manager, who seemed glad of any pretext for punishing them."

22. As Natalie Zemon Davis argued, drivers had to combine the "political skills of an African chief" with "creole savvy" learned on Caribbean plantations. Davis, "Judges, Masters, Diviners: Slaves' Experience of Criminal Justice in Colonial Suriname," *Law and History Review* 29, no. 4 (2011): 948.

23. "Complaint of the Negro Brutus . . . ," Nov. 25, 1826, CO 116/141, TNA. There were thirty-three enslaved people on plantation Vrouw Johanna in 1825. "Return of Slaves . . . attached to Plantation Vrouw Johanna . . . ," Mar. 26, 1825, T 71/442, 515–16, TNA. McRae had been a driver since at least 1817, when he was registered as a thirty-year-old African. "Return of Slaves the property of J. F. Linde . . . ," Dec. 22, 1817, T 71/437, 208, TNA.

24. "Complaint of Quassie . . . ," Aug. 31, 1821, CO 116/138, 88–89, TNA. In 1823, the owner purchased two female slaves: a thirty-five-year-old woman and her infant daughter. "Return of Slaves . . . attached to Plantation Vrouw Johanna."

25. "Complaint of the Negro Brutus."

26. "Complaint of the Negro Brutus." According to the owner, Brutus said "if there was a white person on the Estate, the coffee would be picked, but as there is no white, never mind, let it remain."

27. "Complaint of the Negro Brutus."

28. "Complaint of the Negro Brutus."

29. "Complaint of the Negro Brutus." At the same time the owner confronted the gang, he called on Brutus to answer for his comments on the previous Thursday. "I can get my coffee home without you," the owner said, and even though he was "a mulatto" he "could just as well call at the Governor's or Fiscal's as any other Inhabitant," insisting that even in a slave society undergirded by white supremacy, his status as a slaveowner gave him the same power as white enslavers. He ordered McRae to take Brutus's basket away at the 11:00 A.M. break and planned to take Brutus to town and ask the fiscal to punish him, but Brutus fled. Several days later, Brutus complained to the fiscal himself, denying that he had said "not to pick coffee because the Estate was belonging to a Mulatto man" and explaining that he had left to escape "a severe punishment."

30. May 28–June 19, 1833, CO 116/161, 473–79, TNA.

31. "Examination of a Complaint Preferred by the Negro Primo," Dec. 29, 1820, CO 116/138, 72–73, TNA. For the management and frequent conflicts on plantation Berenstein and the management of Crown slaves in general, see Alvin O. Thompson, *Unprofitable Servants: Crown Slaves in Berbice, Guyana, 1801–1831* (Kingston: University of the West Indies Press, 2002), esp. 153–56, 217–20.

32. "Examination of a complaint made by the negro woman *Rosetta . . . ,*" Nov. 15, 1820, CO 116/138, 69, TNA.

33. "Complaint Preferred by the Negro Primo"; "Reply of J. Deussen, manager of plantation Beerenstein," Mar. 27, 1822, CO 116/138, 78, TNA. The man who escaped, Thomas, had done so previously. Thompson, *Unprofitable Servants*, 224–25.

34. "Examination of *Primo . . . ,*" June 4, 1819, CO 116/138, 54, TNA. Primo was called as a witness for a driver named Zealand who allegedly beat an enslaved woman so badly that she miscarried. Randy M. Browne, *Surviving Slavery in the British Caribbean* (Philadelphia: University of Pennsylvania Press, 2017), 91–92.

35. "Complaint Preferred by the Negro Primo."

36. Thompson, *Unprofitable Servants*, 220–22 ("reign of terror," 222).

37. John Stewart, *A View of the Past and Present State of the Island of Jamaica* (Edinburgh: Oliver and Boyd, 1823), 262–63.

38. Davis, "Judges, Masters, Diviners," esp. 957–59.

39. Stewart, *Island of Jamaica*, 262–63.

40. Barbados planter Joshua Steele "created a magistracy out of the Negroes themselves, and appointed a court or jury of the elder Negroes or head men, for trial and punishment of all casual offences (and these courts were always to be held in my presence, or in that of my superintendent), which court very soon grew respectable." Seven of his drivers "were also constituted *rulers*, as magistrates over all the gang, and were charged to see, at all times, that nothing should go wrong in the plantations; but that, on all necessary occasions they should

assemble and consult together, how any such wrong should be immediately rectified." Steele, *Mitigation of Slavery* (London: Longman, Hurst, Rees, Orme, and Brown, 1814), 9.

41. For drivers' leadership in African "nations," including their role in adjudicating conflicts, see my chapter 5.

42. Justin Roberts, "The 'Better Sort' and the 'Poorer Sort': Wealth Inequalities, Family Formation and the Economy of Energy on British Caribbean Sugar Plantations, 1750–1800," *S&A* 35, no. 3 (2014): 458–73; Browne, *Surviving Slavery*, 176–77. Sophie White found similar evidence of drivers' roles in "the informal surveillance and policing networks that were pervasive" on French Louisiana plantations. White, *Voices of the Enslaved: Love, Labor, and Longing in French Louisiana* (Chapel Hill: University of North Carolina Press, 2019), 41–42 (quotation, 41).

43. Charles asked the manager for a pass to complain to the plantation's attorney but instead went to the protector of slaves, who ordered Peter and the watchman to return Charles's possessions. Sept. 12, 1833, CO 300/32, 364–65, TNA. For watchmen, see Caitlin Rosenthal and Cameron Black, "Enslaved Watchmen: Surveillance and Sousveillance in Jamaica and the British Atlantic World," in *Surveillance Capitalism in America*, ed. Josh Lauer and Kenneth Lipartitio (Philadelphia: University of Pennsylvania Press, 2021), 27–45.

44. June 4, 1833, CO 300/31, 413, TNA.

45. Relevant here is Guyer and Belinga's discussion of the social composition of knowledge in equatorial Africa and the importance of specialized knowledge. Guyer and Belinga, "Wealth in People as Wealth in Knowledge," 113–14. See also Kodesh, "Networks of Knowledge."

46. Richard B. Sheridan, *Doctors and Slaves: A Medical and Demographic History of Slavery in the British West Indies, 1680–1834* (New York: Cambridge University Press, 1985); Anya Jabour, "Slave Health and Health Care in the British Caribbean: Profits, Racism, and the Failure of Amelioration in Trinidad and British Guiana, 1824–1834," *Journal of Caribbean History* 28 (1994): 1–26; Amanda Thornton, "Coerced Care: Thomas Thistlewood's Account of Medical Practice on Enslaved Populations in Colonial Jamaica, 1751–1786," *S&A* 32, no. 4 (2011): 535–59.

47. On obeah and its prohibition, see, among others, Diana Paton, *The Cultural Politics of Obeah: Religion, Colonialism and Modernity in the Caribbean World* (Cambridge: Cambridge University Press, 2015); Jerome S. Handler and Kenneth M. Bilby, *Enacting Power: The Criminalization of Obeah in the Anglophone Caribbean, 1760–2011* (Kingston: University of the West Indies Press, 2013); Jerome S. Handler, "Slave Medicine and Obeah in Barbados, circa 1650 to 1834," *New West Indian Guide* 74, nos. 1–2 (2000): 57–90; Juanita de Barros, "'Setting Things Right': Medicine and Magic in British Guiana, 1803–38," *S&A* 25, no. 1 (2004): 28–50.

48. Several historians have explored the well-documented Minje Mama cases from 1819 and 1821. See especially Emilia Viotti da Costa, *Crowns of Glory, Tears of Blood: The Demerara Slave Rebellion of 1823* (New York: Oxford University Press, 1994), 107–13; De Barros, "Medicine and Magic"; Randy M. Browne, "The 'Bad Business' of Obeah: Power, Authority, and the Politics of Slave Culture in the British Caribbean," *WMQ* 68, no. 3 (2011): 451–80; Paton,

Cultural Politics, 83–88; Gordon E. A. Gill, "Doing the Minje Mama: A Study of the Evolution of an African/Afro-Creole Ritual in the British Slave Colony of Berbice," *Wadabagei* 12, no. 3 (2010): 7–29. See also my chapter 4.

49. "Trial of a Slave in Berbice, for the Crime of Obeah and Murder . . . ," PP 1823 (348), 22.

50. Stilwell, *Slavery and Slaving*, 24–26, 44, 62; John Illiffe, *Africans: The History of a Continent* (New York: Cambridge University Press, 1995), 96–98.

51. For sex ratios in the transatlantic slave trade and American slave societies, see my chapter 1n86. For male rivalries in American plantation societies, see Randy M. Browne and Trevor Burnard, "Husbands and Fathers: The Family Experience of Enslaved Men in Berbice, 1819–1834," *New West Indian Guide* 91, nos. 3–4 (2017): 193–222; Sarah S. M. Pearsall, *Polygamy: An Early American History* (New Haven: Yale University Press, 2019), 137.

52. Browne and Burnard, "Husbands and Fathers."

53. Higman, *Slave Populations*, 370–71; B. W. Higman, "The Slave Family and Household in the British West Indies, 1800–1834," *Journal of Interdisciplinary History* 6, no. 2 (1975): 275, 284–85; Roberts, "'Better Sort' and the 'Poorer Sort'": 468–69; Philip D. Morgan, *Slave Counterpoint: Black Culture in the Eighteenth-Century Chesapeake and Lowcountry* (Chapel Hill: University of North Carolina Press, 1998), 223; Eugene Genovese, *Roll, Jordan, Roll: The World the Slaves Made* (New York: Vintage, 1972), 370–71; Pearsall, *Polygamy*, 139.

54. Roberts, *Slavery and the Enlightenment*, 252.

55. Roberts, *Slavery and the Enlightenment*, 252.

56. For this "masculine provider role," see David Doddington, *Contesting Slave Masculinity in the American South* (New York: Cambridge University Press, 2018), ch. 2 (esp. 70–75).

57. For drivers and polygyny, see B. W. Higman, "Household Structure and Fertility on Jamaican Slave Plantations: A Nineteenth-Century Example," *Population Studies* 27, no. 3 (1973): 539; Morrissey, *Slave Women*, 89–90; Michael Craton, *Searching for the Invisible Man: Slaves and Plantation Life in Jamaica* (Cambridge, Mass.: Harvard University Press, 1978), 211; Hilary McD. Beckles, *Natural Rebels: A Social History of Enslaved Black Women in Barbados* (New Brunswick: Rutgers University Press, 1990), 121; Michael A. Gomez, *Exchanging Our Country Marks: The Transformation of African Identities in the Colonial and Antebellum South* (Chapel Hill: University of North Carolina Press, 1998), 76, 142; Trevor Burnard, *Mastery, Tyranny, and Desire: Thomas Thistlewood and his Slaves in the Anglo-Jamaican World* (Chapel Hill: University of North Carolina Press, 2004), 203-4; Dunn, *Two Plantations*, 235, 330–31; Pearsall, *Polygamy*, 135, 139; Hilary Beckles, *Centering Women: Gender Discourses in Caribbean Slave Society* (Princeton: Markus Wiener, 1999), 55–56; Anthony E. Kaye, *Joining Places: Slave Neighborhoods in the Old South* (Chapel Hill: University of North Carolina Press, 2007), 79; Marjoleine Kars, *Blood on the River: A Chronicle of Mutiny and Freedom on the Wild Coast* (New York: New Press, 2020), 16.

58. Tessa Murphy, "Centering Slavery in the Age of Abolition: The St. Lucia Registry of Plantation Slaves as Archival Source" (forthcoming).

59. "Return of Slaves attached to Plantation Bath & Naarstigheid . . . ," Dec. 1, 1817, T 71/437, 228, TNA; "Return of Slaves . . . attached to Plantation Bath & Naarstigheid . . . ," Jan. 1, 1819, T 71/438, 75–76, TNA.

60. "Return of Slaves attached to Plantation Bath & Naarstigheid …," Dec. 1, 1817; "Return of Slaves … attached to Plantation Bath & Naarstigheid …," Jan. 1, 1819.

61. "[Return of Slaves attached to] Canelle [plantation] …," Dec. 19, 1815, T 71/379, 194–95, TNA.

62. "[Return of Slaves attached to] Union [plantation] …," Nov. 22, 1815, T 71/379, 685–86, TNA.

63. Gabriel Debien, *Les esclaves aux Antilles françaises, XVIIe–XVIIIe siècles* (Basse-Terre, Guadeloupe: Société d'histoire de la Guadeloupe), 127.

64. "Complaint of twenty two negro men …," Sept. 21, 1824, CO 116/140, TNA. The driver, April, was previously registered as a woodcutter. See "Return of Slaves attached to Plantation Catarinasburg & Fransenburg …," Dec. 14, 1817, T 71/437, 147, TNA. The ratio of males to females was highest in the early nineteenth-century British West Indies, at 128.4 males per 100 females in 1810 and 114.5 males per 100 females in 1831, nearly a quarter of a century after the abolition of the slave trade. Higman, *Slave Populations*, 116.

65. Testimony of James Baillie, "Minutes of the Evidence Taken Before a Committee of the House of Commons …," Feb. 20, 1790, in *House of Commons Sessional Papers of the Eighteenth Century*, vol. 71, ed. Sheila Lambert (Wilmington, Del.: Scholarly Resources, 1975), 201.

66. On this point, see Morrissey, *Slave Women*, 94. For drivers' material advantages, see my chapter 1.

67. Leslie A. Schwalm, *A Hard Fight for We: Women's Transition from Slavery to Freedom in South Carolina* (Urbana: University of Illinois Press, 1997), 62.

68. Will of John Packwood Jennings of Demerary, proved Aug. 30, 1827 (but made in 1823), PROB 11/1729/447, cited in *Centre for the Study of the Legacies of British Slavery*, https://www.ucl.ac.uk/lbs/person/view/2146635100.

69. Henry Nelson Coleridge, *Six Months in the West Indies, in 1825* (London: John Murray, 1826), 137.

70. Peter Thompson, "Henry Drax's Instructions on the Management of a Seventeenth-Century Barbadian Sugar Plantation," WMQ 66, no. 3 (2009): 565–604 (quotation, 600). See also Jennifer L. Morgan, *Laboring Women: Reproduction and Gender in New World Slavery* (Philadelphia: University of Pennsylvania Press, 2004), 120.

71. Roberts, *Slavery and the Enlightenment*, 251–53, 256, 258.

72. Dunn, *Two Plantations*, 166; Dunn, "Betty's Family," at http://twoplantations.com. For the reconstruction of a similar family's genealogy in colonial and antebellum North Carolina, see Robert S. Starobin, "Privileged Bondsmen and the Process of Accommodation: The Role of Houseservants and Drivers as Seen in Their Own Letters," *Journal of Social History* 5, no. 1 (1971): 60. Drivers' children may have taken pride in their fathers' status, too, as suggested by the observation of Jean-Baptiste Labat that a driver's child would not want to marry the child of a field laborer. Debien, *Les esclaves aux Antilles françaises*, 126. See also Hilary Mc.D. Beckles, "Creolisation in Action: The Slave Labour Elite and Anti-Slavery in Barbados," *Caribbean Quarterly* 44, nos. 1–2 (1998): 115.

73. See my chapter 4.

74. Bernard Moitt, *Women and Slavery in the French Antilles, 1635–1848* (Bloomington: Indiana University Press, 2001), 99–100; Daina Ramey Berry, *"Swing the Sickle for the Harvest is Ripe": Gender and Slavery in Antebellum Georgia* (Urbana: University of Illinois Press, 2007), 80–81; Jeff Forret, *Slave Against Slave: Plantation Violence in the Old South* (Baton Rouge: Louisiana State University Press, 2015), 348–49; Leslie Howard Owens, *This Species of Property: Slave Life and Culture in the Old South* (New York: Oxford University Press, 1976), 125; Doddington, *Contesting Slave Masculinity*, 83; Kaye, *Joining Places*, 59–60, 79; Schwalm, *Hard Fight*, 44, 68. For similar dynamics under the apprenticeship system in the British Caribbean (1834–38), see Henrice Altink, "Slavery by Another Name: Apprenticed Women in Jamaican Workhouses in the Period 1834–81," *Social History* 26, no. 1 (2001): 85–89.

75. Marlon James, *The Book of Night Women* (New York: Riverhead Books, 2009), 10–11, 14–17, 20, 124–26. James underscores enslaved women's hatred of drivers during the rebellion they organize, in which they brutally kill and mutilate two drivers. Ibid., 388–89.

76. William Anderson to James Chisholme, Sept. 6, 1809, NLS, Nisbet Papers, MS 5466; Anderson to Chisholme, Feb. 8, 1810, NLS, Nisbet Papers, MS 5466. My analysis of this case is also informed by Paton, *Cultural Politics of Obeah*, 110–14. See also Vincent Brown, "Spiritual Terror and Sacred Authority: The Power of the Supernatural in Jamaican Slave Society," in *New Studies in the History of American Slavery*, ed. Stephanie M. H. Camp and Edward E. Baptist (Athens: University of Georgia Press, 2006), 197–98. For a similar case from Martinique, see *Sugar and Slavery, Family and Race: The Letters and Diary of Pierre Dessalles, Planter in Martinique, 1808–1856*, ed. and trans. Elborg Forster and Robert Forster (Baltimore: Johns Hopkins University Press, 1996), 58.

77. Anderson to Chisholme, Sept. 6, 1809; Anderson to Chisholme, Feb. 8, 1810.

78. Anderson to Chisholme, Sept. 6, 1809; Anderson to Chisholme, Feb. 8, 1810. Johannah and her family apparently believed that Napier had consulted an obeah practitioner (identified by the attorney as "an old hag" from another plantation) to harm her children. The attorney wrote that "it was plain to every person that the children had died of putrid sore throat," rather than through spiritual power, but he was still concerned that Napier had collaborated with a practitioner of obeah. For another case where a (former) driver also used threats of spiritual harm—which white authorities interpreted as obeah—to force multiple enslaved women into sexual relationships, see Sligo to Glenelg No. 315, enclosing notes from trial in St. Dorothy Special Slave Courts, July 28, 1831, CO 137/209, TNA; Paton, *Cultural Politics of Obeah*, 110–13.

79. Gunvor Simonsen, *Slave Stories: Law, Representation, and Gender in the Danish West Indies* (Aarhus, Denmark: Aarhus University Press, 2017), 124–30.

80. Simonsen, *Slave Stories*, 124–30. For a similar case from Berbice, see J. H. Lean, "The Secret Lives of Slaves: Berbice, 1819 to 1827," Ph.D. diss., University of Canterbury (2002), 168.

81. John Wray to [David?] Langton, July 4, 1815, Box 1A, London Missionary Society Archives, quoted in Alvin O. Thompson, *Documentary History of Slavery in Berbice, 1796-1834* (Georgetown, Guyana: Free Press, 2002), 187–88.

82. May 28–June 19, 1833, CO 116/161, 473–79, TNA. According to King, the accusation that he had taken the rum and syrup for himself was "a lie" motivated by the long-standing

"quarrel" between him and the other enslaved men about his relationship with Carolina, a "girl" that King "kept," or, as the overseer identified her, King's "wife."

83. Quoted in Debien, *Les esclaves aux Antilles françaises*, 129.

84. "No. 46," April 1, 1831, in *Protectors of Slaves Reports . . .* , PP 1830–31 (262), 175–76.

85. For such incidents in the United States, see Shirley M. Jackson, "Black Slave Drivers in the Southern United States," Ph.D. diss., Bowling Green State University (1977), 162n33.

86. According to Thistlewood, Johnnie's wife had a puzzling reaction when she learned that Johnnie complained to Thistlewood. She tore Johnnie's coats to pieces, which suggests that she may not have wanted to continue her relationship with him. Thistlewood flogged her three times and put her into the bilboes. Soon after Thistlewood's nephew took a canoe onto a river to go fishing and shooting, the canoe was seen drifting upside down. The next day, his body was discovered floating in the river. Burnard, *Mastery, Tyranny, and Desire*, 138, 162; Dunn, *Two Plantations*, 168. For Thistlewood, see also Heather V. Vermeulen, "Thomas Thistlewood's Libidinal Linnaean Project: Slavery, Ecology, and Knowledge Production," *Small Axe* 22, no. 1 (2018): 18–38.

87. Davis, "Judges, Masters, Diviners," 969–70. The interrogation of Coridon and the other rebels revealed several competing explanations for the murder. One story, which Davis judged "the most likely," was that Eva had indeed been Coridon's wife. Another was that when Thoma had sex with Coridon's other wife, Bellona, Coridon began an intimate relationship with Eva out of revenge. Coridon himself claimed "he had no part in [Eva's] pregnancy" and that his jealously had been aroused when Thoma had taken another of his wives, Bessolina, and given her to another enslaved man.

88. Dunn, *Two Plantations*, 78, 152, 236–38.

89. "Examination of the negro Samuel . . . ," Jan. 2, 1821, CO 116/138, 74, TNA. For the owner's response, see "Answer of Mr. Spangenburg to the complaint of Samuel," CO 116/138, 18, TNA. Samuel appealed to the fiscal alongside Esterre, an African man who may have been his brother. For the September 1821 sale to the owner of plantation Anna Clementia, see "Return of Slaves the Property of F. Alidus Spangenberg . . . ," Feb. 27, 1822, T 71/440, 637, TNA. Samuel and a woman named Princess, presumably his wife, had previously been owned by Maria Burgers. "Return of Slaves the Property of Maria Burgers," Dec. 22, 1817, T 71/437, 57, TNA.

90. Fairbairn to Seaforth, Jan. 17, 1805, plantation Brahan, GD46/17/27, quoted in Gordon Eton Gill, "Labor, Material Welfare, and Culture in Hydrologic Plantation Enterprises: A Study of Slavery in the British Colony of Berbice (Guyana)," Ph.D. diss., Howard University (2004), 118.

91. Enslavers' recognition of drivers' skills was also reflected in the higher material values they assigned to drivers compared to other enslaved people, even into old age. See, among others, Paquette, "Drivers Shall Lead," 50; Dubois, *Avengers*, 37; Morgan, *Slave Counterpoint*, 222; Gert Oostindie, *Roosenburg en Mon Bijou; Twee Surinaamse plantages, 1720–1870* (Dordrecht: Foris, 1989), 105–6.

92. See, for example, "No. 42," in *Protectors of Slaves Reports . . .* , March 5, 1830, PP 1830–31 (262), 171–72; Feb. 23, 1831, CO 258/8, 186–92, TNA; "RESULT of an Inquiry in the

Complaint of Mitchel . . . ," Jan. 27, 1823, in *Third Report of the Commissioner of Inquiry into the Administration of Civil and Criminal Justice in the West Indies . . .* , PP 1826–27 (36), 278–80; Viotti da Costa, *Crowns of Glory*, 328n134.

93. Aisha K. Finch, *Rethinking Slave Rebellion in Cuba: La Escalera and the Insurgencies of 1841–1844* (Chapel Hill: University of North Carolina Press, 2015), 174.

94. For natal alienation and social death as threats, see Vincent Brown, "Social Death and Political Life in the Study of Slavery," AHR 114, no. 5 (2009): 1231–49. See also Orlando Patterson, *Slavery and Social Death: A Comparative Study* (Cambridge, Mass.: Harvard University Press, 1982); Michael L. Dickinson, *Almost Dead: Slavery and Social Rebirth in the Black Urban Atlantic, 1680–1807* (Athens: University of Georgia Press, 2020).

95. As Jennifer L. Morgan has noted, colonial laws were not the only source of the presumption that an enslaved mother's child would inherit her status. Morgan, "Partus sequitur ventrem: Law, Race, and Reproduction in Colonial Slavery," *Small Axe* 22, no. 1 (2018): 1–17.

96. Mary Turner, *Slaves and Missionaries: The Disintegration of Jamaican Slave Society, 1787–1834* (Kingston: University of West Indies Press, 1998), 156; Edward B. Rugemer, *Slave Law and the Politics of Resistance in the Early Atlantic World* (Cambridge, Mass.: Harvard University Press, 2018), 290–91; Tom Zoellner, *Island on Fire: The Revolt that Ended Slavery in the British Empire* (Cambridge, Mass.: Harvard University Press, 2020), 106-07.

97. Turner, *Slaves and Missionaries*, 156; Rugemer, *Slave Law*, 290–91; Zoellner, *Island on Fire*, 106–7.

CHAPTER 4. UNBOUNDED AUTHORITY

1. "Complaint of the Slave January belonging to Plant. Deutichem," Mar. 9, 1829, CO 116/142, 76–97, TNA. Deutichem was previously owned by "Nathaniel Winter & Co." Nathaniel Winter died in London in 1824, and by 1828, if not earlier, the plantation was owned by "Winter, Innes, and Baillie." The Winter that arrived in 1829 was presumably Nathaniel Winter's son, Thomas Bassel Winter (1805–1875). See Tikwis Begbie, "British Guiana Colonists," at https://www.vc.id.au/tb/bgcolonistsW.html; "Thomas Bassell Winter," at https://www.geni.com/people/Thomas-Bassell-Winter/6000000014614463010. This incident is also analyzed in Gordon Eton Gill, "Labor, Material Welfare, and Culture in Hydrologic Plantation Enterprises: A Study of Slavery in the British Colony of Berbice (Guyana)," Ph.D. diss., Howard University (2004), 287–93. Gill writes that Winter was the plantation's attorney (rather than owner) and "the brother of Nathaniel Winter" but provides no evidence (288n37).

2. "Complaint of the Slave January." Boas recalled a gathering of "upwards of 200." In 1828 there were 275 enslaved people registered on Deutichem. "Return of Slaves . . . attached to Pln. Deutichem," Feb. 25, 1828, T 71/443, 379–82, TNA.

3. "Complaint of the Slave January."

4. "Complaint of the Slave January."

5. "Complaint of the Slave January."

6. "Complaint of the Slave January."

7. Mary Turner, "Slave Workers, Subsistence and Labour Bargaining: Amity Hall, Jamaica, 1805–1832," S&A 12, no. 1 (1991): 101; Michael Craton, *Testing the Chains: Resistance to Slavery in the British West Indies* (Ithaca: Cornell University Press, 1983), 54–55.

8. Thomas Roughley, *The Jamaica Planter's Guide* ... (London: Longman, Hurst, Rees, Orme, and Brown, 1823), 82.

9. May 10, 1833, CO 300/31, 357–58, TNA.

10. Feb. 21, 1832, CO 300/29, 230–32, TNA. Jamaican overseer Thomas Thistlewood recalled a similar confrontation on the Egypt sugar plantation in December 1752, soon after his arrival. The driver, Quashie, told him in the field "before all ye Negroes" that Thistlewood would not last long on Egypt. When Thistlewood asked if Quashie was threatening to murder or poison him, Quashie paused and then said no, "but he intended to invent Some good lye, and go tell his Master, Mr. Dorril, to get me turned away &c &c." Thistlewood diary, entry for Dec. 27, 1752, quoted in Miles Ogborn, *The Freedom of Speech: Talk and Slavery in the Anglo-Caribbean World* (Chicago: University of Chicago Press, 2019), 2.

11. Sept. 26, 1830, CO 116/146, 208–10, TNA.

12. "At a meeting of the Magistrates, held in Charlestown ...," Jan. 23, 1830, in *Slaves, Relating to Slaves; Slave Laws; Slave Manumissions and Population; Maltreatment of Slaves*, vol. 2, PP 1830–31 (16).

13. Charles Lewsey to William (?) Fitzherbert, Aug. 22, 1826, quoted in Mary Turner, "Chattel Slaves into Wage Slaves: A Jamaican Case Study," in *From Chattel Slaves to Wage Slaves: The Dynamics of Labour Bargaining in the Americas*, ed. Mary Turner (Bloomington: Indiana University Press, 1995), 43.

14. Journal of Pierre Dessalles, July 26, 1823 entry, excerpted in *Sugar and Slavery, Family and Race: The Letters and Diary of Pierre Dessalles, Planter in Martinique, 1808–1856* , ed. and trans. Elborg Forster and Robert Forster (Baltimore: Johns Hopkins University Press, 1996), 58.

15. "RESULT of an Inquiry into the Complaint of Mitchel ...," Jan. 27, 1823, in *Third Report of the Commissioner of Inquiry into the Administration of Civil and Criminal Justice in the West Indies*, PP 1826–27 (24), 278–80.

16. "Complaint of the Negro Fielding ...," Aug. 18, 1824, CO 116/140, TNA.

17. Mar. 27, 1832, CO 300/29, 53–55, TNA.

18. Oct. 14, 1830, CO 116/157, 242–47, TNA. According to slave registration returns, there were 115 enslaved people on plantation Orangestein in 1826 and 97 in 1832. "Return of Slaves in the lawful possession of Peter Vertike [sp?] ...," 1826, T 71/416 1058–60, TNA; "Return of Slaves belonging to Pl. Orangestein ...," 1832, T 71/431, 1104–6, TNA.

19. Oct. 14, 1830.

20. Oct. 14, 1830.

21. Scholarship on obeah is vast, but some of the most influential work has been done by Kenneth M. Bilby, Jerome S. Handler, and Diana Paton. See especially Handler and Bilby, "Obeah: Healing and Protection in West Indian Slave Life," *Journal of Caribbean History* 38, no. 2 (2004): 153–83; Paton, *The Cultural Politics of Obeah: Religion, Colonialism and Modernity in the Caribbean World* (New York: Cambridge University Press, 2015); Handler and Bilby, *Enacting Power: The Criminalization of Obeah in the Anglophone Caribbean, 1760–2011*

(Kingston: University of the West Indies Press, 2013). Several historians have analyzed the 1819 incident in which January collaborated with a practitioner of obeah. See, among others, Emilia Viotti da Costa, *Crowns of Glory, Tears of Blood: The Demerara Slave Rebellion of 1823* (New York: Oxford University Press, 1994), 107–13; Juanita de Barros, "'Setting Things Right': Medicine and Magic in British Guiana, 1803–38," S&A 25, no. 1 (2004): 28–50; Randy M. Browne, *Surviving Slavery in the British Caribbean* (Philadelphia: University of Pennsylvania Press, 2017), ch. 5; Alvin O. Thompson, *Unprofitable Servants: Crown Slaves in Berbice, Guyana, 1803–1831* (Kingston: University of West Indies Press, 2002), 197–200; Gordon E. Gill, "Doing the Minje Mama: A Study in the Evolution of an African/Afro-Creole Ritual in the British Slave Colony of Berbice," *Wadabagei* 12, no. 3 (2009): 7–29.

22. "Proclamation of the Court of Criminal Justice concerning Hans," Aug. 7, 1819, enclosed in James Walker to Stephern Lushington, Dec. 6, 1819, quoted in Alvin O. Thompson, *A Documentary History of Slavery in Berbice, 1796–1834* (Georgetown, Guyana: Free Press, 2002), 149–50. For the 1810 ban on obeah, see "Proclamation of the Governor and Court of Policy Against the Practice of Obeah," April 2, 1810, repr. in part in Thompson, *Documentary History*, 149. See also Handler and Billy, *Enacting Power*, 123–24n21.

23. Da Costa, *Crowns of Glory*, 107–12; De Barros, "'Setting Things Right'"; Browne, *Surviving Slavery*, 140–43; John Wray to William Wilberforce, Oct. 29, 1819, in Council for World Mission/London Missionary Society Archives, West Indies, B. Guiana–Berbice, Incoming Letters, box 1A, 1813–1822, folder 5, SOAS.

24. Five deaths were recorded on Deutichem between early May and mid-June, 1819, though infants who died during or immediately after childbirth may not have been documented. "Return of Slaves . . . attached to Plantn Deutichem," Mar. 23, 1822, T 71/440, 735–36, TNA. For mortality rates in Berbice and the wider British Caribbean, see B. W. Higman, *Slave Populations in the British Caribbean, 1807–1834* (Baltimore: Johns Hopkins University Press, 1984), 314–47.

25. De Barros, "'Setting Things Right.'"

26. There were three hundred and eight enslaved people registered on Deutichem in 1819. "Return of Slaves attached to Plantation Deutichem . . . ," Feb. 19, 1819, T 71/438, 669–76, TNA.

27. Conflicting information makes it difficult to know where Hans lived and worked in 1819. John Wray said Hans had "always been employed at the fort," meaning Fort St. Andrews, where the Berbice River meets the Atlantic Ocean. Wray to Wilberforce. The Deutichem attorney's complaint against Hans to the fiscal, however, identified him as "belonging to [plantation] Beerenstein," owned by the Crown. "*W. Ross*, attorney, plantation Deutichem, complaint, against the negro *Hans*, belonging to Beerenstein, on charge of Obiah," June 17, 1819, CO 116/138, 60–63, TNA. For Beerenstein and Crown-owned slaves in Berbice, see Thompson, *Unprofitable Servants*, esp. 153–56, 217–20.

28. Wray to Wilberforce.

29. "Complaint, against the negro *Hans*."

30. For oaths, see Kenneth Bilby, "Swearing by the Past, Swearing to the Future: Sacred Oaths, Alliances, and Treaties Among the Guianese and Jamaican Maroons," *Ethnohistory*

44, no. 4 (1997): 655–89; Rucker, *Gold Coast Diasporas*, 91–92, 184–85; Ogborn, *Freedom of Speech*, 45–48, 92–93; Bradley L. Craig, "Oathbound: The Trelawny Maroons of Jamaica in the Revolutionary Atlantic World," Ph.D. diss., Harvard University (2020).

31. "Complaint, against the negro *Hans*."

32. "Complaint, against the negro *Hans*."

33. For Frederick's age, see "Return of Slaves attached to Plantation Deutichem," T 71/438, 669. See also Browne, *Surviving Slavery*, 142.

34. "Complaint, against the negro *Hans*"; Wray to Wilberforce.

35. "Complaint, against the negro *Hans*."

36. "Complaint, against the negro *Hans*."

37. "Complaint, against the negro *Hans*."

38. The "pot of obeah" contained "a ram's horn, some fluid, and the bones of some animal." When the ram's horn was cut open, it revealed "blood, Negro hair, shaving of nails, the head of a snake," and other objects commonly associated with obeah. "Complaint, against the negro *Hans*."

39. "Complaint, against the negro *Hans*."

40. "Declaration and demand in a Criminal Case …Versus the Negroe January head driver …," Aug. 4, 1819, Court of Policy and Court of Civil and Criminal Justice Proceedings, Berbice, AB 6 1D, 11–14, NAG; "Declaration and demand … Versus The Negroes La Fleur, Benjamin (Driver) and Lindsay Harry …," Aug. 4, 1819, Court of Policy and Court of Civil and Criminal Justice Proceedings, Berbice, AB 6 1C, 3–6, NAG; "Declaration and Demand … Versus the Negro Woman Venus …," Aug. 4, 1819, Court of Policy and Court of Civil and Criminal Justice Proceedings, Berbice, AB 6 1D, 7–10, NAG. Two years later, the fiscal similarly singled out the drivers involved in another Minje Mama case as especially culpable. See Browne, *Surviving Slavery*, 153–54.

41. "Complaint of the Slave January."

42. "Complaint of the Slave January."

43. Robert Q. Mallard, quoted in Leigh Ann Pruneau, "All the Time Is Work Time: Gender and the Task System on Antebellum Lowcountry Rice Plantations," Ph.D. diss., University of Arizona (1997), 188.

44. "Copies of the Quarterly Returns of the Burgher Officers to the Council of Government Berbice From 1st January 1824 to 6th April 1826," Reports of Captain K[eith] Cooper, CO 116/140, TNA. The earliest (1817) slave registration return from Canefield listed Phillip as "Doctor," indicating that he had not been a field laborer for at least seven years at the time of his death. "Return of Slaves attached to Plantation Canefield …," Dec. 19, 1817, T 71/437, 65, TNA. Five years earlier, when he was a sick nurse, Philip had been punished for alleged drunkenness, as documented in a complaint he made to the fiscal. "Complaint of the Negro Philip …," June 14, 1819, CO 116/138, 53–54, TNA. Philip and his wife, Abaneba, were registered as a couple in 1819 along with a son (Gantje, aged six years) and a daughter (Amelia, aged one and a half years). "Return of Slaves, attached to Plantation Canefield …," Feb. 19, 1819, T 71/438, 125, TNA. In September 1821, Abaneba gave birth to a son, named Philip after his father. "Return of Slaves … attached to Plant. Canefield," Apr. 23, 1822, T 71/440, 313, TNA.

45. Mesopotamia diary and Brother Taylor's diary, quoted in Richard S. Dunn, *A Tale of Two Plantations: Slave Life and Labor in Jamaica and Virginia* (Cambridge, Mass.: Harvard University Press, 2014), 250–51.

46. John Smith diary, entries for Oct. 13 and Oct. 16, 1821, in Rodney Van Cooten, "Van Cooten Voices," at https://www.vc.id.au/fh/smithdiary1821.html#r1821. An 1817 slave registration return listed Asia as a fifty-year-old field laborer. "List of Female Slaves belonging to Plant. Le Resouvenir . . . ," May 31, 1817, T 71/392, 1090, TNA. For John Smith and plantation Le Resouvenir, see Da Costa, *Crowns of Glory*, 88, ch. 4.

47. "Complaint of the negro man Willem . . . ," Feb. 1, 1824, CO 116/140, TNA. In 1817, Willem was registered as a forty-year-old "field negro," born in Berbice. "Return of Slaves attached to Plantation Maria & Agnes . . . ," Dec. 29, 1817, T 71/437, 376, TNA. In 1819, he was listed as a gardener. "Return of Slaves, attached to Plantation Maria & Agnes . . . ," Feb. 25, 1819, T 71/438, 563, TNA. Willem may have been appointed as driver after the previous driver, Jantje, died of epilepsy in September 1820. "Return of Slaves . . . attached to Plantn Maria & Agnes . . . ," Feb. 5, 1822, T 71/440, 621, TNA.

48. "Examination of the negro *Peter* . . . ," Aug. 29, 1820, CO 116/138, TNA.

49. "Complaint of the negro man Willem."

50. "Examination of the negro *Peter*."

51. "Complaint of the negro man Willem."

52. Da Costa, *Crowns of Glory*, 73; Browne, *Surviving Slavery*, 59.

53. "Complaint of the negro man Willem."

54. Feb. 17, 1831, CO 258/8, 172–77, TNA.

55. "Complaint of the Slave January."

56. "Complaint of the Slave January."

57. "Complaint of the Slave January."

58. "Complaint of the Slave January."

59. "Complaint of the Slave January."

60. "Complaint of the Slave January."

61. "Complaint of the Slave January."

62. Apr. 30, 1832, CO 300/29, 134–47, TNA.

63. There were sixty-two enslaved people registered on Bel Air in 1831. T 71/517, 158–59, TNA.

64. Apr. 30, 1832. The current driver, perhaps eager to keep his position, told the protector that he had "no complaint to make against Mr. Fletcher" and "that he never told Goyo to make any complaint." Even after he confirmed that Fletcher had beaten him with a pistol, he claimed that Fletcher was not "in the habit of illtreating any of the slaves."

65. Neville A. T. Hall, *Slave Society in the Danish West Indies: St. Thomas, St. John and St. Croix* (Kingston: University of the West Indies Press, 1992), 28.

66. Quoted in Gloria García Rodríguez, *Voices of the Enslaved in Nineteenth-Century Cuba: A Documentary History,* trans. Nancy L. Westgate (Chapel Hill: University of North Carolina Press, 2011), 25.

67. Everton was apparently established in January 1830, when the owners of plantation Warren sold the entire slave population and the new owners renamed the plantation. For the

Jan. 4, 1830, sale to W. Henery, G. Fullarton, and A. MacDonald (the owners of Everton), see "Return of Slaves ... attached to plantation Warren," Feb. 2, 1831, T 71/444, 629–36, TNA. Henery, Fullarton, and MacDonald also purchased many enslaved people from Davidson Barkly and Moens and Dauncey, the owners of plantation Frederick's Lust. Caroline and North were both previously registered as part of the slave population on Warren, where they had lived since at least 1817. "Return of Slaves ... attached to Pln Everton ...," Mar. 1, 1831, T 71/444, 822–24, TNA; "Return of Slaves attached to Plantation Warren ...," Dec. 29, 1817, T 71/437, 318–19, TNA. Among the enslaved people purchased from Warren, North was the only one recorded as a driver in January 1830.

68. For gendered insults in British Caribbean slave society, see Diana Paton, "Gender, Language, Violence and Slavery: Insult in Jamaica, 1800–1838," *Gender and History* 18, no. 2 (2006): 246–65.

69. Nov. 26, 1830, CO 116/147, 130–33, TNA.

70. Dec. 2, 1830, CO 116/147, 148–51, TNA. In the end, the women's protest failed when the protector did not intervene. He only went so far as recommending that the manager stop punishing them (especially as several of them had apparently already begun to complete their work), and the manager agreed. Sometime later, the manager reported "that the Women gang had since completed their task to his satisfaction."

71. "No. 10," Mar. 1, 1831, CO 116/142, 92–98, TNA. The owner tried to minimize the significance of the relationship between Barentje and her partner by referring to him not as her husband but as "a man with whom she cohabits." He further disparaged him by claiming that he was "not her husband" even though he had "abandoned his wife and family for this woman." Barentje herself explained that she was purchased from plantation Cruysburg "without [a] husband" and sometime after being taken to Utile et Paisible she "took one of the men of the Estate for [her] Husband." She added that "he had a wife and children but he disputed with his wife," after which he began living with her, and that he was the father of her child. Utile et Paisible underwent major changes in the late 1820s. First, the plantation's owner transferred the entire slave population (154 slaves) to Balthayock, another plantation he owned, in December 1827. Then, in February 1828, under the new co-owner and former attorney James Culley, the entire labor force was reconstituted with the purchase of 104 enslaved people. In September 1828, Culley and his partner, George Watson, purchased about forty other enslaved people from plantation Cruysburg, including Barentje. See "Return of Slaves ... attached to Plantation Utile et Posible ...," Mar. 30, 1825, T 71/442 43–44, TNA; "Triennial Return of Slaves ... attached to Pln. Utile et Paisible ...," Feb. 29, 1828, T 71/443 509–10, TNA; "Return of Slaves ... attached to Plantation Utile et Paisible ...," Feb. 28, 1828, T 71/443 583–88, TNA; "Return of Slaves ... attached to Plantation Cruysburg ...," Sept. 29, 1828, T 71/444, 112–13, 181, TNA. The first record of Barentje is an 1817 registration return from Cruysburg that listed her as an eighteen-year-old field laborer, born in Berbice. "Return of Slaves attached to Plantation Cruysburg ...," Nov. 7, 1817, T 71/437, 339, TNA.

72. "No. 10."

73. "No. 10."

74. "No. 10." The fiscal agreed granted the owner's request and ordered that Barentje be placed in solitary confinement "for four days and nights."

75. "Complaint of the Slave January."

76. "Complaint of the Slave January."

77. "Complaint of the Slave January."

78. "Complaint of the Slave January."

79. They went to plantation Friends, which, like Deutichem, had previously been owned by "Nathaniel Winter & Co" and administered by the same attorney in charge of Deutichem before 1829, William Ross.

80. "Complaint of the Slave January."

81. "Complaint of the Slave January."

82. "Complaint of the Slave January."

83. "Complaint of the Slave January."

84. "Complaint of the Slave January."

85. "Complaint of the Slave January."

86. For January's age (thirty-six years old in 1817), see "Return of Slaves attached to Plantation Deutichem . . . ," Dec. 30, 1817, T 71/437, 383, TNA.

87. "Complaint of the Slave January."

88. For the problem of social integration in African societies during the era of the transatlantic slave trade, see Suzanne Miers and Igor Kopytoff, "African 'Slavery' as an Institution of Marginality," in *Slavery in Africa: Historical and Anthropological Perspective*s, ed. Miers and Kopytoff (Madison: University of Wisconsin Press, 1977), 3–81. For "social death," see Orlando Patterson, *Slavery and Social Death: A Comparative Study* (Cambridge, Mass.: Harvard University Press, 1982); Vincent Brown, "Social Death and Political Life in the Study of Slavery," AHR 114, no. 5 (2009): 1231–49; Michel Dickinson, *Almost Dead: Slavery and Social Rebirth in the Black Urban Atlantic, 1680–1807* (Athens: University of Georgia Press, 2022).

89. "Complaint of the Slave January."

90. "Complaint of the Slave January."

CHAPTER 5. REBELLION

1. Bacchus, Mar. 9, 1814, Miscellaneous Interrogations (Examinations), Berbice: Court of Policy and Court of Criminal Justice, AZ.1.5, NAN; "Report of Alexander . . . ," Feb. 15, 1814, Miscellaneous minutes of proceedings, Berbice: Court of Policy and Court of Criminal Justice, AB.6.40A, 216–17, NAN (all quotations). For Alexander's birthplace and age (forty-one years in 1813), see "Return of Slaves attached to Plantations Bath and Naarstigheid . . . ," Dec. 2, 1817, T 71/437, 228, TNA.

2. Bacchus, Mar. 9, 1814, AB.6.40A ("enter into," "so as"); "Report of Alexander" ("all that").

3. For different perspectives on "nation" and ethnicity in the African diaspora, see Douglas B. Chambers, "Ethnicity in the Diaspora: The Slave-Trade and the Creation of African

'Nations' in the Americas," S&A 22, no. 3 (2001): 25–39; Paul E. Lovejoy, "Ethnic Designations of the Slave Trade and the Reconstruction of the History of Trans-Atlantic Slavery,"
in *Trans-Atlantic Dimensions of Ethnicity in the African Diaspora*, ed. Paul E. Lovejoy and
David Trotman (New York: Continuum, 2003), 9–42; Gwendolyn Midlo Hall, *Slavery and
African Ethnicities in the Americas: Restoring the Links* (Chapel Hill: University of North
Carolina Press, 2005); Michael A. Gomez, *Exchanging Our Country Marks: The Transformation of African Identities in the Colonial and Antebellum South* (Chapel Hill: University of
North Carolina Press, 1998); Alexander X. Byrd, "Eboe, Country, Nation, and Gustavus Vas-
sa's 'Interesting Narrative,'" WMQ 63, no. 1 (2006): 123–48; James H. Sweet, "Defying Social
Death: The Multiple Configurations of African Slave Family in the Atlantic World," WMQ
70, no. 2 (2013): 258–59; Jason Sharples, *The World That Fear Made: Slave Revolts and Conspiracy Scares in Early America* (Philadelphia: University of Pennsylvania Press, 2020), ch. 4.
For the African origins of Berbice's slave population, see B. W. Higman, *Slave Populations in
the British Caribbean, 1807–1834* (Baltimore: Johns Hopkins University Press, 1984), 454-55.

4. "Report of Alexander."

5. Women may have had less visible roles as informal advisers to male leaders, as they did
in the 1763 rebellion. Marjoleine Kars, *Blood on the River: A Chronicle of Mutiny and Freedom
on the Wild Coast* (New York: New Press, 2000), 83–85. In sharp contrast to the 1814 investigation, more than a third of those questioned after the 1763 rebellion were women. Marjoleine Kars, "Dodging Rebellion: Politics and Gender in the Berbice Slave Uprising of 1763,"
AHR 121, no. 1 (2016): 51. For enslaved women's strategic silence, see Aisha Finch, "'What
Looks Like a Revolution': Enslaved Women and the Gendered Terrain of Slave Insurgencies
in Cuba, 1843–1844," *Journal of Women's History* 26, no. 2 (2014): 112–34 (esp. 116, 122–24);
Vanessa M. Holden, *Surviving Southampton: African American Women and Resistance in Nat
Turner's Community* (Champaign: University of Illinois Press, 2021). See also Sharples, *World
That Fear Made*, 156–58. Berbice had one of the highest male-to-female sex ratios in the West
Indies, with 128.4 males per 100 females in 1817, when the collection of records to assess sex
ratios began. Higman, *Slave Populations*, 116.

6. Historians have not explored these records or the 1813–14 conspiracy in much detail.
The most thorough treatment is David Alston, *Slaves and Highlanders: Silenced Histories of
Scotland and the Caribbean* (Edinburgh: Edinburgh University Press, 2021), 147–54. Brief
mentions also appear in Alvin O. Thompson, *Unprofitable Servants: Crown Slaves in Berbice,
Guyana, 1803–1831* (Kingston: University of the West Indies Press, 2002), 74, 96; Gordon
Eton Gill, "Labor, Material Welfare, and Culture in Hydrologic Plantation Enterprises: A
Study of Slavery in the British Colony of Berbice (Guyana)," Ph.D. diss., Howard University
(2004), 295–300.

7. For some of the many rebellions that drivers led, see Robert L. Paquette, "The Drivers
Shall Lead Them: Image and Reality in Slave Resistance," in *Slavery, Secession and Southern
History*, ed. Robert Louis Paquette and Louis A. Ferleger (Charlottesville: University of Vir-
ginia Press, 2000), 43–49.

8. For rebellions organized around "national" or "ethnic" groups, see Monica Schuler,
"Ethnic Slave Rebellions in the Caribbean and the Guianas," *Journal of Social History* 3, no. 4

(1970): 374–85; Michael Mullin, *Africa in America: Slave Acculturation and Resistance in the American South and the British Caribbean, 1736–1831* (Urbana: University of Illinois Press, 1992); Sandra E. Greene, "From Whence They Came: A Note on the Influence of West African Ethnic and Gender Relations on the Organizational Character of the 1733 St. John Slave Rebellion," in *The Danish West Indian Slave Trade: Virgin Islands Perspectives*, ed. George F. Tyson and Arnold R. Highfield (St. Croix: Antilles Press, 1994), 47–67; Ray A. Kea, "'When I die, I shall return to my own land': An 'Amina' Slave Rebellion in the Danish West Indies, 1733–1734," in *The Cloth of Many Colored Silks*, ed. John Hunwick and Nancy Lawler (Evanston, Ill.: Northwestern University Press, 1996), 159–93. For a critique of such interpretations (focused on the Coromantees), see Walter C. Rucker, *Gold Coast Diasporas: Identity, Culture, and Power* (Bloomington: Indiana University Press, 2015), 118–19. Other important studies that stress the specific African backgrounds of rebels include John K. Thornton, "'I Am the Subject of the King of Congo': African Political Ideology and the Haitian Revolution," *Journal of World History* 4, no. 2 (1993): 181–214; Manuel Barcia, *The Great African Slave Revolt of 1825: Cuba and the Fight for Freedom in Matanzas* (Baton Rouge: Louisiana State University Press, 2012). For the importance of African rebels' military experience in Africa, see Manuel Barcia, *West African Warfare in Bahia and Cuba: Soldier Slaves in the Atlantic World, 1807–1844* (New York: Oxford University Press, 2014); Vincent Brown, *Tacky's Revolt: The Story of an Atlantic Slave War* (Cambridge, Mass.: Harvard University Press, 2020); Kars, *Blood on the River.*

9. John K. Thornton, "The Coromantees: An African Cultural Group in North America and the Caribbean," *Journal of Caribbean History* 32, no. 1 (1998): 171.

10. For coronation or ennobling ceremonies, national assemblies, and the connections colonial authorities drew to rebellion, see Rucker, *Gold Coast Diasporas*, 152–55, 158–61; Sharples, *World That Fear Made*, 41, 109, 159–61; Thornton, "Coromantees," 170; Thornton, "War, the State, and Religious Norms in 'Coromantee' Thought: The Ideology of an African American Nation," in *Possible Pasts: Becoming Colonial in Early America*, ed. Robert Blair St. George (Ithaca: Cornell University Press, 2000), 194–95; Miles Ogborn, *The Freedom of Speech: Talk and Slavery in the Anglo-Caribbean World* (Chicago: University of Chicago Press, 2019), 98–105.

11. As Walter Rucker argued, "The ethnic labels attached to particular diasporic groupings, however problematic and inaccurate, held meaning for those who identified with those labels and who redefined them over time." Rucker, *Gold Coast Diasporas*, 7. See also Hall, *Slavery and African Ethnicities*, 38–54. For ethnogenesis, see "Forum: Ethnogenesis," WMQ 68, no. 2 (2011), esp. the introductory essay by James Sidbury and Jorge Cañizares-Esguerra, "Mapping Ethnogensis in the Early Modern Atlantic," 181–208; John Thornton, *Africa and Africans in the Making of the Atlantic World, 1400–1800*, 2nd ed. (New York: Cambridge University Press, 1998), ch. 7 (esp. 196–205); Chambers, "Ethnicity in the Diaspora"; Lovejoy and Trotman, eds., *Ethnicity in the African Diaspora*; James Sidbury, *Becoming African in America: Race and Nation in the Early Black Atlantic* (New York: Oxford University Press, 2007).

12. Sharples, *World That Fear Made*, 150–52, 155–56; Thornton, "Coromantees," 169–72; Thornton, "War, the State, and Religious Norms," 183; Rucker, *Gold Coast Diasporas*, 159;

Vincent Brown, *The Reaper's Garden: Death and Power in the World of Atlantic Slavery* (Cambridge, Mass.: Harvard University Press, 2008), 212–13.

13. For the Coromantees, see Rucker, *Gold Coast Diasporas*; Thornton, "Coromantees"; Robin Law "Ethnicities of Enslaved Africans in the Diaspora: On the meanings of 'Mina' (Again)," *History in Africa* 32 (2005): 247–67; Brown, *Tacky's Revolt*, 91–92, 234–35. For the Akans, see Kwasi Konadu, *The Akan Diaspora in the Americas* (New York: Oxford University Press, 2010); Rebecca Shumway, *The Fante and the Transatlantic Slave Trade* (Rochester: University of Rochester Press, 2011), esp. 17–21. For Tacky's Revolt, see Brown, *Tacky's Revolt*. For similar fears in Antigua in 1736, when colonial authorities believed that they had uncovered a rebel plot, see Sharples, *World That Fear Made*, ch. 4 (esp. 155, 158–62). For funeral "plays," see Rucker, *Gold Coast Diasporas*, 123, 159–62.

14. Edward Long, *The History of Jamaica . . .* (London: T. Lowndes, 1774), vol. 2, 470–75.

15. Many witnesses acknowledged that they knew that nightly meetings and the appointment of officers were illegal and "contrary to the orders" of their enslavers. Nighttime gatherings of enslaved people had similarly been prohibited since 1811 in Demerara in response to concerns that meetings held "avowedly for religious purposes" were "productive of disorder" and "dangerous." May 25, 1811, *Essequibo and Demerara Gazette*, quoted in David Alston, "The Guyana Maroons, 1796–1834: Persistent and Resilient Until the End of Slavery," S&A 2023 (online ahead of print): 14.

16. Dick, Feb. 22, 1814, AZ.1.5; Lambert, Feb. 22, 1814, AZ.1.5.

17. "Interrogatories to be put to the negroe Monday . . . ," Mar. 12, 1814, AZ.1.5 ("Big Man"); Lambert, Feb. 22 ("head man"); Ganges, Feb. 21, 1814, AZ.1.5. In January of 1814, there were 239 enslaved people on Washington. "List of Negroes on the following Estates . . . ," Oct. 1, 1814, *Berbice Gazette*.

18. "Interrogatories to be put to the Negro Sam alias Congo Sam . . . ," Mar. 11, 1814, AZ.1.5; Trim, Feb. 24, 1814, AZ.1.5 ("the story"). "The Grove" was in the Mahaica region of Demerara, near the border with Berbice. For the office of the fiscal, see Randy M. Browne, *Surviving Slavery in the British Caribbean* (Philadelphia: University of Pennsylvania Press, 2017), 5–6, 34–36.

19. "Examination of Johannes . . . ," Feb. 15, 1814, AZ.1.5; Ganges, Feb. 21.

20. "Report of the Commissaries of the Honble Court of Criminal and Civil Justice of Demerary, concerning the examination of the afternamed negroes lately arrested," Aug. 10, 1808, AB.1.8, (all quotations); David Alston, "'Die Houw Worte'" (unpublished paper).

21. Ganges, Feb. 21.

22. Dick, Feb. 22 ("head man"); Foulis, Feb. 23, 1814, AZ.1.5 ("King—father—at top"). Pompey supposedly said he would not be king because he was a driver but agreed to "assist and advise" the others. Fordyce, Mar. 19, 1814, AZ.1.5.

23. For Bambara (or Bamana), see Hall, *Slavery and African Ethnicities*, 96–100.

24. Margaret, Mar. 19, 1814, AZ.1.5.

25. Pompey, Mar. 2, 1814, AZ.1.5; Jupiter, Feb. 26, 1814, AZ.1.5; Fordyce, Mar. 19; "Examination Greenock," Mar. 12, 1814, Greenock, Feb. 26.

26. Fordyce, Mar. 19.

27. Greenock, Feb. 26.

28. "Examination Greenock," Mar. 12 ("to take care"); Hercules, Feb. 23, 1814, AZ.1.5 ("that as no new," "they must take"); Ganges, Feb. 21 ("they are obliged"); Dick, Feb. 22.

29. Hercules, Feb. 23 ("his house"); "Interrogatories to be put to the Negroe Pompey . . . ," Mar. 12, 1814, AZ.1.5; Fordyce, Mar. 19; Sam, Feb. 21, 1814, AZ.1.5.

30. Greenock, Feb. 26.

31. "Reexamination Pompey," Mar. 19, 1814, AZ.1.5 ("he was"); "Reexamination Greenock," Mar. 19, 1814, AZ.1.5. Other witnesses offered a different explanation. Alexander (Weldaad), who said he helped catch Greenock on Pompey's orders, claimed Pompey "rebuked Greenock for beating his wife." Alexander, Mar. 19, 1814, AZ.1.5. Dick (Washington) similarly said that Pompey had Greenock tied up "until he paid a guilder for disputing with his wife." "Reexamination Dick," Mar. 19, 1814, AZ.1.5.

32. Den[d?]a, Mar. 19, 1814, AZ.1.5.

33. Greenock, Feb. 26.

34. "Reexamination Greenock," Mar. 19.

35. "Interrogatories to be put to the Negro Sam."

36. "Interrogatories to be put unto the Negroe Romeo . . . ," Mar. 12, 1814, AZ.1.5.

37. Greenock, Feb. 26, 1814.

38. "Interrogatories to be put to the Negroe Pompey."

39. Thomas, Mar. 2, 1814, AZ.1.5 ("the cause"); "Interrogatories to be put unto the negroe Cudjoe . . . ," Mar. 8, 1814, AZ.1.5; "Interrogatories put to the negroe Joe . . . ," Mar. 8, 1814, AZ.1.5. In January 1814, seventy-five slaves were registered on Trafalgar and 132 on Union. "List of Negroes."

40. Thomas said Archy called the Coromantees together "as soon as" he came back from the United Kingdom, which suggests a late 1813 return (Thomas, Mar. 2, 1814). But Fraser and Archy arrived in Berbice in late September 1812 on the *Kingsmill*. Fraser of Reelig, Lewis Cameron to Edward Fraser snr, October 3, 1812, National Register of Archives Scotland. The *Kingsmill* left Liverpool on July 28, 1812. *Royal Gazette of Jamaica*, Sept. 19, 1812.

41. Thomas, Mar. 2, 1814 ("he was"). According to some witnesses, Agar (or King) was appointed governor, but Archy "took the title of governor for himself." "Interrogatories . . . to be put unto the Negroe George . . . ," Mar. 1, 1814, AZ.1.5. I have been unable to determine the origin of the Viah people, who were referred to elsewhere as "Vashee." See "Report of Alexander"; February, Feb. 15, 1814, AB.6.40, 217; Strap, Mar. 19 [?], 1814, AZ.1.5. One possibility is the Mande-speaking Vai people from what is now Liberia. See Adam Jones, "Who Were the Vai?" *Journal of African History* 22, no. 2 (1981): 159–78.

42. Quashie was also known as George.

43. "Interrogatories . . . to be put unto the Negroe Barrington . . . ," Mar. 8, 1814, AZ.1.5.

44. Archy, Feb. 21, 1814, AZ.1.5.

45. "Interrogatories to be put unto the negroe Cudjoe."

46. "Interrogatories . . . to be put unto the Negroe George." See also "Interrogatories to be put unto the negroe Cudjoe."

47. Some witnesses also said that Archy's motivation was "merely to appoint officers of his nation to beat the others in play." See, for example, "Interrogatories put to the negroe Joe."

48. "Interrogatories . . . to be put unto the Negroe George."

49. "Interrogatories put to the negroe Joe."

50. Archy, Feb. 21, 1814.

51. "Interrogatories put to the Negroe George . . . ," Mar. 8, 1814, AZ.1.5.

52. Joe, Mar. 10, 1814, AZ.1.5.

53. Caesar said that "they began to call him king soon after Mr. Hobson left Lancaster and came to Gibraltar," referring to Hobson's June 1812 sale of the plantation Lancaster and subsequent purchase of plantation Gibraltar. Caesar, Mar. 15, 1814, Miscellaneous Letters and Letter books, Berbice: Court of Policy and Court of Criminal Justice, Society of Berbice and Successors, AB.6.3C (quotation); "Webbe Hobson," at *Legacies of British Slavery*, https://www.ucl.ac.uk/lbs/person/view/2146644861 (last accessed Apr. 5, 2023], citing *London Gazette* 16609 02/06/1812, p. 1076; "Examination of the Negroe Henry . . . ," Jun. 1, 1814, AB.6.3C ("yanga").

54. Caesar, Mar. 15, 1814.

55. Jack, AB.6.3C; "Apollo or Palla," May 12, 1814, AB.6.3C ("Caesar said"); "Examination of the Negroe Henry . . . ," Jun. 1, 1814.

56. John, Mar. 5, 1814, AB.6.3C ("aid de camp"); Archer, Mar. 5, 1814, AB.6.3 ("a stick," "countrymen," "in the Courantine"); "Apollo or Palla," May 12, 1814 ("send and give"). According to Mark, Apollo was not present at Dick's funeral, when Caesar appointed him commissary, and when he heard about the appointment, "he objected, saying he was but newly come to this coast." "Examination Negroe Mark . . . ," June 1, 1814, AB.6.3C.

57. "Examination of the Negroe John . . . ," May 11, 1814, AB.6.3C.

58. "Examination of the woman Nano . . . ," May 16, 1814, AB.6.3C.

59. "Examination of the woman Nano . . . ," May 16, 1814; "Examination of the Negroe John . . . ," May 11, 1814; Sibly, May 11, 1814, AB.6.3C ("big man"); Sibly, Mar. 5, 1814, AB.6.3C ("head man"); Michael, Mar. 9, 1814, AB.6.3C.

60. Drummer, May 31, 1814, AB.6.3C.

61. Frank, Mar. 15, 1814, AB.6.3C ("as the Congos"); Maria, Apr. 12, 1814, AB.6.3C ("arrangements"); Sibly, May 31, 1814, AB.6.3C.

62. Sibly, May 11, 1814 ("fowls"); Sibly, May 31, 1814 ("Con had"); North, Mar. 9, 1814, AB.6.3C; "Examination of the Negroe Con . . . ," May 31, 1814, AB.6.3C. Sibly also testified that after the funeral on Kendalls, Michael "told him to contribute fowls, bitts, & hogs for the funeral, and proposed that he should be a Big Man" (May 11, 1814).

63. Cuffy, Mar. 12, 1814, AB.6.3C ("there were"); Sibeley [Sibly], Mar. 10, 1814, AB.6.3C (all other quotations).

64. Jem, Mar. 9, 1814, AB.6.3C.

65. "Examination of the Negroe John . . . ," May 11, 1814.

66. Caesar, Mar. 15, 1814; John, Mar. 9, 1814, AB.6.3C (quotations); Susannah, Mar. 5, 1814, AB.6.3C; "Examination of the Negroe John . . . ," May 11, 1814. For the connection between social gatherings hosted by women and rebellious conspiracies, see Sharples, *World That Fear Made*, 156–58.

67. Scipio, Mar. 5, 1814, AB.6.3C ("governor"); John, Mar. 9, 1814, ("toast," "Congo language"); "Examination of the Negroe John . . . ," May 11, 1814 ("strong hand," "I can

take"); "Examination of the Negroe Carban," June 1, 1814, AB.6.3C ("unfit person"); Caesar, Mar. 15, 1814.

68. Susannah, Mar. 5, 1814 ("king business"); "Examination of the Negroe Carban," Jun. 1, 1814 ("drove them"); Caesar, Mar. 15, 1814.

69. Susannah, Mar. 10, 1814, AB.6.3C. For an argument that keeping such gatherings secret was an important part of rebel organizing, see Finch, "Gendered Terrain," 123–24, 127.

70. Sibly, Mar. 5, 1814 ("many people"); Carban, Mar. 5, 1814, AB.6.3C ("great dance").

71. Susannah, Mar. 5, 1814 ("attendants"); Toby, Mar. 5, 1814, AB.6.3C ("a little"); Cudjo, Mar. 5, 1814, AB.6.3C; Caesar, Mar. 15, 1814.

72. Jem, Mar. 10, 1814, AB.6.3C ("began to"); Carban, Mar. 5, 1814 ("rings," "all the"); Toby, Mar. 5, 1814 ("went to"); Cudjo, Mar. 5, 1814. Caesar clearly saw the New Year's dance as his coup de grâce. The following day, when everyone resumed work, Caesar told the field laborers he supervised on Lancaster that although Jem had wanted to be king on the east coast, "he had overruled it" and "was to be sole King." "Examination of the Negroe Kendall . . . ," Mar. 15, 1814, AB.6.3C. When Caesar was later interrogated by colonial authorities, he said that he was "King from Kewley's place" (likely plantation Mary's Hope, on the eastern Corentyne Coast) "to Mourants" (Port Mourant). Caesar, Mar. 15, 1814. Nevertheless, after New Year's John continued his efforts to resolve the struggle between Caesar and Jem, hosting a "great dinner" on plantation Kendalls a week later. Yet again, no resolution was reached. Archer, Mar. 5, 1814.

73. John Ross to M. S. Bennett, Mar. 14, 1814, AZ.1.5 ("in the habit"); John McLennan to M. S. Bennett, Mar. 15, 1814, AZ.1.5; "Demand . . . against Caesar," June 3, 1814, AB.6.3C; "Criminal Demand . . . versus the Negroe Archy," Mar. 23, 1814, AB.6.3C.

74. Kars, "Dodging Rebellion."

75. Rebellions in Demerara also took place in 1772 and 1795. Bram Hoonhout, *Borderless Empire: Dutch Guiana in the Atlantic World, 1750–1800* (Athens: University of Georgia Press, 2020), 96–109.

76. "Report of the Commissaries"; May 1, 1804, Miscellaneous minutes of proceedings and Attachments, Essequibo and Demerara: Court of Policy, AB.1.5, 349–50 (quotations), 357–59; May 3, 1804, AB.1.5, 375–78; May 29, 1804, AB.1.5, 399–403; May 30, 1804, AB.1.5, 435–41; Alston, "'Die Houw Worte.'"

77. "Report of the Commissaries"; Robert Nicholson to Lord Castlereagh, June 6, 1808, CO 111/8, 23; Sept. 3, 1808, *St. James's Chronicle*; Alston, *Slaves and Highlanders*, 151–52; Thomas Staunton St. Clair, *A Residence in the West Indies and America* (London: Richard Bentley, 1834), 142–49. As Alston observed, St. Clair left Demerara on June 10, 1808—before the rebel conspiracy was investigated—and thus his account, written more than twenty-five years later, contained several errors, including that the rebel plot was uncovered in December 1807 and that Valentine and eight others were executed. Alston, "'Die Houw Worte.'"

78. "Interrogatories put to the negroe Joe."

79. Jem, Mar. 9, 1814.

80. Susannah, Mar. 5, 1814 ("remembered," "king business," "she would"); John, Mar. 9, 1814 ("trouble").

81. Michael, Mar. 23, 1814, AZ.1.5.

82. Apollo, Mar. 12, 1814, AB.6.3C.

83. "Confession of Joseph . . . ," Mar. 19, 1814, AZ.1.5 ("they spoke," "white man"); Joseph, Feb. 19, 1814, AZ.1.5 ("nothing to do"); Boatswain, Feb. 22, 1814, AZ.1.5.

84. "Questions to Romeo," Feb. 21, 1814, AZ.1.5 ("head men," "intended to make him"); "Information given by Sandy, James and Thomas . . . ," Mar. 28, 1814, AZ.1.5 ("they all"); Sam, Feb. 21, 1814, AZ.1.5 ("gentlemen," "began to talk"); James, Mar. 28, 1814, AZ.1.5 ("principal").

85. Trim, Feb. 24, 1814 ("drove them"); Romeo, Feb. 19, 1814, AZ.1.5 ("their own"); "Information given by Sandy, James and Thomas" ("to sup"); Monday, Feb. 24, 1814, AZ.1.5; "Interrogatories to be put to the Negro Sam."

86. Quamina was a common derivation of the Akan name Kwame or Kwamina for males born on Saturday, and he was officially known as Oxford. He was not explicitly identified as a driver during the investigation but was described by John as having supervised and punished enslaved children and, later, being sent into the field without a whip, which together suggest that he had a role as a driver of the third, or children's, gang. John, Mar. 1, 1814, AZ.1.5. For Cape Lahoo (Lahou), a major slave-trading site on the eastern Windward Coast that could just as easily be considered part of the Gold Coast, see Jelmer Vos, "The Slave Trade from the Windward Coast: The Case of the Dutch, 1740–1805," *African Economic History* 38 (2010): 29–51; Hall, *Slavery and African Ethnicities*, 31–32. In Berbice in this period, Cape Lahoo seems to have been an identity with some flexibility and to overlap with Canga and Coromantee, which were linked to nearby regions in the Windward and Gold Coasts.

87. Dorset, Mar. 21, 1814, AZ.1.5.

88. "Interrogatories to be put unto the negroe Cudjoe" ("rid of," "side dam"); "Interrogatories put to . . . Queen . . . ," Mar. 8, 1814, AZ.1.5 ("wizard," "country woman," "some hogs"); "Interrogatories . . . put unto the Negroe Barrington . . . ," Mar. 8, 1814, AZ.1.5.

89. Wilson alias Wah, Feb. 23, 1814, AZ.1.5; Banaba, Feb. 19, 1814, AZ.1.5.

90. "Reexamination Oxford," Mar. 11, 1814, AZ.1.5.

91. "Reexamination Oxford" (quotation); Bacchus, Mar. 9.

92. Dorset, Mar. 21.

93. Bacchus, Mar. 9.

94. Jean Baart, Feb. 19, 1814, AZ.1.5.

95. For "Namouay," see Pidores, Mar. 21, 1814, AZ.1.5.

96. Pidores, Mar. 21, 1814; Quashie, Feb. 22, 1814, AZ.1.5 ("too old"); Quamina, Feb. 22, 1814, AZ.1.5; Goodluck, Feb. 19, 1814, AZ.1.5; Primo, Feb. 22, 1814, AZ.1.5.

97. "Interrogatories . . . put unto the Negroe Banaba . . . ," Feb. 28, 1814, AZ.1.5. Officials referred to "the two last revolts"—one in 1763 and the other in 1783. "Declaration and Demand . . . versus The Negroe Banaba . . . ," Mar. 23, 1814, AB.6.3C; "Criminal Demand . . . versus The Negroe Pompey . . . ," Mar. 23, 1814, AB.6.3C. I have not been able to identify any revolt in 1783, nor has Marjoleine Kars, an expert on eighteenth-century Berbice. Kars, email to author, Oct. 1, 2020. There was, however, a small revolt in 1782. See Miscellaneous Interrogations (Examinations), Berbice: Court of Policy and Court of Criminal Justice, AB.3.82, NAN.

98. The details of Banaba's participation in the 1763 rebellion are obscure. He was not among those interrogated by Dutch officials at the time, nor was he mentioned by other

witnesses. Kars, email to author, May 22, 2021. His young age at the time may help explain his absence in surviving records.

99. Quamina, Apr. 12, 1814, AB.6.3C.

100. Kars, *Blood on the River*, 254–55.

101. Banaba, Feb. 19.

102. For the impact of the Haitian Revolution on other slave societies, see Julius S. Scott, *The Common Wind: Afro-American Currents in the Age of the Haitian Revolution* (New York: Verso Books, 2020); Ada Ferrer, "Speaking of Haiti: Slavery, Revolution and Freedom in Cuban Slave Testimony," in *The World of the Haitian Revolution*, ed. David Geggus and Norman Fiering (Bloomington: Indiana University Press, 2009), 223–47; Linda Rupert, "Inter-Colonial Networks and Revolutionary Ferment in Eighteenth Century Curaçao and Tierra Firme," in *Curaçao in the Age of Revolutions, 1795–1800*, ed. Wim Klooster and Gert Oostindie (Leiden: KITLV Press, 2011), 75–96; João José Reis and Flavio dos Santos Gomes, "Repercussions of the Haitian Revolution in Brazil, 1791–1850," in Geggus and Fiering, eds., *World of the Haitian Revolution*, 284–313.

103. For oaths, see Kenneth Bilby, "Swearing by the Past, Swearing to the Future: Sacred Oaths, Alliances, and Treaties Among the Guianese and Jamaican Maroons," *Ethnohistory* 44, no. 4 (1997): 655–89; Rucker, *Gold Coast Diasporas*, 91–92, 184–85; Ogborn, *Freedom of Speech*, 45–48, 92–93; Bradley L. Craig, "Oathbound: The Trelawny Maroons of Jamaica in the Revolutionary Atlantic World," Ph.D. diss., Harvard University (2020).

104. "Reexamination Oxford," Mar. 11.

105. According to the governor, the rebellion was also delayed by "the Illness of the newly elected King," presumably Banaba—a factor not mentioned by witnesses. Henry Bentinck to Earl Bathurst, Apr. 29, 1814, CO 111/81, 21–22, in Alvin O. Thompson, *A Documentary History of Slavery in Berbice, 1796–1834* (Georgetown, Guyana: Free Press, 2002), 134.

106. Kars, *Blood on the River*, 88; Carolyn Fick, *The Making of Haiti: The Saint Domingue Revolution from Below* (Knoxville: University of Tennessee Press, 1990), 86, 100. Drivers in Cuba were similarly targeted by rebels in the 1840s. See Robert L. Paquette, *Sugar Is Made with Blood: The Conspiracy of La Escalera and the Conflict Between Empires over Slavery in Cuba* (Middletown, Conn.: Wesleyan University Press, 1988), 67; Manuel Barcia, "Los contramayorales negros y mulatos en la Cuba decimonónica," *Boletín del Gabinete de Arqueología* 2, no. 2 (2002): 91; Aisha K. Finch, *Rethinking Slave Rebellion in Cuba: La Escalera and the Insurgencies of 1841–1844* (Chapel Hill: University of North Carolina Press, 2015), 82.

107. According to John, when Quamina had been put in charge of supervising enslaved children on Bath, he "licked," or whipped, Alexander's child, "which occasioned a quarrel" between the two of them. John told Alexander that Quamina "only did his duty," but Alexander decided to punish Quamina by sending him into the field without a whip. John, Mar. 1.

108. "Return of Slaves attached to Plantations Bath and Naarstigheid," Dec. 2, 1817; "Return of Slaves … attached to Plantations Bath and Naarstigheid …," Feb. 25, 1819, T 71/438, 75–76.

109. Kars, *Blood on the River*.

110. For a compelling argument that historians of slave rebellions ought to pay more attention to the many enslaved people who "were neither purposeful rebels nor committed collaborators or loyalists," see Kars, "Dodging Rebellion" (quotation, 41).

111. Feb. 15, 1814, AB.6.40A, 216–18.

112. Bentinck to Bathurst, Apr. 29 ("all that"); Feb. 15, 1814, AB.6.40A, 218–29 ("full & careful").

113. For the challenges involved in interpreting such evidence and the strategies enslaved people used to navigate the legal process, see, among others, Natalie Zacek, "Voices and Silences: The Problem of Slave Testimony in the English West Indian Law Court," S&A 24, no. 3 (2003): 24–39; Emilia Viotti da Costa, *Crowns of Glory, Tears of Blood: The Demerara Slave Rebellion of 1823* (New York: Oxford University Press, 1997), 170–71, 234–38; Barcia, *Great African Slave Revolt*, 19–22; Finch, "Gendered Terrain"; Kars, "Dodging Rebellion," 51–52; Sharples, *World That Fear Made*; Sophie White, *Voices of the Enslaved: Love, Labor, and Longing in French Louisiana* (Chapel Hill: University of North Carolina Press, 2019), 11–23, 27–47; Gunvor Simonsen, *Slave Stories: Law, Representation, and Gender in the Danish West Indies* (Aarhus, Denmark: Aarhus University Press, 2017).

114. Jean Baart, Feb. 19, 1814; 1814 Journal of John Wray, Council for World Mission/London Missionary Society Archives, West Indies and British Guiana journals, box 2, folder 4, SOAS. For these features as common tropes in conspiracy scares, see Sharples, *World That Fear Made*. Other rumors circulated that discussion of amelioration and missionary activity had sparked the rebellion. Thompson, *Unprofitable Servants*, 96.

115. Maroon communities in Berbice were located relatively close—ten to fifteen miles—from coastal plantations, and Maroons were regularly blamed for uprisings, especially between the 1790s and 1810s. Alston, "Guyana Maroons," 3.

116. The 1816 Barbados Rebellion—led in part by a driver, or "ranger," named Bussa (or Busso)—was similarly "organised and led almost exclusively by élite slaves," mainly drivers, who reportedly had to coerce others into joining the rebellion. As Hilary Beckles observed, the rebellion thus revealed "the persistence of ideological fracture within the slave community" and the resulting difficulty of political mobilization. Beckles, "Creolisation in Action: The Slave Labour Élite and Anti-Slavery in Barbados," *Caribbean Quarterly* 44, nos. 1–2 (1998): 124. See also Beckles, "The Slave-Drivers' War: Bussa and the 1816 Barbados Slave Rebellion," *Boletín de Studios Latinoamericanos y del Caribe*, no. 29 (1985): 85–110 (esp. 107–8); Michael Craton, *Testing the Chains: Resistance to Slavery in the British West Indies* (Ithaca: Cornell Univertsity Press), 1982), 254–66 (esp. 260). In 2000, Jerome S. Handler and Beckles engaged in a heated debate in Barbadian newspapers regarding Bussa's identity and role in the rebellion. Their articles are archived on Handler's website: https://jeromehandler.org/wp-content/uploads/2009/07/1816-Revolt-2000.pdf (accessed Aug. 1, 2022).

117. Liverpool, Mar. 12, 1814, AZ.1.5.

118. Kars, *Blood on the River*, 156–57, 166–70, 186. Coromantees were the "instigators" of the rebellion and "formed the senior leadership," though "Africans of many nations as well as some Creoles" also participated. Ibid., 78. See also Rucker, *Gold Coast Diasporas,* 122.

119. After the rebellion, there were only about thirty-three hundred enslaved people in Berbice. The slave population declined further in subsequent years, as enslaved people died at horrific rates and transatlantic slave traders preferred to do business in more lucrative markets. Only toward the end of the eighteenth century, when the British began an informal takeover, did Berbice's slave population and plantation economy grow. From just 1796 to 1807, slave traders imported as many African captives as they had during the entire previous century. The slave population grew rapidly—from about eight thousand slaves in 1796 to more than twenty-eight thousand by 1807—almost entirely due to the transatlantic and intercolonial slave trades. After the transatlantic slave trade ended, the population declined once again, due to high death rates and low birth rates. In 1814, there were about twenty thousand enslaved people. Kars, *Blood on the River*, 260, 263; Browne, *Surviving Slavery*, 20, 26.

120. Enslaved people in Jamaica similarly took inspiration from their predecessors. In the early nineteenth century, recently arrived African captives learned from other enslaved people about rebellions dating back to the 1760s. As Vincent Brown writes, "An oppositional political history taught and learned on Jamaican plantations—a radical pedagogy of the enslaved—shaped the slaves' goals, strategies, and tactics as they rehearsed bygone battles and considered future possibilities." Brown, *Tacky's Revolt*, 238–43 (quotation, 242).

121. Goodluck, for example, explained that the rebels' goal was "to renew the disturbances which took place once here & in Demerara." Mar. 11, 1814, AB.6.40A.

122. Cedric J. Robinson, *Black Marxism: The Making of the Black Radical Tradition*, 3rd ed. (Chapel Hill: University of North Carolina Press, 2020 [1983]), l.

123. "Examination of Johannes." Similar dynamics emerged in other rebel conspiracies, including one in 1736 on Antigua, where Coromantees included Creoles and Igbos in their planning, and one on Jamaica in 1776, where Igbo, Coromantee, and Creole rebel groups each elected their own "king." For Antigua, see David Barry Gaspar, *Bondmen and Rebels: A Study of Master-Slave Relations in Antigua* (Durham, N.C.: Duke University Press, 1993); Sharples, *World That Fear Made*, chs. 3–4. For Jamaica, see Sharples, *World That Fear Made*, 226–35; Edward B. Rugemer, *Slave Law and the Politics of Resistance in the Early Atlantic World* (Cambridge, Mass.: Harvard University Press, 2018), 193–99; Brown, *Tacky's Revolt*, 237–38; Ogborn, *Freedom of Speech*, 100, 270n134.

124. "Confession of the Negroe Thomas . . . ," Apr. 11, 1814, AB.6.3C.

125. "Criminal Demand . . . versus The Negroe Pompey . . . ," Mar. 23, 1814.

126. Mar. 9, 1814, AB.6.40A (quotation); Mar. 11, 1814, AB.6.40A.

127. The rumored plot on Essequibo's Arabian Coast resulted in the arrest of several "Ring leaders" suspected of having "proposed a revolt against the Whites at Christmas." Edward Codd to Henry Bentinck, Nov. 8, 1813, quoted in Alston, "Guyana Maroons," 14.

128. Joe, Feb. 19, 1814, AZ.1.5.

129. Jean Baart, Feb. 19.

130. "Report of Alexander."

131. "Confession of the Negroe Thomas."

132. "Interrogatories put to the negroe Joe . . . ," Mar. 11, 1814, AZ.1.5.

133. Mar. 9, 1814, AB.6.40A.

134. "Confession of the Negroe Thomas."

135. Bone, Mar. 23, 1814, AZ.1.5 ("field people"); Ned, Mar. 11, 1814, AZ.1.5 ("low class"); Paris, Mar. 23, 1814, AZ.1.5.

136. Mandingo Joe, Mar. 19, 1814, AZ.1.5; Joe, Mar. 10, 1814, AZ.1.5; "Interrogatories put to the Negroe Joe . . . ," Mar. 11, AZ.1.5.

137. "Interrogatories to be put to the Negro Sam . . . ," Mar. 12, 1814, AZ.1.5. About two decades earlier, British physician and soldier George Pinckard described similar divisions among Maroons in Demerara. They "subjected themselves to a sort of regular discipline under their captains and lieutenants," Pinckard wrote, and leaders forced the "lower orders" to conduct dangerous night raids on plantations and to work harder even than they had under slavery. George Pinckard, *Notes on the West Indies . . .* , vol. 1 (London: Baldwin, Cradock, and Joy, 1816 [1806]), 370.

138. Fragmentary evidence suggests that women both "dodged" the rebellion themselves and encouraged their husbands to do the same. "Examination of the woman Nano . . . ," May 16, 1814; Cyrus, Mar. 2, 1814, AZ.1.5. See also Kars, "Dodging Rebellion."

139. Kars, *Blood on the River*, 5, 9, 93–94, 187. For a different perspective, see Rucker, *Gold Coast Diasporas*, 174. In 1733, enslaved people from the Gold Coast organized a rebellion on the Danish island of St. John with similar goals under the leadership of several drivers. Kea, "'Amina' Slave Rebellion"; Rucker, *Gold Coast Diasporas*, 147–51.

140. Cudjo, an enslaved watchman on plantation Success, was "considered by the Coromanti negroes of the East Coast as their Chief," or "King," and was said to have "taken up . . . the runaway Coromantis, and to have kept them as slaves for his own use." Morris, formerly enslaved, had purchased his freedom from his owner by 1808 but continued to live on Success, where he owned three slaves. May 30, 1804, AB.1.5, 436. See also Alston, "'Die Houw Worte.'"

141. Carolyn Fick, "Emancipation in Haiti: From Plantation Labour to Peasant Proprietorship," *S&A* 21, no. 2 (2000): 11–40. For oral communication networks in the Age of Revolution, see Scott, *Common Wind*.

142. Walter Rucker has described this sort of political vision—in reference to the 1733–34 Akwamu revolt on St. John—as the result of an "elite consciousness" that was, he argues, less common than the antislavery, egalitarian "commoner consciousness" that Coromantees in American slave societies developed. Rucker, *Gold Coast Diasporas*, 8 (quotation), 15–16, ch. 4. See also Beckles, "Slave-Drivers' War," 107–8; Kars, "Dodging Rebellion," 88–94.

143. https://www.noonans.co.uk/auctions/archive/lot-archive/results/202378/?keywords=berbice&discipline=&category=&date_on=&date_start=&date_end=&lot_no= (accessed Aug. 10, 2022). In July 2011, the medal was purchased by a private collector in the United States for £4,000. Jan. 28, 2021, and Jan. 29, 2021 emails from Peter Preston-Morley, associate director of Dix Noonan Webb (now Noonans), to author.

144. https://www.dnw.co.uk/auction-archive/past-catalogues/lot.php?auction_id=233&lot_uid=202378 (accessed Oct. 19, 2021); https://www.noonans.co.uk/auctions/archive/lot-archive/results/202378/?keywords=berbice&discipline=&category=&date_on=&date_start=&date_end=&lot_no=. For a sketch of the medal given to February, see Sotheby,

Wilkinson, and Hodge, *Catalogue of the Valuable Collection of Coins and Medals, the Property of the late John G. Murdoch* . . . (London: Dryden Press, 1904), 49.

145. The idea of rewarding Alexander and the others came from John McCamon, the co-owner of Bath and Catharinasburg and a member of the court. May 14, 1814, and Aug. 10, 1814, Miscellaneous Letters and Letter books, Berbice: Court of Policy and Court of Criminal Justice, Society of Berbice and Successors, AB.6.3B, NAN. In addition to the medal, Alexander received twelve Johanneses (Portuguese gold coins) per year "for the term of his natural life"; a silver-headed cane; and an annual set of clothes that included a red jacket, blue pantaloons, a hat, a silk handkerchief, and a white shirt. The other men who were rewarded were: February and Joe, both from Catharinasburg; and Bacchus, Quashie, and Liverpool, all from Bath. May 14, 1814, Miscellaneous minutes of proceedings, Berbice: Court of Policy and Court of Criminal Justice, AB.1.11, 631, NAN.

146. May 14, 1814, AB.6.3B; May 14, 1814, AB.1.11, 631. Colonial authorities had issued similar medals in the past, such as one given to an African man named Vigaro (or Figaro) in January 1810 for the "fidelity" he showed in participating in an attack against Maroons under the command of his owner. Alston, "'Die Houw Worte'."

147. Aug. 10, 1814, AB.6.3B.

148. Jean Baart, Feb. 19.

149. Brown, *Tacky's Revolt*, 248.

150. For white authorities supposedly being surprised by drivers' participation in rebellions, see Craton, *Testing the Chains*, 158, 172; Laurent Dubois, *Avengers of the New World: The Story of the Haitian Revolution* (Cambridge, Mass.: Harvard University Press, 2004), 112; Sharples, *World that Fear Made*, 80.

151. McCammon, AB.6.3C.

152. This reaction echoed colonizers' response to the Haitian Revolution as an "unthinkable" event. Michel-Rolph Trouillot, *Silencing the Past: Power and the Production of History* (Boston: Beacon Press, 1995), ch. 3.

153. AB.6.3C, 53–54 (Archy), 61–62 (Congo Sam), 63–64 (Monday), 65–66 (Romeo), 67–68 (Hercules), 69–70 (Greenock), 71–72 (Joe), 91–92 (Harry), 150 (Joe), 242–43 (John), 244–46 (Caesar).

154. AB.6.3C, 55-56 (Ned), 57–58 (Pompey [plantation Union]) 73–74 (Jupiter and Dick), 87 (Congo), 89–90 (Sam, Foulis, and Trim), 93–94 (Benus, Alfred, Brutus, Harlow, Ganges), 95–96 (Romeo and Joseph), 97–98 (Boatswain, Peter Henery, Vrydag, Lambert, Adam, and Alexander), 240–41 (Con, Sibly, Henery, Apollo [plantation Liverpool], Apollo [plantation Belvedere], and Jem). Berbice's colonial government also enacted other measures designed to prevent future rebellions, including a reorganization and expansion of the militia (Mar. 19, 1814, *Berbice Gazette*); a ban on "any and all" dancing by enslaved people until 1815 (Mar. 26, 1814, *Berbice Gazette*); the prohibition of "all Assemblies for wakes, feasts or *dancing at funerals*" (John Wray to Burder, Feb. 20, 1826, referring a Mar. 8, 1814 law, box 1B, London Missionary Society, in Thompson, *Documentary History*, 159); and proclamations that suspended all holidays, prohibited enslaved people from leaving the plantations where they worked without written passes, and criminalized "singing, shouting, or making outcry

in boats, within the River and Creeks of this colony" (July 16, 1814, *Berbice Gazette*; Mar. 8, AB.6.40A; July 6, 1814, AB.6.3B).

155. AB.6.3C, 43–44 (George/Quashie), 45–47 (John), 47–48 (Quamina/Oxford), 49–50 (Banaba), 51–52 (Thomas), 59–60 (Pompey), 99–100, 169–72. For the symbolic power of such violence and the terror it was meant to incite, see Diana Paton, "Punishment, Crime, and the Bodies of Slaves in Eighteenth-Century Jamaica," *Journal of Social History* 34, no. 4 (2001): 923–54 (esp. 939–40); Brown, *Reaper's Garden*, 130–43.

CONCLUSION

1. Quoted in Richard S. Dunn, *A Tale of Two Plantations: Slave Life and Labor in Jamaica and Virginia* (Cambridge, Mass.: Harvard University Press, 2014), 81. I have modernized the spelling from the original.

2. For slavery as a state of perpetual war, see Vincent Brown, *Tacky's Revolt: The Story of an Atlantic Slave War* (Cambridge, Mass.: Harvard University Press, 2020).

3. Vincent Brown, "Social Death and Political Life in the Study of Slavery," AHR 114, no. 5 (2009): 1235.

4. Relevant here is the argument that enslaved people's struggles and politics were shaped and "compelled by the very conditions that slaves have been described as resisting." Brown, "Social Death and Political Life," 1246. See also Marisa J. Fuentes, *Dispossessed Lives: Enslaved Women, Violence, and the Archive* (Philadelphia: University of Pennsylvania Press, 2016), 85; Walter Johnson, *River of Dark Dreams: Slavery and Empire in the Cotton Kingdom* (Cambridge, Mass.: Harvard University Press, 2013), 214.

5. For enslaved people's politics of survival, see Randy M. Browne, *Surviving Slavery in the British Caribbean* (Philadelphia: University of Pennsylvania Press, 2017); Brown, "Social Death and Political Life."

6. For "social death" and natal alienation, see Orlando Patterson, *Slavery and Social Death: A Comparative Study* (Cambridge, Mass.: Harvard University Press, 1982); Brown, "Social Death and Political Life"; Stephanie E. Smallwood, *Saltwater Slavery: A Middle Passage from Africa to American Diaspora* (Cambridge, Mass.: Harvard University Press, 2007); Michael L. Dickinson, *Almost Dead: Slavery and Social Rebirth in the Black Urban Atlantic, 1680–1807* (Athens: University of Georgia Press, 2020).

7. For a critique of scholarship that emphasizes solidarity among the enslaved, see Aviva Ben-Ur, "Bound Together? Reassessing the 'Slave Community' and 'Resistance' Paradigms," *Journal of Global Slavery* 3, no. 1 (2018): 195–210.

8. James Stephen, *The Slavery of the British West India Colonies Delineated*, vol. 2 (London: Saunders and Benning, 1830), 192 ("odious"), 214 ("most peculiar").

9. Some self-styled reformist planters shared similar fantasies. See Justin Roberts, *Slavery and the Enlightenment in the British Atlantic, 1750–1807* (New York: Cambridge University Press, 2013); Christa Dierksheide, *Amelioration and Empire: Progress and Slavery in the Plantation Americas* (Charlottesville: University of Virginia Press, 2014).

10. For similar arguments and elaboration on these points, see Caitlin Rosenthal, *Accounting for Slavery: Masters and Management* (Cambridge, Mass.: Harvard University Press, 2018); Roberts, *Slavery and the Enlightenment*; Edward E. Baptist, *The Half Has Never Been Told: Slavery and the Making of American Capitalism* (New York: Basic Books, 2014); Trevor Burnard, "Introduction: The Management of Enslaved People on Anglo-American Plantations, 1700–1860," special issue of *Journal of Global Slavery* 6, no. 1 (2021): 1–9.

11. "In modern capitalist society," Rodney wrote, "rules are drawn up to protect members of the possessing class from devouring each other raw; but on the Upper Guinea Coast and the West African littoral as a whole, capitalism paraded without even a loin-cloth to hide its nakedness." Walter Rodney, *A History of the Upper Guinea Coast 1545–1800* (Oxford: Clarendon Press, 1970), 254. Marcus Rediker, drawing on Rodney, similarly described the slave ship as "the new, modern economic system in all its horrifying nakedness, capitalism without a loincloth." Rediker, *The Slave Ship: A Human History* (New York: Viking, 2007), 339.

INDEX

Locators in italics indicate a figure

ACKNOWLEDGMENTS

I am very grateful for the generous support so many people and institutions provided during the long process of researching and writing this book.

Thank you to the staff of the many libraries and archives I used, including the McDonald Library at Xavier University (especially Anne Ryckbost and Sidnie Reed), the British National Archives, the Library Company of Philadelphia (where Krystal Appiah and Jim Green were particularly helpful), the National Archives of Guyana (also known as the Walter Rodney Archives), the Huntington Library (especially Steve Hindle, Vanessa Wilkie, Natalie Serrano, and Juan Gomez), the National Archives of Cuba, and the National Archives of the Netherlands (especially Johan van Langen).

Generous financial support provided essential time to work on this project. I am very grateful to have received Faculty Development Research Sabbatical Fellowships from Xavier University in the spring of 2016 and fall of 2021. A Fletcher Jones Foundation Long-Term Fellowship from the Huntington Library in 2020–21 was also extraordinarily helpful, not least of all because it allowed me to learn from the other fellows in my cohort and because the infectious enthusiasm of Steve Hindle, director of research, kept my spirits up despite the many disruptions caused by the COVID-19 pandemic.

For the past twelve years, I have been privileged to work with many thoughtful, supportive colleagues at Xavier University. Thanks to my colleagues in the Department of History, especially my chairs, Karim Tiro, Kathleen Smythe, and Amy Whipple, who advocated for me to get the resources I needed to work on this book and worked hard to maintain a supportive, collegial department. I also want to thank my fellow historians in the administration: David Mengel, dean of the College of Arts and Sciences, and Rachel Chrastil, provost and chief academic officer.

Many kind friends and colleagues took time away from their own commitments to answer questions, read drafts, write recommendations, share references and documents, and offer other kinds of help. I am particularly grateful to Armando Azmitia, Fernanda Bretones, Vibert Cambridge, Chris Cameron, Meghan Cohorst, Juanita Cox, Nick Crawford, Sharika Crawford, Matt D'Antonio, Natalie Zemon Davis, David Doddington, Richard Dunn, Jeff Erbig, Misha Ewan, Karwan Fatah-Black, Rob Ferguson, Corey Gibson, Jorge Giovannetti, Frank Gullo, Deborah Hamer, Jared Hardesty, Stefanie Hunt-Kenendy, Tara Inniss, Marjoleine Kars, Thiago Kruse, Jane Landers, Jeremy Lange, Scott Licardi, Chris Luessen, Stephen Mullen, Tessa Murphy, Greg O'Malley, Nick Radburn, Matt Price, Justin Roberts, Casey Schmitt, Gunvor Simonsen, Kathleen Smythe, Jason Sharples, Karim Tiro, and Erika Wilson. At crucial stages, Lisa Lindsay and Rachel Walker offered incisive comments and much-needed encouragement. David Alston shared his own exciting works in progress and archival finds with unusual generosity and always made time to consult.

Two dear friends have stuck with this project—and its author—from the very beginning. I thank John Fairfield and John Sweet for the many conversations we have had about this project, for their honest and at times bracing feedback, and for helping me figure out what this book was about and how to write it. Their friendship has sustained me through various personal and professional challenges.

My thinking about drivers and their world has been enriched by the feedback I received at several seminars, conferences, and lectures. Many thanks to the organizers and participants of the Race and Slavery in the Atlantic World Working Group at Yale University; the Slavery and Freedom Studies Working Group at Rutgers University; the Omohundro Institute of Early American History and Culture Colloquium at the College of William and Mary; the Washington Early America Seminar at the University of Maryland, College Park; the Slavery, Memory, and African Diasporas Seminar at Howard University; the Caribbean Seminar at the Institute of the Americas, University College London; the Carter G. Woodson Institute for African American and African Studies Colloquium at the University of Virginia; the Kentucky Early American Seminar; the annual meetings of the North American Conference on British Studies and Association of Caribbean Historians; the "(En)Gendering the Atlantic World Conference" at New York University; and the Berkshire Conference on the History of Women, Genders, and Sexualities. I am also grateful for opportunities to speak at Eckerd College and Bowdoin College. For invitations, questions, comments, and critiques, I am particularly grateful to Laura Rosanne Adderley, Ana Lucia Araujo, Patrick Barker, Yesenia Barragan, Rick Bell, Lissa Bolletino, Chris Bonner, Bridget Brereton, Holly Brewer, Bradley Craig, Kate de Luna, Dusty Dye, Anne Eller, Claudius Fergus, Lin Fisher, Bethan Fisk, Marisa Fuentes, Dexter Gabriel, Rebecca Goetz,

Isaac Guzman, Jerry Handler, Scott Heerman, Gad Heuman, Rosemarijn Hoefte, Nate Jéréme-Brink, Carolyn Johnston, Marjoleine Kars, Daniel Livesay, Clare Lyons, Michelle McDonald, Roderick McDonald, Deborah McDowell, Warren Milteer, Elise Mitchell, Kathleen Monteith, Jennifer Morgan, Brooke Newman, Kwame Otu, Clara Palmiste, Josh Piker, Nick Popper, Laura Premack, Ed Rugemer, Kelly Ryan, Sasha Turner, Rachel Walker, Brad Wood, and Karin Wulf.

I owe an especially large debt to Kathleen Brown, Vincent Brown, and Diana Paton. They made time to read the entire manuscript closely, asked hard questions and made incisive suggestions, and, ultimately, pushed me to produce a more ambitious book. I hope the end result reflects my respect for their judgment and deep gratitude for their careful engagement.

Long before this project started to take shape, Bob Lockhart at Penn Press was a pivotal figure in its development. Bob has been an enthusiastic and crucial interlocutor from start to finish, always encouraging me to sharpen my analysis and more clearly explain the implications of my arguments. I thank him for the significant time and energy he invested in this book.

Thanks, above all, to my family for their steadfast support. I thank my parents, Kim and Randy Browne, and my parents-in-law, Martha Velasquez and Juan Torres. I continue to miss those who died while I worked on this book: R. M. Browne III, Elizabeth Browne, and Raja Torres Browne. Thanks, too, to the wider Escobar, Ness, Pfeifer, Torres, and Velasquez families. This book is dedicated to the two people who mean the most to me: Mafe, who has given me more support, laughter, and joy than I could have ever imagined, and Pedro, who has distracted me from this project in the best of ways and, in the process, changed the way I see the world.